ABOUT THIS PUBLICATION

FOR SERVICE ASSISTANCE

Customer Service
1.704.898.0770

North Carolina General Statues is published by The Muliti-Media Group of Greater Charlotte in Charlotte, North Carolina. Copyright 2015 by the Multi-Media Group of Greater Charlotte. This book or parts thereof may not be reproduced in any form, stored in a retrieval system, or transmitted in any form by any means—electronic, mechanical, photocopy, recording or otherwise—without prior written permission of the publisher, except as provided by United States of America copyright law.

The records required by U.S. Code 2257(a) through (c) and the pertinent regulations 28 C.F.R. Cli. 1, Part 75 with respect to this publication and all materials associated with such records are maintained by The Multi-Media Group of Greater Charlotte, Publisher and available for review by Attorney General.

www.visionbooks.org

Copyright © 2015 by MMGGC
All rights reserved!

TID: 5109401
ISBN (10) digit: 1503255409
ISBN (13) digit: 978-1503255401

123-4-56789-01239-Paperback
123-4-56789-01239-Hardback

First Edition

090520140547

Printed in the United States of America

2015 EDITION

North Carolina Criminal Law And Procedure-Pamphlet # 72

Printed In conjunction with the Administration of the Courts

North Carolina Criminal Law and Procedure
Pamphlet Reference Guide

Chapters	Pamphlet
Chapter 1 Civil Procedure	1
Chapter 1 Civil Procedure (Continue)	2
Chapter 1A Rules of Civil Procedure	2
Chapter 1B Contribution.	2
Chapter 1C Enforcement of Judgments.	2
Chapter 1D Punitive Damages.	2
Chapter 1E Eastern Band of Cherokee Indians.	2
Chapter 1F North Carolina Uniform Interstate Depositions and Discovery Act.	2
Chapter 2 - Clerk of Superior Court [Repealed and Transferred.]	3
Chapter 3 - Commissioners of Affidavits and Deeds [Repealed.]	3
Chapter 4 - Common Law	3
Chapter 5 - Contempt [Repealed.]	3
Chapter 5A - Contempt	3
Chapter 6 - Liability for Court Costs	3
Chapter 7 - Courts [Repealed and Transferred.]	3
Chapter 7A – Judicial Department	3
Chapter 7A – Continuation (Judicial Department)	4
Chapter 7A – Continuation (Judicial Department)	5
Chapter 7B - Juvenile Code	5
Chapter 8 - Evidence	6
Chapter 8A - Interpreters for Deaf Persons [Recodified.]	6
Chapter 8B - Interpreters for Deaf Persons	6
Chapter 8C - Evidence Code	6
Chapter 9 - Jurors	6
Chapter 10 - Notaries [Repealed.]	6
Chapter 10A - Notaries [Recodified.]	6
Chapter 10B - Notaries	6
Chapter 11 - Oaths	6
Chapter 12 - Statutory Construction	6
Chapter 13 - Citizenship Restored	6
Chapter 14 - Criminal Law	7
Chapter 14 –Criminal Law (Continuation)	8
Chapter 15 - Criminal Procedure	9
Chapter 15A - Criminal Procedure Act (Continuation)	10
Chapter 15A - Criminal Procedure Act (Continuation)	11
Chapter 15B - Victims Compensation	11
Chapter 15C - Address Confidentiality Program	11
Chapter 16 - Gaming Contracts and Futures	11
Chapter 17 - Habeas Corpus	11

Chapter 17A - Law-Enforcement Officers [Recodified.]	11
Chapter 17B - North Carolina Criminal Justice Education and Training System [Recodified.] Chapter 17C - North Carolina Criminal Justice Education and Training Standards Commission	11
	11
Chapter 17D - North Carolina Justice Academy	11
Chapter 17E - North Carolina Sheriffs' Education and Training Standards Commission	11
Chapter 18 - Regulation of Intoxicating Liquors [Repealed.]	12
Chapter 18A - Regulation of Intoxicating Liquors [Repealed.]	12
Chapter 18B - Regulation of Alcoholic Beverages	12
Chapter 18C - North Carolina State Lottery	12
Chapter 19 - Offenses against Public Morals	12
Chapter 19A - Protection of Animals	12
Chapter 20 - Motor Vehicles	13
Chapter 20 - Motor Vehicles (Continuation)	14
Chapter 20 - Motor Vehicles (Continuation)	15
Chapter 20 - Motor Vehicles (Continuation)	16
Chapter 21 - Bills of Lading	17
Chapter 22 - Contracts Requiring Writing	17
Chapter 22A - Signatures	17
Chapter 22B - Contracts Against Public Policy	17
Chapter 22C - Payments to Subcontractors	17
Chapter 23 - Debtor and Creditor	17
Chapter 24 – Interest	17
Chapter 25 – Uniform Commercial Code	18
Chapter 25 – Uniform Commercial Code (Continuation)	19
Chapter 25A – Retail Installment Sales Act	20
Chapter 25B - Credit	20
Chapter 25C - Sales of Artwork	20
Chapter 26 - Suretyship	20
Chapter 27 - Warehouse Receipts [Repealed.]	20
Chapter 28 - Administration [Repealed.]	20
Chapter 28A - Administration of Decedents' Estates	20
Chapter 28B - Estates of Absentees in Military Service	20
Chapter 28C - Estates of Missing Persons	20
Chapter 29 - Intestate Succession	21
Chapter 30 - Surviving Spouses	21
Chapter 31 - Wills	21
Chapter 31A - Acts Barring Property Rights	21
Chapter 31B - Renunciation of Property and Renunciation of Fiduciary Powers Act	21
Chapter 31C - Uniform Disposition of Community Property Rights at Death Act	21
Chapter 32 - Fiduciaries	21
Chapter 32A - Powers of Attorney	21
Chapter 33 - Guardian and Ward [Repealed and Recodified.]	21

Chapter 33A - North Carolina Uniform Transfers to Minors Act	21
Chapter 33B - North Carolina Uniform Custodial Trust Act	21
Chapter 34 - Veterans' Guardianship Act	22
Chapter 35 - Sterilization Procedures	22
Chapter 35A - Incompetency and Guardianship	22
Chapter 36 - Trusts and Trustees [Repealed.]	22
Chapter 36A - Trusts and Trustees	22
Chapter 36B - Uniform Management of Institutional Funds Act [Repealed.]	22
Chapter 36C - North Carolina Uniform Trust Code	22
Chapter 36D - North Carolina Community Third Party Trusts, Pooled Trusts	23
Chapter 36E - Uniform Prudent Management of Institutional Funds Act	23
Chapter 37 - Allocation of Principal and Income [Repealed.]	23
Chapter 37A - Uniform Principal and Income Act	23
Chapter 38 - Boundaries	23
Chapter 38A - Landowner Liability	23
Chapter 39 - Conveyances	23
Chapter 39A - Transfer Fee Covenants Prohibited	23
Chapter 40 - Eminent Domain [Repealed.]	23
Chapter 40A - Eminent Domain	23
Chapter 41 - Estates	23
Chapter 41A - State Fair Housing Act	23
Chapter 42 - Landlord and Tenant	23
Chapter 42A - Vacation Rental Act	23
Chapter 43 - Land Registration	23
Chapter 44 - Liens	24
Chapter 44A - Statutory Liens and Charges	24
Chapter 45 - Mortgages and Deeds of Trust	24
Chapter 45A - Good Funds Settlement Act	24
Chapter 46 - Partition	24
Chapter 47 - Probate and Registration	25
Chapter 47A - Unit Ownership	25
Chapter 47B - Real Property Marketable Title Act	25
Chapter 47C - North Carolina Condominium Act	25
Chapter 47D - Notice of Settlement Act [Expired.]	25
Chapter 47E - Residential Property Disclosure Act	25
Chapter 47F - North Carolina Planned Community Act	25
Chapter 47G - Option to Purchase Contracts	25
Chapter 47H - Contracts for Deed	25
Chapter 48 - Adoptions	26
Chapter 48A - Minors	26
Chapter 49 - Bastardy	26
Chapter 49A - Rights of Children	26
Chapter 50 - Divorce and Alimony	26
Chapter 50A - Uniform Child-Custody Jurisdiction and	

Enforcement Act	26
Chapter 50B - Domestic Violence	26
Chapter 50C - Civil No-Contact Orders	26
Chapter 51 - Marriage	26
Chapter 52 - Powers and Liabilities of Married Persons	27
Chapter 52A - Uniform Reciprocal Enforcement of Support Act [Repealed.]	27
Chapter 52B - Uniform Premarital Agreement Act	27
Chapter 52C - Uniform Interstate Family Support Act	27
Chapter 53 - Banks	27
Chapter 53A - Business Development Corporations and North Carolina Capital Resource Corporations	28
Chapter 53B - Financial Privacy Act	28
Chapter 54 - Cooperative Organizations	28
Chapter 54A - Capital Stock Savings and Loan Associations [Repealed.]	28
Chapter 54B - Savings and Loan Associations	29
Chapter 54C - Savings Banks	29
Chapter 55 - North Carolina Business Corporation Act	30
Chapter 55A - North Carolina Nonprofit Corporation Act	31
Chapter 55B - Professional Corporation Act	31
Chapter 55C - Foreign Trade Zones	31
Chapter 55D - Filings, Names, and Registered Agents for Corporations, Nonprofit Corporations, and Partnerships	31
Chapter 56 - Electric, Telegraph and Power Companies [Repealed.]	31
Chapter 57 - Hospital, Medical and Dental Service Corporations [Recodified.]	31
Chapter 57A - Health Maintenance Organization Act [Recodified.]	31
Chapter 57B - Health Maintenance Organization Act [Recodified.]	31
Chapter 57C - North Carolina Limited Liability Company Act.	31
Chapter 58 - Insurance.	32
Chapter 58 - Insurance (Continuation)	33
Chapter 58 - Insurance (Continuation)	34
Chapter 58 - Insurance (Continuation)	35
Chapter 58 - Insurance (Continuation)	36
Chapter 58 - Insurance (Continuation)	37
Chapter 58 - Insurance (Continuation)	38
Chapter 58A - North Carolina Health Insurance Trust Commission [Recodified.]	38
Chapter 59 - Partnership.	39
Chapter 59B - Uniform Unincorporated Nonprofit Association Act.	39
Chapter 60 - Railroads and Other Carriers [Repealed and Transferred.]	39
Chapter 61 - Religious Societies	39
Chapter 62 - Public Utilities	39

Chapter 62 - Public Utilities (Continuation)	40
Chapter 62A - Public Safety Telephone Service And Wireless Telephone Service	40
Chapter 63 - Aeronautics	40
Chapter 63A - North Carolina Global TransPark Authority	40
Chapter 64 - Aliens	40
Chapter 65 – Cemeteries	40
Chapter 66 - Commerce and Business	41
Chapter 67 - Dogs	41
Chapter 68 - Fences and Stock Law	41
Chapter 69 - Fire Protection	41
Chapter 70 - Indian Antiquities, Archaeological Resources and Unmarked Human Skeletal Remains Protection	42
Chapter 71 - Indians [Repealed.]	42
Chapter 71A - Indians	42
Chapter 72 - Inns, Hotels and Restaurants	42
Chapter 73 - Mills	42
Chapter 74 - Mines and Quarries	42
Chapter 74A - Company Police [Repealed.]	42
Chapter 74B - Private Protective Services Act [Repealed.]	42
Chapter 74C - Private Protective Services	42
Chapter 74D - Alarm Systems	42
Chapter 74E - Company Police Act	42
Chapter 74F - Locksmith Licensing Act	42
Chapter 74G - Campus Police Act	42
Chapter 75 - Monopolies, Trusts and Consumer Protection	42
Chapter 75A - Boating and Water Safety	43
Chapter 75B - Discrimination in Business	43
Chapter 75C - Motion Picture Fair Competition Act	43
Chapter 75D - Racketeer Influenced and Corrupt Organizations	43
Chapter 75E - Unlawful Activities in Connection With Certain Corporate Transactions	43
Chapter 76 - Navigation	43
Chapter 76A - Navigation and Pilotage Commissions	43
Chapter 77 - Rivers, Creeks, and Coastal Waters	43
Chapter 78 - Securities Law [Repealed.]	43
Chapter 78A - North Carolina Securities Act	43
Chapter 78B - Tender Offer Disclosure Act [Repealed.]	43
Chapter 78C - Investment Advisers	43
Chapter 78D - Commodities Act	43
Chapter 79 - Strays [Repealed.]	43
Chapter 80 - Trademarks, Brands, etc.	44
Chapter 81 - Weights and Measures [Recodified.]	44
Chapter 81A - Weights and Measures Act of 1975.	44
Chapter 82 - Wrecks [Repealed.]	44
Chapter 83 - Architects [Recodified.]	44

Chapter 83A - Architects	44
Chapter 84 - Attorneys-at-Law	44
Chapter 84A - Foreign Legal Consultants	44
Chapter 85 - Auctions and Auctioneers [Repealed.]	44
Chapter 85A - Bail Bondsmen and Runners [Recodified.]	44
Chapter 85B - Auctions and Auctioneers	44
Chapter 85C - Bail Bondsmen and Runners [Recodified.]	44
Chapter 86 - Barbers [Recodified.]	44
Chapter 86A - Barbers	44
Chapter 87 - Contractors	44
Chapter 88 - Cosmetic Art [Repealed.]	44
Chapter 88A - Electrolysis Practice Act	44
Chapter 88B - Cosmetic Art	45
Chapter 89 - Engineering and Land Surveying [Recodified.]	45
Chapter 89A - Landscape Architects	45
Chapter 89B - Foresters	45
Chapter 89C - Engineering and Land Surveying	45
Chapter 89D - Landscape Contractors	45
Chapter 89E - Geologists Licensing Act	45
Chapter 89F - North Carolina Soil Scientist Licensing Act	45
Chapter 89G - Irrigation Contractors	45
Chapter 90 - Medicine and Allied Occupations	45
Chapter 90 - Medicine and Allied Occupations (Continuation)	46
Chapter 90 - Medicine and Allied Occupations (Continuation)	47
Chapter 90 - Medicine and Allied Occupations (Continuation)	48
Chapter 90A - Sanitarians and Water and Wastewater Treatment Facility Operators	48
Chapter 90B - Social Worker Certification and Licensure Act	48
Chapter 90C - North Carolina Recreational Therapy Licensure Act	48
Chapter 90D - Interpreters and Transliterators	48
Chapter 91 - Pawnbrokers [Repealed.]	48
Chapter 91A - Pawnbrokers Modernization Act of 1989	48
Chapter 92 - Photographers [Deleted.]	48
Chapter 93 - Certified Public Accountants	48
Chapter 93A - Real Estate License Law	49
Chapter 93B - Occupational Licensing Boards	49
Chapter 93C - Watchmakers [Repealed.]	49
Chapter 93D - North Carolina State Hearing Aid Dealers and Fitters Board.	49
Chapter 93E - North Carolina Appraisers Act	49
Chapter 94 - Apprenticeship	49
Chapter 95 - Department of Labor and Labor Regulations	49
Chapter 95 - Department of Labor and Labor Regulations (Continuation)	50
Chapter 96 - Employment Security	50
Chapter 97 - Workers' Compensation Act	50
Chapter 97 - Workers' Compensation Act (Continuation)	51

Chapter 98 - Burnt and Lost Records	51
Chapter 99 - Libel and Slander	51
Chapter 99A - Civil Remedies for Criminal Actions	51
Chapter 99B - Products Liability	51
Chapter 99C - Actions Relating to Winter Sports Safety and Accidents	51
Chapter 99D - Civil Rights	51
Chapter 99E - Special Liability Provisions	51
Chapter 100 - Monuments, Memorials and Parks	51
Chapter 101 - Names of Persons	51
Chapter 102 - Official Survey Base	51
Chapter 103 - Sundays, Holidays and Special Days	51
Chapter 104 - United States Lands	51
Chapter 104A - Degrees of Kinship	51
Chapter 104B - Hurricanes or Other Acts of Nature	51
Chapter 104C - Atomic Energy, Radioactivity and Ionizing Radiation [Repealed and Recodified.]	51
Chapter 104D - Southern States Energy Compact	51
Chapter 104E - North Carolina Radiation Protection Act	51
Chapter 104F - Southeast Interstate Low-Level Radioactive Waste Management Compact [Repealed]	51
Chapter 104G - North Carolina Low-Level Radioactive Waste Management Authority Act of 1987 [Repealed]	51
Chapter 105 - Taxation	51
Chapter 105 - Taxation (Continuation)	52
Chapter 105 - Taxation (Continuation)	53
Chapter 105 - Taxation (Continuation)	54
Chapter 105A - Setoff Debt Collection Act	55
Chapter 105B - Defaulted Student Loan Recovery Act	55
Chapter 106 - Agriculture	55
Chapter 106 - Agriculture (Continue)	56
Chapter 106 - Agriculture (Continue)	57
Chapter 107 - Agricultural Development Districts [Repealed.]	57
Chapter 108 - Social Services [Repealed and Recodified.]	57
Chapter 108A - Social Services	57
Chapter 108B - Community Action Programs	58
Chapter 108C Medicaid and Health Choice Provider Requirements.	58
Chapter 108D Medicaid Managed Care for Behavioral Health Services.	58
Chapter 109 - Bonds [Recodified.]	58
Chapter 110 - Child Welfare	58
Chapter 111 - Aid to the Blind	58
Chapter 112 - Confederate Homes and Pensions [Repealed.]	58
Chapter 113 - Conservation and Development	58
Chapter 113 - Conservation and Development (Continuation)	59

Chapter 113A - Pollution Control and Environment	59
Chapter 113A - Pollution Control and Environment (Continuation)	60
Chapter 113B - North Carolina Energy Policy Act of 1975	60
Chapter 114 - Department of Justice	60
Chapter 115 - Elementary and Secondary Education [Repealed.]	60
Chapter 115A - Community Colleges, Technical Institutes, and Industrial Education Centers [Repealed.]	60
Chapter 115B - Tuition and Fee Waivers	60
Chapter 115C - Elementary and Secondary Education	60
Chapter 115C - Elementary and Secondary Education (Continuation)	61
Chapter 115C - Elementary and Secondary Education (Continuation)	62
Chapter 115C - Elementary and Secondary Education (Continuation)	63
Chapter 115D - Community Colleges	63
Chapter 115E - Private Educational Facilities Finance Act [Recodified]	63
Chapter 116 - Higher Education	63
Chapter 116 - Higher Education (Continuation)	63
Chapter 116A - Escheats and Abandoned Property [Repealed.]	64
Chapter 116B - Escheats and Abandoned Property	64
Chapter 116C - Continuum of Education Programs	64
Chapter 116D - Higher Education Bonds	64
Chapter 116E -Education Longitudinal Data System	64
Chapter 117 - Electrification	64
Chapter 118 - Firemen's and Rescue Squad Workers' Relief and Pension Funds [Recodified.]	64
Chapter 118A - Firemen's Death Benefit Act [Repealed.]	64
Chapter 118B - Members of a Rescue Squad Death Benefit Act [Repealed.]	64
Chapter 119 - Gasoline and Oil Inspection and Regulation	64
Chapter 120 - General Assembly	65
Chapter 120 - General Assembly (Continuation)	66
Chapter 120 - General Assembly (Continuation)	67
Chapter 120C - Lobbying	67
Chapter 121 - Archives and History	67
Chapter 122 - Hospitals for the Mentally Disordered [Repealed.]	67
Chapter 122A - North Carolina Housing Finance Agency	67
Chapter 122B - North Carolina Agricultural Facilities Finance Act [Repealed.]	67
Chapter 122C - Mental Health, Developmental Disabilities, and Substance Abuse Act of 1985	67
Chapter 122C - Mental Health, Developmental Disabilities, and Substance Abuse Act of 1985 (Continuation)	68

Chapter 122D - North Carolina Agricultural Finance Act	68
Chapter 122E - North Carolina Housing Trust and Oil Overcharge Act	68
Chapter 123 - Impeachment	69
Chapter 123A - Industrial Development [Repealed.]	69
Chapter 124 - Internal Improvements	69
Chapter 125 - Libraries	69
Chapter 126 - State Personnel System	69
Chapter 127 - Militia [Repealed.]	69
Chapter 127A - Militia	69
Chapter 127B - Military Affairs	69
Chapter 127C - Advisory Commission on Military Affairs	69
Chapter 128 - Offices and Public Officers	69
Chapter 128 - Offices and Public Officers (Continuation)	70
Chapter 129 - Public Buildings and Grounds	70
Chapter 130 - Public Health [Repealed.]	70
Chapter 130A - Public Health	70
Chapter 130A - Public Health (Continuation)	71
Chapter 130A - Public Health (Continuation)	72
Chapter 130B - Hazardous Waste Management Commission [Repealed.]	72
Chapter 131 - Public Hospitals [Repealed.]	72
Chapter 131A - Health Care Facilities Finance Act	72
Chapter 131B - Licensing of Ambulatory Surgical Facilities [Repealed.]	72
Chapter 131C - Charitable Solicitation Licensure Act [Repealed.]	72
Chapter 131D - Inspection and Licensing of Facilities	72
Chapter 131E - Health Care Facilities and Services	72
Chapter 131E - Health Care Facilities and Services (Continuation)	73
Chapter 131F - Solicitation of Contributions	73
Chapter 132 - Public Records	73
Chapter 133 - Public Works	74
Chapter 134 - Youth Development [Recodified.]	74
Chapter 134A - Youth Services [Repealed.]	74
Chapter 135 - Retirement System for Teachers and State Employees; Social Security; Health Insurance Program for Children	74
Chapter 135 - Retirement System for Teachers and State Employees; Social Security; Health Insurance Program for Children	75
Chapter 136 - Transportation	75
Chapter 136 - Transportation (Continuation)	76
Chapter 137 - Rural Rehabilitation [Repealed.]	76
Chapter 138 - Salaries, Fees and Allowances	76
Chapter 138A - State Government Ethics Act	76

Chapter 139 - Soil and Water Conservation Districts	76
Chapter 140 - State Art Museum; Symphony and Art Societies	76
Chapter 140A - State Awards System	76
Chapter 141 - State Boundaries	76
Chapter 142 - State Debt	76
Chapter 143 - State Departments, Institutions, and Commissions	77
Chapter 143 - State Departments, Institutions, and Commissions (Continuation)	78
Chapter 143 - State Departments, Institutions, and Commissions (Continuation)	79
Chapter 143 - State Departments, Institutions, and Commissions (Continuation)	80
Chapter 143A - State Government Reorganization	80
Chapter 143B - Executive Organization Act of 1973	80
Chapter 143B - Executive Organization Act of 1973 (Continuation)	81
Chapter 143B - Executive Organization Act of 1973 (Continuation)	82
Chapter 143C - State Budget Act	83
Chapter 143D - The State Governmental Accountability and Internal Control Act	83
Chapter 144 - State Flag, Official Governmental Flags, Motto, and Colors	83
Chapter 145 - State Symbols and Other Official Adoptions.	83
Chapter 146 - State Lands	83
Chapter 147 - State Officers	83
Chapter 148 - State Prison System	84
Chapter 149 - State Song and Toast	84
Chapter 150 - Uniform Revocation of Licenses [Repealed.]	84
Chapter 150A - Administrative Procedure Act [Recodified.]	84
Chapter 150B - Administrative Procedure Act	84
Chapter 151 - Constables [Repealed.]	84
Chapter 152 - Coroners	84
Chapter 152A - County Medical Examiner [Repealed.]	84
Chapter 152A - County Medical Examiner [Repealed.] (Continuation)	85
Chapter 153 - Counties and County Commissioners [Repealed.]	85
Chapter 153A - Counties	85
Chapter 153B - Mountain Resources Planning Act	85
Chapter 153C - Uwharrie Regional Resources Act	85
Chapter 154 - County Surveyor [Repealed.]	85
Chapter 155 - County Treasurer [Repealed.]	85
Chapter 156 - Drainage	85

Chapter 156 – Drainage (Continuation)	86
Chapter 157 - Housing Authorities and Projects	86
Chapter 157A - Historic Properties Commissions [Transferred.]	86
Chapter 158 - Local Development	86
Chapter 159 - Local Government Finance	86
Chapter 159 - Local Government Finance (Continuation)	87
Chapter 159A - Pollution Abatement and Industrial Facilities Financing Act [Unconstitutional.]	87
Chapter 159B - Joint Municipal Electric Power and Energy Act	87
Chapter 159C - Industrial and Pollution Control Facilities Financing Act	87
Chapter 159D - The North Carolina Capital Facilities Financing Act	87
Chapter 159E - Registered Public Obligations Act	87
Chapter 159F - North Carolina Energy Development Authority [Repealed.]	87
Chapter 159G - Water Infrastructure	87
Chapter 159H - [Reserved.]	87
Chapter 159I - Solid Waste Management Loan Program and Local Government Special Obligation Bonds	87
Chapter 160 - Municipal Corporations [Repealed And Transferred.]	87
Chapter 160A - Cities and Towns	88
Chapter 160A - Cities and Towns (Continuation)	89
Chapter 160B - Consolidated City-County Act	89
Chapter 160C - Baseball Park Districts [Repealed.]	90
Chapter 161 - Register of Deeds	90
Chapter 162 - Sheriff	90
Chapter 162A - Water and Sewer Systems	90
Chapter 162B Continuity of Local Government in Emergency.	90
Chapter 163 Elections and Election Laws.	90
Chapter 163 Elections and Election Laws. (Continuation)	91
Chapter 164 Concerning the General Statutes of North Carolina.	92
Chapter 165 Veterans.	92
Chapter 166 Civil Preparedness Agencies [Repealed.]	92
Chapter 166A North Carolina Emergency Management Act.	92
Chapter 167 State Civil Air Patrol [Repealed.]	92
Chapter 168 Persons with Disabilities.	92
Chapter 168A Persons With Disabilities Protection Act.	92

§ 130A-373. Authority and duties.

(a) The State Center for Health Statistics is authorized to:

(1) Collect, maintain and analyze health data on:

a. The extent, nature and impact of illness and disability on the population of the State;

b. The determinants of health and health hazards;

c. Health resources, including the extent of available work power and resources;

d. Utilization of health care;

e. Health care costs and financing; and

f. Other health or health-related matters; and

(2) Undertake and support research, demonstrations and evaluations respecting new or improved methods for obtaining data.

(b) The State Center for Health Statistics may collect health data on behalf of other governmental or nonprofit organizations.

(c) The State Center for Health Statistics shall collect data only on a voluntary basis except when there is specific legal authority to compel mandatory reporting of the health data. In collecting health data on a voluntary basis, the State Center for Health Statistics shall give the person a statement in writing:

(1) That the data is being collected on a voluntary basis and that the person is not required to respond; and

(2) The purposes for which the health data is being collected.

(d) Subject to the provisions of G.S. 130A-374, the State Center for Health Statistics may share health data with other persons, agencies and organizations.

(e) The State Center for Health Statistics shall:

(1) Take necessary action to assure that statistics developed under this Article are of high quality, timely and comprehensive, as well as specific and adequately analyzed and indexed; and

(2) Publish, make available and disseminate statistics on as wide a basis as practical.

(f) The State Center for Health Statistics shall coordinate health data activities within the State in order to eliminate unnecessary duplication of data collection and to maximize the usefulness of data collected by:

(1) Participating with State and local agencies in the design and implementation of a cooperative system for producing comparable and uniform health information and statistics at the State and local levels; and

(2) Undertaking and supporting research, development, demonstration and evaluation respecting the cooperative system. (1983, c. 891, s. 2).

§ 130A-374. Security of health data.

(a) Medical records of individual patients shall be confidential and shall not be public records open to inspection. The State Center for Health Statistics may disclose medical records of individual patients which identify the individual described in the record only if:

(1) The individual described in the medical record has authorized the disclosure; or

(2) The disclosure is for bona fide research purposes. The Commission shall adopt rules providing for the use of the medical records for research purposes.

(b) The State Center for Health Statistics shall take appropriate measures to protect the security of health data collected by the Center, including:

(1) Limiting the access to health data to authorized individuals who have received training in the handling of this data;

(2) Designating a person to be responsible for physical security; and

(3) Developing and implementing a system for monitoring security. (1983, c. 891, s. 2.)

§§ 130A-375 through 130A-376. Reserved for future codification purposes.

Article 16.

Postmortem Investigation and Disposition.

Part 1. Postmortem Medicolegal Examinations and Services.

§ 130A-377. Establishment and maintenance of central and district offices.

The Department shall establish and maintain a central office with appropriate facilities and personnel for postmortem medicolegal examinations. District offices, with appropriate facilities and personnel, may also be established and maintained if considered necessary by the Department for the proper management of postmortem examinations. (1955, c. 972, s. 1; 1957, c. 1357, s. 1; 1967, c. 1154, s. 1; 1973, c. 476, s. 128; 1983, c. 891, s. 2.)

§ 130A-378. Qualifications and appointment of the Chief Medical Examiner.

The Chief Medical Examiner shall be a forensic pathologist certified by the American Board of Pathology and licensed to practice medicine. The Chief Medical Examiner shall be appointed by the Secretary. (1983, c. 891, s. 2.)

§ 130A-379. Duties of the Chief Medical Examiner.

The Chief Medical Examiner shall perform postmortem medicolegal examinations as provided in this Part. The Chief Medical Examiner may, upon request, provide instruction in health science, legal medicine and other subjects related to his duties at The University of North Carolina, the North Carolina Justice Academy and other institutions of higher learning. (1983, c. 891, s. 2.)

§ 130A-380. The Chief Medical Examiner's staff.

The Chief Medical Examiner may employ qualified pathologists to serve as Associate and Assistant Medical Examiners in the central and district offices. The Associate and Assistant Medical Examiners shall perform duties assigned by the Chief Medical Examiner. Forensic chemists may be employed by the Chief Medical Examiner to provide toxicological and related support. (1983, c. 891, s. 2.)

§ 130A-381. Additional services and facilities.

In order to provide proper facilities for investigating deaths as authorized in this Part, the Chief Medical Examiner may arrange for the use of existing public or private laboratory facilities. Each county shall provide or contract for an appropriate facility for the examination and storage of bodies under Medical Examiner jurisdiction. The Chief Medical Examiner may contract with qualified persons to perform or to provide support services for autopsies and other studies and investigations. (1967, c. 1154, s. 1; 1973, c. 476, s. 128; 1983, c. 891, s. 2; 2007-187, s. 5.)

§ 130A-382. County medical examiners; appointment; term of office; vacancies.

One or more county medical examiners for each county shall be appointed by the Chief Medical Examiner for a three-year term. County medical examiners shall be appointed from a list of physicians licensed to practice medicine in this State submitted by the medical society of the county in which the appointment is to be made. If no names are submitted by the society, the Chief Medical Examiner shall appoint one or more medical examiners from physicians in the county licensed to practice medicine in this State. In the event no licensed physician in a county accepts an appointment, the Chief Medical Examiner may appoint as acting county medical examiner one or more physicians licensed to practice medicine in this State from other counties, a licensed physician assistant, a nurse, a coroner, or an individual who has taken an approved course of training as required by the Chief Medical Examiner. The acting county medical examiner shall have all the duties and authority of the physician medical examiner except to perform autopsies. A medical examiner may serve more than one county. The Chief Medical Examiner may take jurisdiction in any case or appoint another medical examiner to do so. (1955, c. 972, s. 1; 1957, c. 1357, s. 1; 1963, c. 492, s. 4; 1967, c. 1154, s. 1; 1973, c. 476, s. 128; 1981, c. 187, ss. 2-4; 1983, c. 891, s. 2; 2007-187, s. 4.)

§ 130A-383. Medical examiner jurisdiction.

(a)   Upon the death of any person resulting from violence, poisoning, accident, suicide or homicide; occurring suddenly when the deceased had been in apparent good health or when unattended by a physician; occurring in a jail, prison, correctional institution or in police custody; occurring in State facilities operated in accordance with Part 5 of Article 4 of Chapter 122C of the General Statutes; occurring pursuant to Article 19 of Chapter 15 of the General Statutes; or occurring under any suspicious, unusual or unnatural circumstance, the medical examiner of the county in which the body of the deceased is found shall be notified by a physician in attendance, hospital employee, law-enforcement officer, funeral home employee, emergency medical technician, relative or by any other person having suspicion of such a death. No person shall disturb the body at the scene of such a death until authorized by the medical examiner unless in the unavailability of the medical examiner it is determined by the appropriate law enforcement agency that the presence of the body at the scene would risk the integrity of the body or provide a hazard to the safety of others. For the limited purposes of this Part, expression of opinion that death has occurred may be made by a nurse, an emergency medical technician or any other competent person in the absence of a physician.

(b)   The discovery of anatomical material suspected of being part of a human body shall be reported to the medical examiner of the county in which the material is found.

(c)   Upon completion of the investigation and in accordance with the rules of the Commission, the medical examiner shall release the body to the next of kin or other interested person who will assume responsibility for final disposition. (1955, c. 972, s. 1; 1957, c. 1357, s. 1; 1963, c. 492, s. 4; 1967, c. 1154, s. 1; 1983, c. 891, s. 2; 1989, c. 353, s. 1; 2008-131, s. 2.)

§ 130A-384. Notification concerning out-of-state body.

When a body is brought into this State for disposal and there is reason to believe either that the death was not investigated properly or that there is not an adequate certificate of death, the body shall be reported to a medical examiner in the county where the body resides or to the Chief Medical Examiner. These deaths may be investigated by the same procedure as deaths occurring in this State under G.S. 130A-383. (1983, c. 891, s. 2.)

§ 130A-385. Duties of medical examiner upon receipt of notice; reports; copies.

(a)   Upon receipt of a notification under G.S. 130A-383, the medical examiner shall take charge of the body, make inquiries regarding the cause and manner of death, reduce the findings to writing and promptly make a full report to the Chief Medical Examiner on forms prescribed for that purpose.

The Chief Medical Examiner or the county medical examiner is authorized to inspect and copy the medical records of the decedent whose death is under investigation. In addition, in an investigation conducted pursuant to this Article, the Chief Medical Examiner or the county medical examiner is authorized to inspect all physical evidence and documents which may be relevant to determining the cause and manner of death of the person whose death is under investigation, including decedent's personal possessions associated with the death, clothing, weapons, tissue and blood samples, cultures, medical equipment, X rays and other medical images. The Chief Medical Examiner or county medical examiner is further authorized to seek an administrative search warrant pursuant to G.S. 15-27.2 for the purpose of carrying out the duties imposed under this Article. In addition to the requirements of G.S. 15-27.2, no administrative search warrant shall be issued pursuant to this section unless the Chief Medical Examiner or county medical examiner submits an affidavit from the office of the district attorney in the district in which death occurred stating that the death in question is not under criminal investigation.

The Chief Medical Examiner shall provide directions as to the nature, character and extent of an investigation and appropriate forms for the required reports. The facilities of the central and district offices and their staff services shall be available to the medical examiners and designated pathologists in their investigations.

(b)   The medical examiner shall complete a certificate of death, stating the name of the disease which in his opinion caused death. If the death was from external causes, the medical examiner shall state on the certificate of death the means of death, and whether, in the medical examiner's opinion, the manner of death was accident, suicide, homicide, execution by the State, or undetermined. The medical examiner shall also furnish any information as may be required by the State Registrar of Vital Statistics in order to properly classify the death.

(c)   The Chief Medical Examiner shall have authority to amend a medical examiner death certificate.

(d)   A copy of the report of the medical examiner investigation may be forwarded to the appropriate district attorney.

(e)   In cases where death occurred due to an injury received in the course of the decedent's employment, the Chief Medical Examiner shall forward to the Commissioner of Labor a copy of the medical examiner's report of the investigation, including the location of the fatal injury and the name and address of the decedent's employer at the time of the fatal injury. The Chief Medical Examiner shall forward this report within 30 days of receipt of the information from the medical examiner.

(f)   If a death occurred in a facility licensed subject to Article 2 or Article 3 of Chapter 122C of the General Statutes, or Articles 1 or 1A of Chapter 131D of the General Statutes, and the deceased was a client or resident of the facility or a recipient of facility services at the time of death, then the Chief Medical Examiner shall forward a copy of the medical examiner's report to the Secretary of Health and Human Services within 30 days of receipt of the report from the medical examiner. (1955, c. 972, s. 1; 1957, c. 1357, s. 1; 1967, c. 1154, s. 1; 1973, c. 476, s. 128; 1977, 2nd Sess., c. 1145; 1983, c. 891, s. 2; 1989, c. 353, s. 2; c. 797; 1991 (Reg. Sess., 1992), c. 894, s. 6; 2000-129, s. 4.)

§ 130A-386. Subpoena authority.

The Chief Medical Examiner and the county medical examiners are authorized to issue subpoenas for the attendance of persons and for the production of documents as may be required by their investigation. (1983, c. 891, s. 2.)

§ 130A-387. Fees.

For each investigation and prompt filing of the required report, the medical examiner shall receive a fee paid by the State. However, if the deceased is a resident of the county in which the death or fatal injury occurred, that county shall pay the fee. The fee shall be one hundred dollars ($100.00). (1983, c. 891, s. 2; 1991, c. 463, s. 1; 2005-368, s. 1.)

§ 130A-388. Medical examiner's permission necessary before embalming, burial and cremation.

(a) No person knowing or having reason to know that a death may be under the jurisdiction of the medical examiner pursuant to G.S. 130A-383 or 130A-384, shall embalm, bury or cremate the body without the permission of the medical examiner.

(b) A dead body shall not be cremated or buried at sea unless a medical examiner certifies that he has inquired into the cause and the manner of death and has the opinion that no further examination is necessary. This subsection shall not apply to deaths occurring less than 24 hours after birth or to deaths of patients resulting only from natural disease and occurring in a licensed hospital unless the death falls within the jurisdiction of the medical examiner under G.S. 130A-383 or 130A-384. The Commission is authorized to adopt rules creating additional exceptions to this subsection. For making this certification, the medical examiner shall be entitled to a fee in an amount determined reasonable and appropriate by the Secretary, not to exceed fifty dollars ($50.00), to be paid by the applicant. (1955, c. 972, s. 1; 1957, c. 1357, s. 1; 1963, c. 492, s. 4; 1967, c. 1154, s. 1; 1971, c. 444, s. 7; 1973, c. 873, s. 7; 1983, c. 891, s. 2.)

§ 130A-389. Autopsies.

(a) If, in the opinion of the medical examiner investigating the case or of the Chief Medical Examiner, it is advisable and in the public interest that an autopsy or other study be made; or, if an autopsy or other study is requested by the district attorney of the county or by any superior court judge, an autopsy or other study shall be made by the Chief Medical Examiner or by a competent pathologist designated by the Chief Medical Examiner. A complete autopsy report of findings and interpretations, prepared on forms designated for the purpose, shall be submitted promptly to the Chief Medical Examiner. Subject to the limitations of G.S. 130A-389.1 relating to photographs and video or audio recordings of an autopsy, a copy of the report shall be furnished to any person upon request. A fee for the autopsy or other study shall be paid by the State. However, if the deceased is a resident of the county in which the death or fatal injury occurred, that county shall pay the fee. The fee shall be one thousand two hundred fifty dollars ($1,250).

(b)   In deaths where the Chief Medical Examiner and the medical examiner investigating the case do not deem it advisable and in the public interest that an autopsy be performed, but the next-of-kin of the deceased requests that an autopsy be performed, the Chief Medical Examiner or a designated pathologist may perform the autopsy, unless the deceased's health care power of attorney granted authority for such decisions to the health care agent. If the Chief Medical Examiner or a designated pathologist performs the autopsy at the request of the next of kin, the cost shall be paid by the next of kin.

(c)   When the next-of-kin of a decedent whose death does not fall under G.S. 130A-383 or 130A-384 requests that an autopsy be performed, the Chief Medical Examiner or a designated pathologist may perform that autopsy and the cost shall be paid by the next-of-kin.

(d)   The report of autopsies performed pursuant to subsections (b) and (c) shall be a part of the decedents' medical records and therefore not public records open to inspection. (1955, c. 972, s. 1; 1957, c. 1357, s. 1; 1967, c. 1154, s. 1; 1973, c. 47, s. 2; c. 476, s. 128; 1975, c. 9; 1981, c. 187, s. 7; c. 562, p. 5; 1983, c. 891, s. 2; 1991, c. 463, s. 2; 1998-212, s. 29A.10(a); 2005-351, s. 4; 2005-393, s. 2; 2006-226, s. 32; 2013-360, s. 12E.8(a).)

§ 130A-389.1. Photographs and video or audio recordings made pursuant to autopsy.

(a)   Except as otherwise provided by law, any person may inspect and examine original photographs or video or audio recordings of an autopsy performed pursuant to G.S. 130A-389(a) at reasonable times and under reasonable supervision of the custodian of the photographs or recordings. Except as otherwise provided by this section, no custodian of the original recorded images shall furnish copies of photographs or video or audio recordings of an autopsy to the public. For purposes of this section, the Chief Medical Examiner shall be the custodian of all autopsy photographs or video or audio recordings unless the photographs or recordings were taken by or at the direction of an investigating medical examiner and the investigating medical examiner retains the original photographs or recordings. If the investigating medical examiner has retained the original photographs or recordings, then the investigating medical examiner is the custodian of the photographs or video or audio recordings and must allow the public to inspect and examine them in accordance with this subsection.

(b)   The following public officials may obtain copies of autopsy photographs or video or audio recordings for official use only. These public officials shall not disclose the photographs or video or audio recordings to the public except as provided by law:

(1)   The Chief Medical Examiner or a pathologist designated by the Chief Medical Examiner.

(2)   Investigating Medical Examiner.

(3)   District attorney.

(4)   Superior court judge.

(5)   Law enforcement officials conducting an investigation relating to the death.

A public official authorized by this subsection to obtain copies may provide a copy of the photograph or videotape to another person for the sole purpose of aiding in the identification of the deceased through publication of the photograph or videotape.

(c)   The following persons may obtain copies of autopsy photographs or video or audio recordings but may not disclose the photographs or video or audio recordings to the public unless otherwise authorized by law:

(1)   The personal representative of the estate of the deceased.

(2)   A person authorized by an order issued in a special proceeding pursuant to subsection (d) of this section.

(3) A physician licensed to practice in North Carolina who uses a copy of the photographs or video or audio recording to confer with attorneys or others with a bona fide professional need to use or understand forensic science, provided that the physician promptly returns the copy to the custodian.

(4) After redacting all information identifying the decedent, including name, address, and social security number, and after anonymizing any physical recognition, a medical examiner, coroner, physician, or their designee who uses such material for:

a. Medical or scientific teaching or training purposes;

b. Teaching or training of law enforcement personnel;

c. Teaching or training of attorneys or others with a bona fide professional need to use or understand forensic science;

d. Conferring with medical or scientific experts in the field of forensic science; or

e. Publication in a scientific or medical journal or textbook.

A medical examiner, coroner, or physician who has in good faith complied with this subsection shall not be subject to any penalty under this section.

Any person who lawfully obtains a copy of a photograph or video or audio recording pursuant to this subsection shall be required to sign a statement acknowledging that they have received notice that any unauthorized disclosure of the photograph or video or audio recording is a Class 2 misdemeanor.

(d) A person who is denied access to copies of photographs or video or audio recordings, or who is restricted in the use the person may make of the photographs or video or audio recordings under this section, may commence a special proceeding in accordance with Article 33 of Chapter 1 of the General Statutes. Upon a showing of good cause, the clerk may issue an order authorizing the person to copy or disclose a photograph or video or audio recording of an autopsy and may prescribe any restrictions or stipulations that the clerk deems appropriate. In determining good cause, the clerk shall consider whether the disclosure is necessary for the public evaluation of governmental performance; the seriousness of the intrusion into the family's right to privacy and whether the disclosure is the least intrusive means available; and the availability of similar information in other public records, regardless of form. In all cases, the viewing, copying, listening to, or other handling of a photograph or video or audio recording of an autopsy shall be under the direct supervision of the Chief Medical Examiner or the Chief Medical Examiner's designee. A party aggrieved by an order of the clerk may appeal to the appropriate court in accordance with Article 27A of Chapter 1 of the General Statutes.

(e)   The petitioner shall provide reasonable notice of the commencement of a special proceeding, as authorized by subsection (d) of this section, and reasonable notice of the opportunity to be present and heard at any hearing on the matter in accordance with Rule 5 of the Rules of Civil Procedure. The notice shall be provided to the personal representative of the estate of the deceased, if any, and to the surviving spouse of the deceased. If there is no surviving spouse, then the notice shall be provided to the deceased's parents, and if the deceased has no living parent, then to the adult child of the deceased or to the guardian or custodian of a minor child of the deceased.

(f)   This section does not apply to the use of autopsy photographs or video or audio recordings in a criminal, civil, or administrative proceeding except that nothing in this section prohibits a court or presiding officer, upon good cause shown, from restricting or otherwise controlling the disclosure to persons other than the parties and attorneys to the proceeding of an autopsy, crime scene, or similar photograph or video or audio recordings in the manner provided under this section.

(g)   Any person who willfully and knowingly violates this section is guilty of a Class 2 misdemeanor, provided that more than one disclosure of the same item by the same person is not a separate offense.

(h)   Any person not authorized by this section to obtain a copy of an autopsy photograph or video or audio recording, who knowingly and willfully removes, copies, or otherwise creates an image of an autopsy photograph or video or audio recording with intent to steal the same, is guilty of a Class 1 misdemeanor. (2005-393, s. 3.)

§ 130A-390. Exhumations.

(a) In any case of death described in G.S. 130A-383 or 130A-384 where the body is buried without investigation by a medical examiner as to the cause and manner of death or where sufficient cause develops for further investigation after a body is buried as determined by a county medical examiner or the Chief Medical Examiner, the Chief Medical Examiner shall authorize an investigation and send a report of the investigation with recommendations to the appropriate district attorney. The district attorney may forward the report to the superior court judge and petition for disinterment. The judge may order that the body be exhumed and that an autopsy be performed by the Chief Medical Examiner. A report of the autopsy and other pathological studies shall be delivered to the judge. The cost of the exhumation, autopsy, transportation and disposition of the body shall be paid by the State. However, if the deceased is a resident of the county in which death or fatal injury occurred, that county shall pay the cost.

(b) Any person may petition a judge of the superior court for an order of exhumation. Upon showing of sufficient cause, the judge may order the body exhumed. The cost incurred shall be assigned to the petitioner.

(c) Without applying for a judicial exhumation order, the next-of-kin of a deceased person may have the remains exhumed, examined by the Chief Medical Examiner and redisposed. The cost shall be paid by the next-of-kin. (1983, c. 891, s. 2; 1991, c. 463, s. 3.)

§ 130A-391: Repealed by Session Laws 2008-153, s. 3, effective August 2, 2008.

§ 130A-392. Reports and records as evidence.

Reports of investigations made by a county medical examiner or by the Chief Medical Examiner and toxicology and autopsy reports made pursuant to this Part may be received as evidence in any court or other proceeding. Copies of records, photographs, laboratory findings and records in the Office of the Chief Medical Examiner, any county medical examiner or designated pathologist, when duly certified, shall have the same evidentiary value as the original. (1967, c. 1154, s. 1; 1973, c. 476, s. 128; 1981, c. 187, s. 8; 1983, c. 891, s. 2.)

§ 130A-393. Rules.

The Commission shall adopt rules to carry out the intent and purpose of this Part. (1967, c. 1154, s. 1; 1973, c. 476, s. 128; 1981, c. 614, s. 15; 1983, c. 891, s. 2.)

§ 130A-394. Coroner to hold inquests.

In every case requiring the medical examiner to be notified, as provided by G.S. 130A-383, the coroner shall be notified by the medical examiner, and the coroner shall hold an inquest and preliminary hearing in those instances as required in G.S. 152-7. The coroner shall file a written report of his investigation with the district attorney of the superior court and the medical examiner. The body shall remain in the custody and control of the medical examiner. However, if a county has abolished the office of coroner pursuant to the provisions of Chapter 152A at a time when Chapter 152A was in effect in the county: (i) The provisions of this Article relating to coroner shall not be applicable to the county, (ii) the provisions of G.S. 152A-9 shall remain in full force and effect in the county, and (iii) Chapter 152 of the General Statutes shall not be applicable in the county. (1955, c. 972, s. 1; 1957, c. 1357, s. 1; 1967, c. 1154, s. 1; 1969, c. 299; 1973, c. 47, s. 2; 1983, c. 891, s. 2; 1985, c. 462, s. 1.)

§ 130A-395. Handling and transportation of bodies.

(a)   It shall be the duty of the physician licensed to practice medicine under Chapter 90 attending any person who dies and is known to have smallpox, plague, HIV infection, hepatitis B infection, rabies, or Jakob-Creutzfeldt to provide written notification to all individuals handling the body of the proper precautions to prevent infection. This written notification shall be provided to funeral service personnel at the time the body is removed from any hospital, nursing home, or other health care facility. When the patient dies in a location other than a health care facility, the attending physician shall notify the funeral service personnel verbally of the precautions required in subsections (b) and (c) as soon as the physician becomes aware of the death.

(b)   The body of a person who died from smallpox or plague shall not be embalmed. The body shall be enclosed in a strong, tightly sealed outer case which will prevent leakage or escape of odors as soon as possible after death and before the body is removed from the hospital room, home, building, or other premises where the death occurred. This case shall not be reopened except with the consent of the local health director.

(c)   Persons handling bodies of persons who died and were known to have HIV infection, hepatitis B infection, Jakob-Creutzfeldt, or rabies shall be provided written notification to observe blood and body fluid precautions. (1989, c. 698, s. 4.)

§§ 130A-396 through 130A-397: Reserved for future codification purposes.

Part 2. Autopsies.

§ 130A-398. Limitation on right to perform autopsy.

The right to perform an autopsy shall be limited to those cases in which:

(1)   The Chief Medical Examiner or a county medical examiner, acting pursuant to G.S. 130A-389, directs that an autopsy be performed;

(2)   The Commission of Anatomy, acting pursuant to G.S. 130A-415, has given written consent for an autopsy to be performed on an unclaimed body;

(3)   A prosecuting officer or district attorney, acting pursuant to G.S. 15-7 in case of homicide, directs that an autopsy be performed;

(4)   The decedent directs in writing prior to death that an autopsy be performed upon the occurrence of the decedent's death;

(4a)   The health care agent under a health care power of attorney with authority to make decisions with respect to autopsies requests that an autopsy be performed upon the deceased principal;

(5)   The personal representative of the estate of the decedent requests that an autopsy be performed upon the decedent; or

(6) Any of the following persons, in order of priority, when persons in prior classes are not available at the time of death, and in the absence of actual notice of contrary indications by the decedent or actual opposition by a member of the same or prior class, authorizes an autopsy to be performed:

a. The spouse;

b. Any adult child or stepchild;

c. Any parent or stepparents;

d. Any adult sibling;

e. A guardian of the person of the decedent at the time of the decedent's death;

f. Any relative or person who accepts responsibility for final disposition of the body by other customary and lawful procedures;

g. Any person under obligation to dispose of the body. (1931, c. 152; 1933, c. 209; 1967, c. 1154, s. 4; 1969, c. 444; 1973, c. 47, s. 2; 1983, c. 891, s. 2; 2005-351, s. 5; 2006-226, s. 32.)

§ 130A-399. Postmortem examination of inmates of certain public institutions.

Upon the death of any inmate of an institution maintained by the State, or a city, county or other political subdivision of the State, for the care of the sick, mentally ill or mentally retarded, the administrator of the institution in which the death occurs is empowered to authorize a postmortem examination of the deceased person. The examination shall be of a scope and nature necessary to promote knowledge of the human organism and its disorders. (1943, c. 87, s. 1; 1983, c. 891, s. 2.)

§ 130A-400. Written consent for postmortem examinations required.

An administrator of an institution shall not authorize a postmortem examination described in G.S. 130A-399 without first securing the written consent of the deceased person's spouse, one of the next-of-kin or nearest known relative, or other person charged by law with the duty of burial, in the order named and as known. A copy of the written consent shall be filed in the office of the administrator of the institution where the inmate died. (1943, c. 87, s. 3; 1983, c. 891, s. 2.)

§ 130A-401. Postmortem examinations in certain medical schools.

The postmortem examinations and studies authorized by G.S. 130A-399 may be made in the laboratories of medical schools of colleges and universities on conditions established by the administrator. (1943, c. 87, s. 2; 1983, c. 891, s. 2.)

Part 3. Uniform Anatomical Gift Act.

§ 130A-402: Repealed by Session Laws 2007-538, s. 3(b), effective October 1, 2007.

§ 130A-403: Repealed by Session Laws 2007-538, s. 3(b), effective October 1, 2007.

§ 130A-404: Repealed by Session Laws 2007-538, s. 3(b), effective October 1, 2007.

§ 130A-405: Repealed by Session Laws 2007-538, s. 3(b), effective October 1, 2007.

§ 130A-406: Repealed by Session Laws 2007-538, s. 3(b), effective October 1, 2007.

§ 130A-407: Repealed by Session Laws 2007-538, s. 3(b), effective October 1, 2007.

§ 130A-408: Repealed by Session Laws 2007-538, s. 3(b), effective October 1, 2007.

§ 130A-409: Repealed by Session Laws 2007-538, s. 3(b), effective October 1, 2007.

§ 130A-410: Repealed by Session Laws 2007-538, s. 3(b), effective October 1, 2007.

§ 130A-411: Repealed by Session Laws 2007-538, s. 3(b), effective October 1, 2007.

§ 130A-412: Repealed by Session Laws 2007-538, s. 3(b), effective October 1, 2007.

§ 130A-412.1: Repealed by Session Laws 2007-538, s. 3(b), effective October 1, 2007.

§ 130A-412.2: Repealed by Session Laws 2007-538, s. 3(b), effective October 1, 2007.

Part 3A. Revised Uniform Anatomical Gift Act.

§ 130A-412.3. Short title.

This Part may be cited as the Revised Uniform Anatomical Gift Act. (2007-538, s. 1.)

§ 130A-412.4. Definitions.

The following definitions apply in this Part:

(1) "Adult" means an individual who is at least 18 years of age.

(2) "Agent" means an individual:

a. Authorized to make an anatomical gift on the principal's behalf under a power of attorney for health care; or

b. Expressly authorized to make an anatomical gift on the principal's behalf by any other record signed by the principal.

(3) "Anatomical gift" means a donation of all or part of a human body to take effect after the donor's death for the purpose of transplantation, therapy, research, or education.

(4) "Body part" means an organ, an eye, or tissue of a human being. The term does not include the whole body.

(5) "Decedent" means a deceased individual whose body or body part is or may be the source of an anatomical gift. The term includes a stillborn infant and, subject to restrictions imposed by law other than this Article, a fetus.

(6) "Disinterested witness" means any individual except for the following:

a. The donor's: spouse, child, parent, sibling, grandchild, grandparent, or guardian.

b. An adult who exhibited special care and concern for the donor.

c. A person to whom an anatomical gift could pass under G.S. 130A-412.13.

(7) "Document of gift" means a donor card or other record used to make an anatomical gift. The term includes a statement or symbol on a drivers license, identification card, or donor registry.

(8) "Donor" means an individual whose body or body part is the subject of an anatomical gift.

(9) "Donor registry" means a database that contains records of anatomical gifts and amendments to or revocations of anatomical gifts.

(10) "Drivers license" means a license or permit issued by the North Carolina Department of Transportation, Division of Motor Vehicles, to operate a vehicle, whether or not conditions are attached to the license or permit.

(11) "Eye bank" means an entity that is licensed, accredited, or regulated under federal or state law to engage in the recovery, screening, testing, processing, storage, or distribution of human eyes or portions of human eyes.

(12) "Guardian" means a person appointed by a court to make decisions regarding the support, care, education, health, or welfare of an individual. The term does not include a guardian ad litem.

(12a) "Health care decision" means any decision made regarding the health care of the prospective donor.

(13) "Hospital" means a facility licensed as a hospital under the law of any state or a facility operated as a hospital by the United States, a state, or a subdivision of a state.

(14) "Identification card" means an identification card issued by the North Carolina Department of Transportation, Division of Motor Vehicles.

(15) "Know" means to have actual knowledge.

(16) "Minor" means an individual who is under 18 years of age.

(17) "Organ procurement organization" means a person designated by the Secretary of the United States Department of Health and Human Services as an organ procurement organization.

(18) "Parent" means a parent whose parental rights have not been terminated.

(19) "Person" means an individual, corporation, business trust, estate, trust, partnership, limited liability company, association, joint venture, public corporation, government or governmental subdivision, agency, or instrumentality, or any other legal or commercial entity.

(20) "Physician" means an individual authorized to practice medicine or osteopathy under the law of any state.

(21) "Procurement organization" means an eye bank, organ procurement organization, or tissue bank.

(22) "Prospective donor" means an individual who is dead or near death and has been determined by a procurement organization to have a body part that could be medically suitable for transplantation, therapy, research, or education. The term does not include an individual who has made a refusal.

(23) "Reasonably available" means able to be contacted by a procurement organization without undue effort and willing and able to act in a timely manner consistent with existing medical criteria necessary for the making of an anatomical gift.

(24) "Recipient" means an individual into whose body a decedent's body part has been or is intended to be transplanted.

(25) "Record" means information that is inscribed on a tangible medium or that is stored in an electronic or other medium and is retrievable in perceivable form.

(26) "Refusal" means a record created under G.S. 130A-412.9 that expressly states an intent to bar other persons from making an anatomical gift of an individual's body or body part.

(27) "Sign" means, with the present intent to authenticate or adopt a record:

a. To execute or adopt a tangible symbol; or

b. To attach to or logically associate with the record an electronic symbol, sound, or process.

(28) "State" means a state of the United States, the District of Columbia, Puerto Rico, the United States Virgin Islands, or any territory or insular possession subject to the jurisdiction of the United States.

(29) "Technician" means an individual determined to be qualified to remove or process body parts by an appropriate organization that is licensed, accredited, or regulated under federal or state law. The term includes an enucleator.

(30) "Tissue" means a portion of the human body other than an organ or an eye. The term does not include blood unless the blood is donated for the purpose of research or education.

(31) "Tissue bank" means a person that is licensed, accredited, or regulated under federal or state law to engage in the recovery, screening, testing, processing, storage, or distribution of tissue.

(32) "Transplant hospital" means a hospital that furnishes organ transplants and other medical and surgical specialty services required for the care of transplant patients. (2007-538, s. 1.)

§ 130A-412.5. Applicability.

This act applies to an anatomical gift or amendment to, revocation of, or refusal to make an anatomical gift, whenever made. (2007-538, s. 1.)

§ 130A-412.6. Who may make an anatomical gift before donor's death.

Subject to G.S. 130A-412.10, an anatomical gift of a donor's body or body part may be made during the life of the donor for the purpose of transplantation, therapy, research, or education in the manner provided in G.S. 130A-412.7 by:

(1) The donor, if the donor is an adult or if the donor is a minor and is:

a. Emancipated; or

b. Authorized under State law to apply for a drivers license because the donor is at least 16 years of age;

(2) An agent of the donor to the extent authorized under a power of attorney for health care or other record;

(3) A parent of the donor, if the donor is an unemancipated minor; or

(4) The donor's guardian. (2007-538, s. 1.)

§ 130A-412.7. Manner of making anatomical gift before donor's death.

(a) A donor may make an anatomical gift by any of the following methods:

(1) By authorizing that a statement or symbol be imprinted on the donor's drivers license or identification card indicating that the donor has made an

anatomical gift. Anatomical gifts made by this method shall not include a donation of tissue or the donor's body.

(2)   In a will.

(3)   During a terminal illness or injury of the donor, by any form of communication addressed to at least two adults, at least one of whom is a disinterested witness.

(4)   As provided in subsection (b) of this section.

(b)   A donor or other person authorized to make an anatomical gift under G.S. 130A-412.6 may make a gift by a signed donor card or other record signed by the donor or other person making the gift or by authorizing that a statement or symbol indicating that the donor has made an anatomical gift be included on a donor registry. If the donor or other person is physically unable to sign a record, the record may be signed by another individual at the direction of the donor or other person and must:

(1)   Be witnessed by at least two adults, at least one of whom is a disinterested witness, who have signed at the request of the donor or the other person; and

(2)   State that it has been signed and witnessed as provided in subdivision (1) of this subsection.

(c)   Revocation, suspension, expiration, or cancellation of a drivers license or identification card upon which an anatomical gift is indicated does not invalidate the gift.

(d)   An anatomical gift made by will takes effect upon the donor's death whether or not the will is probated. Invalidation of the will after the donor's death does not invalidate the gift. (2007-538, s. 1.)

§ 130A-412.8. Amending or revoking anatomical gift before donor's death.

(a)   Subject to G.S. 130A-412.10, a donor or other person authorized to make an anatomical gift under G.S. 130A-412.6 may amend or revoke an anatomical gift by:

(1) A record signed by:

a. The donor;

b. The other person; or

c. Subject to subsection (b) of this section, another individual acting at the direction of the donor or the other person if the donor or other person is physically unable to sign; or

(2) A later-executed document of gift that amends or revokes a previous anatomical gift or portion of an anatomical gift, either expressly or by inconsistency.

(b) A record signed pursuant to sub-subdivision c. of subdivision (1) of subsection (a) of this section must:

(1) Be witnessed by at least two adults, at least one of whom is a disinterested witness, who have signed at the request of the donor or the other person; and

(2) State that it has been signed and witnessed as provided in subdivision (1) of this subsection.

(c) Subject to G.S. 130A-412.10, a donor or other person authorized to make an anatomical gift under G.S. 130A-412.6 may revoke an anatomical gift by the destruction or cancellation of the document of gift, or the portion of the document of gift used to make the gift, with the intent to revoke the gift.

(d) A donor may amend or revoke an anatomical gift that was not made in a will by any form of communication during a terminal illness or injury addressed to at least two adults, at least one of whom is a disinterested witness.

(e) A donor who makes an anatomical gift in a will may amend or revoke the gift in the manner provided for amendment or revocation of wills or as provided in subsection (a) of this section. (2007-538, s. 1.)

§ 130A-412.9. Refusal to make anatomical gift; effect of refusal.

(a) An individual may refuse to make an anatomical gift of the individual's body or body part by:

(1) A record signed by:

a. The individual; or

b. Subject to subsection (b) of this section, another individual acting at the direction of the individual if the individual is physically unable to sign;

(2) The individual's will, whether or not the will is admitted to probate or invalidated after the individual's death; or

(3) Any form of communication made by the individual during the individual's terminal illness or injury addressed to at least two adults, at least one of whom is a disinterested witness.

(b) A record signed pursuant to sub-subdivision b. of subdivision (1) of subsection (a) of this section must:

(1) Be witnessed by at least two adults, at least one of whom is a disinterested witness, who have signed at the request of the individual; and

(2) State that it has been signed and witnessed as provided in subdivision (1) of this subsection.

(c) An individual who has made a refusal may amend or revoke the refusal:

(1) In the manner provided in subsection (a) of this section for making a refusal;

(2) By subsequently making an anatomical gift pursuant to G.S. 130A-412.7 that is inconsistent with the refusal; or

(3) By destroying or canceling the record evidencing the refusal, or the portion of the record used to make the refusal, with the intent to revoke the refusal.

(d) Except as otherwise provided in G.S. 130A-412.10(h), in the absence of an express, contrary indication by the individual set forth in the refusal, an individual's unrevoked refusal to make an anatomical gift of the individual's body or body part bars all other persons from making an anatomical gift of the individual's body or body part. (2007-538, s. 1.)

§ 130A-412.10. Preclusive effect of an anatomical gift, amendment, or revocation.

(a) Except as otherwise provided in subsection (g) of this section and subject to subsection (f) of this section, in the absence of an express, contrary indication by the donor, a person other than the donor is barred from making, amending, or revoking an anatomical gift of a donor's body or body part if either of the following apply:

(1) The donor made an anatomical gift of the donor's body or body part under G.S. 130A-412.7.

(2) The donor made an amendment to an anatomical gift of the donor's body or body part under G.S. 130A-412.8.

(b) A donor's revocation of an anatomical gift of the donor's body or body part under G.S. 130A-412.8 is not a refusal and does not bar another person specified in G.S. 130A-412.6 or G.S. 130A-412.11 from making an anatomical gift of the donor's body or body part under G.S. 130A-412.7 or G.S. 130A-412.12.

(c) If a person other than the donor makes an unrevoked anatomical gift of the donor's body or body part under G.S. 130A-412.7 or an amendment to an anatomical gift of the donor's body or body part under G.S. 130A-412.8, another person may not make, amend, or revoke the gift of the donor's body or body part under G.S. 130A-412.12.

(d) A revocation of an anatomical gift of a donor's body or body part under G.S. 130A-412.8 by a person other than the donor does not bar another person from making an anatomical gift of the body or body part under G.S. 130A-412.7 or G.S. 130A-412.12.

(e) In the absence of an express, contrary indication by the donor or other person authorized to make an anatomical gift under G.S. 130A-412.6, an anatomical gift of a body part is neither a refusal to give another body part nor a limitation on the making of an anatomical gift of another body part at a later time by the donor or another person.

(f)   In the absence of an express, contrary indication by the donor or other person authorized to make an anatomical gift under G.S. 130A-412.6, an anatomical gift of a body part for one or more of the purposes set forth in G.S. 130A-412.6 is not a limitation on the making of an anatomical gift of the body part for any of the other purposes by the donor or any other person under G.S. 130A-412.7 or G.S. 130A-412.12.

(g)   If a donor who is an unemancipated minor dies, a parent of the donor who is reasonably available may revoke or amend an anatomical gift of the donor's body or body part.

(h)   If an unemancipated minor who signed a refusal dies, a parent of the minor who is reasonably available may revoke the minor's refusal. (2007-538, s. 1.)

§ 130A-412.11. Who may make an anatomical gift of decedent's body or body part.

(a)   Subject to subsections (b) and (c) of this section, and unless barred by G.S. 130A-412.9 or G.S. 130A-412.10, an anatomical gift of a decedent's body or body part for purpose of transplantation, therapy, research, or education may be made by any member of the following classes of persons who is reasonably available, in the order of priority listed:

(1)   An agent of the decedent at the time of death who could have made an anatomical gift under G.S. 130A-412.6(2) immediately before the decedent's death;

(2)   The spouse of the decedent;

(3)   Adult children of the decedent;

(4)   Parents of the decedent;

(5)   Adult siblings of the decedent;

(6) Adult grandchildren of the decedent;

(7) Grandparents of the decedent;

(8) An adult who exhibited special care and concern for the decedent;

(9) The persons who were acting as the guardians of the person of the decedent at the time of death; and

(10) Any other person having the authority to dispose of the decedent's body.

(b) If there is more than one member of a class listed in subdivision (a)(1), (3), (4), (5), (6), (7), or (9) of this section entitled to make an anatomical gift, an anatomical gift may be made by a member of the class unless that member or a person to which the gift may pass under G.S. 130A-412.13 knows of an objection by another member of the class. If an objection is known, the gift may be made only by a majority of the members of the class who are reasonably available.

(c) A person may not make an anatomical gift if, at the time of the decedent's death, a person in a prior class under subsection (a) of this section is reasonably available to make or to object to the making of an anatomical gift. (2007-538, s. 1.)

§ 130A-412.12. Manner of making, amending, or revoking anatomical gift of decedent's body or body part.

(a) A person authorized to make an anatomical gift under G.S. 130A-412.11 may make an anatomical gift by a document of gift signed by the person making the gift or by that person's oral communication that is electronically recorded or is contemporaneously reduced to a record and signed by the individual receiving the oral communication.

(b) Subject to subsection (c) of this section, an anatomical gift by a person authorized under G.S. 130A-412.11 may be amended or revoked orally or in a record by any member of a prior class who is reasonably available. If more than one member of the prior class is reasonably available, the gift made by a person authorized under G.S. 130A-412.11 may be:

(1) Amended only if a majority of the reasonably available members agrees to the amending of the gift; or

(2) Revoked only if a majority of the reasonably available members agrees to the revoking of the gift or if they are equally divided as to whether to revoke the gift.

(c) A revocation under subsection (b) of this section is effective only if, before an incision has been made to remove a body part from the donor's body or before invasive procedures have begun to prepare the recipient, the procurement organization, transplant hospital, or physician or technician knows of the revocation. (2007-538, s. 1.)

§ 130A-412.13. Persons that may receive anatomical gift; purpose of anatomical gift.

(a) An anatomical gift may be made to the following persons named in the document of gift:

(1) A hospital; accredited medical school, dental school, college, or university; organ procurement organization; or other appropriate person, including the Commission on Anatomy, for research or education;

(2) Subject to subsection (b) of this section, an individual designated by the person making the anatomical gift if the individual is the recipient of the body part;

(3) An eye bank or tissue bank.

(b) If an anatomical gift to an individual under subdivision (a)(2) of this section cannot be transplanted into the individual, the body part passes in accordance with subsection (g) of this section in the absence of an express, contrary indication by the person making the anatomical gift.

(c) If an anatomical gift of one or more specific body parts or of all body parts is made in a document of gift that does not name a person described in subsection (a) of this section but identifies the purpose for which an anatomical gift may be used, the following rules apply:

(1) If the body part is an eye and the gift is for the purpose of transplantation or therapy, the gift passes to the appropriate eye bank.

(2) If the body part is tissue and the gift is for the purpose of transplantation or therapy, the gift passes to the appropriate tissue bank.

(3) If the body part is an organ and the gift is for the purpose of transplantation or therapy, the gift passes to the appropriate organ procurement organization as custodian of the organ.

(4) If the body part is an organ, an eye, or tissue and the gift is for the purpose of research or education, the gift passes to the appropriate procurement organization.

(d) For the purpose of subsection (c) of this section, if there is more than one purpose of an anatomical gift set forth in the document of gift but the purposes are not set forth in any priority, the gift must be used for transplantation or therapy, if suitable. If the gift cannot be used for transplantation or therapy, the gift may be used for research or education.

(e) If an anatomical gift of one or more specific body parts is made in a document of gift that does not name a person described in subsection (a) of this section and does not identify the purpose of the gift, the gift may be used only for transplantation or therapy, and the gift passes in accordance with subsection (g) of this section.

(f) If a document of gift specifies only a general intent to make an anatomical gift by words such as "donor," "organ donor," or "body donor," or by a symbol or statement of similar import, the gift may be used only for transplantation or therapy, and the gift passes in accordance with subsection (g) of this section.

(g) For purposes of subsections (b), (e), and (f) of this section, the following rules apply:

(1) If the body part is an eye, the gift passes to the appropriate eye bank.

(2) If the body part is tissue, the gift passes to the appropriate tissue bank.

(3) If the body part is an organ, the gift passes to the appropriate organ procurement organization as custodian of the organ.

(h) An anatomical gift of an organ for transplantation or therapy, other than an anatomical gift under subdivision (a)(2) of this section, passes to the organ procurement organization as custodian of the organ.

(i) If an anatomical gift does not pass pursuant to subsections (a) through (h) of this section or the decedent's body or body part is not used for transplantation, therapy, research, or education, then custody of the body or body part passes to the person under obligation to dispose of the body or body part.

(j) A person may not accept an anatomical gift if the person knows that the gift was not effectively made under G.S. 130A-412.7 or G.S. 130A-412.12 or if the person knows that the decedent made a refusal under G.S. 130A-412.9 that was not revoked. For purposes of this subsection, if a person knows that an anatomical gift was made on a document of gift, the person is deemed to know of any amendment or revocation of the gift or any refusal to make an anatomical gift on the same document of gift.

(k) Except as otherwise provided in subdivision (a)(2) of this section, nothing in this act affects the allocation of organs for transplantation or therapy. (2007-538, s. 1.)

§ 130A-412.14. Search and notification.

A search of an individual who is reasonably believed to be dead or near death for a document of gift or other information identifying the individual as a donor or as an individual who made a refusal, and, if applicable, notification of the hospital to which the individual is taken, shall be governed by G.S. 90-602. (2007-538, s. 1; 2008-153, s. 2.)

§ 130A-412.15. Delivery of document of gift not required; right to examine.

(a) A document of gift need not be delivered during the donor's lifetime to be effective.

(b) Upon or after an individual's death, a person in possession of a document of gift or a refusal to make an anatomical gift with respect to the individual shall allow examination and copying of the document of gift or refusal by a person authorized to make or object to the making of an anatomical gift with respect to the individual or by a person to which the gift could pass under G.S. 130A-412.13. (2007-538, s. 1.)

§ 130A-412.16. Rights and duties of procurement organization and others.

(a) When a hospital refers an individual at or near death to a procurement organization, the organization shall make a reasonable search of the records of the North Carolina Department of Transportation, Division of Motor Vehicles, and any donor registry that it knows exists for the geographical area in which the individual resides to ascertain whether the individual has made an anatomical gift.

(b) A procurement organization must be allowed reasonable access to information in the records of the North Carolina Department of Transportation, Division of Motor Vehicles, to ascertain whether an individual at or near death is a donor.

(c) When a hospital refers an individual at or near death to a procurement organization, the organization may conduct any reasonable examination necessary to ensure the medical suitability of a body part that is or could be the subject of an anatomical gift for transplantation, therapy, research, or education from a donor or a prospective donor. During the examination period, measures necessary to ensure the medical suitability of the body part may not be withdrawn unless the hospital or procurement organization knows that the individual expressed a contrary intent.

(d) Unless prohibited by law other than this Part, at any time after a donor's death, the person to which a body part passes under G.S. 130A-412.13 may conduct any reasonable examination necessary to ensure the medical suitability of the body or body part for its intended purpose.

(e) Unless otherwise prohibited by law, an examination under subsection (c) or (d) of this section may include an examination of all medical and dental records of the donor or prospective donor.

(f) Upon the death of a minor who was a donor or had signed a refusal, unless a procurement organization knows the minor is emancipated, the procurement organization shall conduct a reasonable search for the parents of the minor and provide the parents with an opportunity to revoke or amend the anatomical gift or revoke the refusal.

(g)   Upon referral by a hospital under subsection (a) of this section, a procurement organization shall make a reasonable search for any person listed in G.S. 130A-412.11 having priority to make an anatomical gift on behalf of a prospective donor. If a procurement organization receives information that an anatomical gift to any other person was made, amended, or revoked, it shall promptly advise the other person of all relevant information.

(h)   Subject to G.S. 130A-412.13(i) and G.S. 130A-412.25, the rights of the person to which a body part passes under G.S. 130A-412.13 are superior to the rights of all others with respect to the body part. The person may accept or reject an anatomical gift in whole or in part. Subject to the terms of the document of gift and this Part, a person that accepts an anatomical gift of an entire body may allow embalming, burial, or cremation, and use of remains in a funeral service. If the gift is of a body part, the person to which the body part passes under G.S. 130A-412.13, upon the death of the donor and before embalming, burial, or cremation, shall cause the body part to be removed without unnecessary mutilation.

(i)   Neither the physician who attends the decedent at death nor the physician who determines the time of the decedent's death may participate in the procedures for removing or transplanting a part from the decedent.

(j)   A physician or technician may remove a donated body part from the body of a donor that the physician or technician is qualified to remove. (2007-538, s. 1.)

§ 130A-412.17. Coordination of procurement and use.

Each hospital in this State shall enter into agreements or affiliations with procurement organizations for coordination of procurement and use of anatomical gifts. (2007-538, s. 1.)

§ 130A-412.18. Sale or purchase of body parts prohibited.

(a) Except as otherwise provided in subsection (b) of this section, a person, that for valuable consideration, knowingly purchases or sells a body part for transplantation or therapy if removal of a body part from an individual is intended to occur after the individual's death commits a Class H felony and upon conviction may be fined up to fifty thousand dollars ($50,000) for each offense.

(b) A person may charge a reasonable amount for the removal, processing, preservation, quality control, storage, transportation, implantation, or disposal of a body part. (2007-538, s. 1.)

§ 130A-412.19. Other prohibited acts.

A person that, in order to obtain a financial gain, intentionally falsifies, forges, conceals, defaces, or obliterates a document of gift, an amendment or revocation of a document of gift, or a refusal commits a Class H felony and upon conviction may be fined up to fifty thousand dollars ($50,000) for each offense. (2007-538, s. 1.)

§ 130A-412.20. Immunity.

(a) A person that acts with due care in accordance with this Part or with the applicable anatomical gift law of another state, or attempts in good faith to do so, is not liable for the act in a civil action, criminal prosecution, or administrative proceeding.

(b) Neither the person making an anatomical gift nor the donor's estate is liable for any injury or damage that results from the making or use of the gift.

(c) In determining whether an anatomical gift has been made, amended, or revoked under this Part, a person may rely upon representations of an individual listed in subdivisions (2) through (8) of G.S. 130A-412.11(a) relating to the individual's relationship to the donor or prospective donor unless the person knows that the representation is untrue. (2007-538, s. 1.)

§ 130A-412.21. Law governing validity; choice of law as to execution of document of gift; presumption of validity.

(a)   A document of gift is valid if executed in accordance with:

(1)   This Part;

(2)   The laws of the state or country where it was executed; or

(3)   The laws of the state or country where the person making the anatomical gift was domiciled, has a place of residence, or was a national at the time the document of gift was executed.

(b)   If a document of gift is valid under this section, the law of this State governs the interpretation of the document of gift.

(c)   A person may presume that a document of gift or amendment of an anatomical gift is valid unless that person knows that it was not validly executed or was revoked. (2007-538, s. 1.)

§ 130A-412.22. Donor registry.

The online Organ Donor Registry Internet site established pursuant to G.S. 20-43.2 shall be the State donor registry for anatomical gifts made pursuant to this Part. Requirements for maintenance and use of the State donor registry shall be as provided under G.S. 20-43.2. (2007-538, s. 1.)

§ 130A-412.23. Cooperation between a medical examiner and the procurement organization.

(a)   The medical examiner shall cooperate with procurement organizations to maximize the opportunity to recover anatomical gifts for the purpose of transplantation, therapy, research, or education.

(b)   If a medical examiner receives notice from a procurement organization that an anatomical gift might be available or was made with respect to a decedent whose body is under the jurisdiction of the medical examiner and a postmortem examination is going to be performed, unless the medical examiner denies recovery in accordance with G.S. 130A-412.24, the medical examiner or designee shall conduct a postmortem examination of the body or the body part in a manner and within a period compatible with its preservation for the purposes of the gift.

(c) A body part may not be removed from the body of a decedent under the jurisdiction of a medical examiner for transplantation, therapy, research, or education unless the body part is the subject of an anatomical gift. The body of a decedent under the jurisdiction of the medical examiner may not be delivered to a person for research or education unless the body is the subject of an anatomical gift. This subsection does not preclude a medical examiner from performing the medicolegal investigation upon the body or body parts of a decedent under the jurisdiction of the medical examiner.

(d) As used in this section and G.S. 130A-412.24, "medical examiner" includes the Chief Medical Examiner, a county medical examiner, or a designee of either. (2007-538, s. 1.)

§ 130A-412.24. Facilitation of anatomical gift from decedent whose body is under the jurisdiction of a medical examiner.

(a) Upon request of a procurement organization, a medical examiner shall release to the procurement organization the name, contact information, and available medical and social history of a decedent whose body is or will come under the jurisdiction of the medical examiner. If the decedent's body or body part is medically suitable for transplantation, therapy, research, or education, the medical examiner shall release postmortem examination results to the procurement organization. The procurement organization may make a subsequent disclosure of the postmortem examination results or other information received from the medical examiner only if relevant to transplantation or therapy.

(b) The medical examiner may conduct a medicolegal examination, including physical examination of a donor or prospective donor and review of all medical records, laboratory test results, X-rays, other diagnostic results, and other information that any person possesses about a donor or prospective donor whose body is under the jurisdiction of the medical examiner or whose body would be under the medical examiner's jurisdiction upon death and that the medical examiner determines may be relevant to the investigation.

(c)   A person that has any information requested by a medical examiner pursuant to subsection (b) of this section shall provide that information as expeditiously as possible to allow the medical examiner to conduct the medicolegal investigation within a period compatible with the preservation of body parts for the purpose of transplantation, therapy, research, or education.

(d)   If an anatomical gift has been or might be made of a body part of a decedent whose body is under the jurisdiction of the medical examiner and a postmortem examination is not required, or the medical examiner determines that a postmortem examination is required but that the recovery of the body part that is the subject of an anatomical gift will not interfere with the examination, the medical examiner and procurement organization shall cooperate in the timely removal of the body part from the decedent for the purpose of transplantation, therapy, research, or education.

(e)   If an anatomical gift of a body part from the decedent under the jurisdiction of the medical examiner has been or might be made, but the medical examiner initially believes that the recovery of the body part could interfere with the postmortem investigation into the decedent's cause or manner of death, the collection of evidence, or the description, documentation, or interpretation of injuries on the body, the medical examiner shall consult with the procurement organization or physician or technician designated by the procurement organization about the proposed recovery. After consultation, the medical examiner may deny or allow the recovery.

(f)   If the medical examiner or designee allows recovery of a body part under subsection (d) or (e) of this section, the procurement organization shall provide the medical examiner or designee with a record describing the condition of the body part signed by the physician or technician who removes the body part and any other information and observations that would assist in the postmortem examination. (2007-538, s. 1.)

§ 130A-412.25: Reserved for future codification purposes.

§ 130A-412.26: Reserved for future codification purposes.

§ 130A-412.27: Reserved for future codification purposes.

§ 130A-412.28: Reserved for future codification purposes.

§ 130A-412.29: Reserved for future codification purposes.

§ 130A-412.30. Use of tissue declared a service; standard of care; burden of proof.

The procurement, processing, distribution or use of whole blood, plasma, blood products, blood derivatives and other human tissues such as corneas, bones or organs for the purpose of injecting, transfusing or transplanting any of them into the human body is declared to be, for all purposes, the rendition of a service by every participating person or institution. Whether or not any remuneration is paid, the service is declared not to be a sale of whole blood, plasma, blood products, blood derivatives or other human tissues, for any purpose. No person or institution shall be liable in warranty, express or implied, for the procurement, processing, distribution or use of these items but nothing in this section shall alter or restrict the liability of a person or institution in negligence or tort in consequence of these services. (1971, c. 836; 1983, c. 891, s. 2; 2007-538, s. 3(a).)

§ 130A-412.31. Giving of blood by persons 16 years of age or more.

A person who is 16 years of age or more may give or donate blood to an individual, hospital, blood bank or blood collection center without the consent of the parent or parents or guardian of the donor. It shall be unlawful for a person under the age of 18 years to sell blood. (1971, c. 10; c. 1093, s. 16; 1977, c. 373; 1983, c. 891, s. 2; 2007-538, s. 3(a); 2008-153, s. 9.)

§ 130A-412.32. Duty of hospitals to establish organ procurement protocols.

(a) In order to facilitate the goals of this Part, each hospital shall establish written protocols that:

(1) Require that only the organ procurement organization designated by the Secretary of Health and Human Services be notified of all deaths or impending

brain deaths meeting criteria for notification as established by the designated organ procurement organization; and

(2) Ensure that notification required under subdivision (1) of this subsection be made as soon as it is determined that brain death is imminent or cardiac death has occurred.

(b) Hospitals shall provide their federally designated organ procurement organizations and tissue banks reasonable access to patients' medical records for the purpose of determining organ or tissue donation potential.

(c) The family of any person whose organ or tissue is donated for transplantation shall not be financially liable for any costs related to the evaluation of the suitability of the donor's organ or tissue for transplantation, or for any costs of retrieval of the organ or tissue.

(d) Each hospital shall provide its federally designated organ procurement organization with reasonable access during regular business hours to the medical records of deceased patients for the following purposes:

(1) Determining the hospital's organ and tissue donation potential;

(2) Assessing the educational needs of the hospital in regard to the organ and tissue donation process; and

(3) Providing documentation to the hospital to evaluate the effectiveness of the hospital's efforts.

(e) Each hospital shall have a signed agreement with its federally designated organ procurement organization that addresses the requirements of this section and the requirements of G.S. 130A-412.33.

(f) The requirements of this section, or of any hospital procurement protocols established pursuant to this section, shall not exceed those provided for by the hospital organ protocol provisions of Title XI of the Social Security Act, except for the purposes of this section the term "organ and tissue donors" shall include cornea and tissue donors for transplantation.

(g) Hospitals and hospital personnel shall not be subject to civil or criminal liability nor to discipline for unprofessional conduct for actions taken in good faith to comply with this section. This subsection shall not provide immunity from civil liability arising from gross negligence. (1987, c. 719, s. 1; 1989, c. 537, s. 4; 1997-192, s. 2; 1997-456, s. 48; 2007-538, ss. 3(a), 4.)

§ 130A-412.33. Duty of designated organ procurement organizations and tissue banks.

(a) After notification regarding an impending brain death, brain death, or cardiac death has been made to the federally designated organ procurement organization, the federally designated organ procurement organization shall evaluate donation potential.

(b) The federally designated organ procurement organization or tissue bank shall assure that families of potential organ and tissue donors are made aware of the option of organ and tissue donation and their option to decline.

(c) The federally designated organ procurement organization or tissue bank shall, working collaboratively with the hospital, request consent for organ or tissue donation in the order of priority established under G.S. 130A-412.11 and shall have designated, trained staff available to perform the consent process 24 hours a day, 365 days a year.

(d) The federally designated organ procurement organization or tissue bank shall encourage discretion and sensitivity with respect to the circumstances, views, and beliefs of the families of potential organ and tissue donors.

(e) All hospital and patient information, interviews, reports, statements, memoranda, and other data obtained or created by a tissue bank or federally designated organ procurement organization from the medical records review described in G.S. 130A-412.33 shall be privileged and confidential and may be used by the tissue bank or federally designated organ procurement organization only for the purposes set forth in G.S. 130A-412.33 and shall not be subject to discovery or introduction as evidence in any civil action, suit, or proceeding. However, hospital and patient information, interviews, reports, statements, memoranda, and other data otherwise available are not immune from discovery or use in a civil action, suit, or proceeding merely because they were obtained or created by a tissue bank or federally designated organ procurement organization from the medical records review described in G.S. 130A-412.33.

(f)   If the hospital is made a party of any action, suit, or proceeding arising out of the failure of a federally designated organ procurement organization or tissue bank to comply with the requirements of this section, the hospital shall be held harmless from any and all liability and costs, including the amounts of judgments, settlements, fines, or penalties, and expenses and reasonable attorneys' fees incurred in connection with the action, suit, or proceeding. (1997-192, s. 3; 2007-538, ss. 3(a), 5, 6.)

Part 4. Human Tissue Donation Program.

§ 130A-413. Coordinated human tissue donation program; legislative findings and purpose; program established.

(a)   The General Assembly finds that there is an increasing need for human tissues for transplantation purposes; that there is a continuing need for human tissues for the purposes of medical education and research; and that these needs are not being sufficiently filled at the present because of a shortage of human tissue donors. The General Assembly establishes a coordinated human tissue donation program to facilitate the acquisition and distribution of human tissues to promote the public health. For the purposes of this Part, the term "human tissue" includes cadavers.

(b)   The Department shall establish and administer a coordinated program among departments and agencies of the State and all groups, both public and private, involved in the acquisition and distribution of human tissue to:

(1)   Increase awareness of the need for human tissue donations and of the methods by which these donations are made;

(2)   Increase awareness of the existing programs of human tissue transplantation and of medical research and education which employs human tissue and share information with the public;

(3)   Study the problems surrounding the acquisition and distribution of human tissue and make suggestions for their solution;

(4)   Disseminate information to health and other professionals concerning the techniques of human tissue retrieval and transplantation, the legalities involved in making anatomical gifts; and

(5) Arrange for the quick and precise transportation of donated human tissue in emergency transplant situations.

(c) All departments and agencies of the State and county and municipal law-enforcement agencies shall cooperate with the coordinated human tissue donation program instituted by the Department. (1983, c. 891, s. 2.)

§ 130A-414. Repealed by Session Laws 1987, c. 719, s. 2.

Part 5. Disposition of Unclaimed Bodies.

§ 130A-415. Unclaimed bodies; bodies claimed by the Lifeguardianship Council of the Association for Retarded Citizens of North Carolina; disposition.

(a) Any person, including officers, employees and agents of the State or of any unit of local government in the State, undertakers doing business within the State, hospitals, nursing homes or other institutions, having physical possession of a dead body shall make reasonable efforts to contact relatives of the deceased or other persons who may wish to claim the body for final disposition. If the body remains unclaimed for final disposition for 10 days, the person having possession shall notify the Commission of Anatomy. Upon request of the Commission of Anatomy, the person having possession shall deliver the dead body to the Commission of Anatomy at a time and place specified by the Commission of Anatomy or shall permit the Commission of Anatomy to take and remove the body.

(b) All dead bodies not claimed for final disposition within 10 days of the decedent's death may be received and delivered by the Commission of Anatomy pursuant to the authority contained in G.S. 130A-33.30 and this Part and in accordance with the rules of the Commission of Anatomy. Upon receipt of a body by the Commission of Anatomy all interests in and rights to the unclaimed dead body shall vest in the Commission of Anatomy. The recipient to which the Commission of Anatomy delivers the body shall pay all expenses for the embalming and delivery of the body, and for the reasonable expenses arising from efforts to notify relatives or others.

(b1)   The 10-day period referenced in subsections (a) and (b) of this section may be shortened by the county director of social services upon determination that a dead body will not be claimed for final disposition within the 10-day period.

(c)   Should the Commission of Anatomy decline to receive a dead body, the person with possession shall inform the director of social services of the county in which the body is located. The director of social services of that county shall arrange for prompt final disposition of the body, either by cremation or burial. Reasonable costs of disposition and of efforts made to notify relatives and others shall be considered funeral expenses and shall be paid in accordance with G.S. 28A-19-6 and G.S. 28A-19-8. If those expenses cannot be satisfied from the decedent's estate, they shall be borne by the decedent's county of residence. If the deceased is not a resident of this State, or if the county of residence is unknown, those expenses shall be borne by the county in which the death occurred.

(d)   No autopsy shall be performed on an unclaimed body without the written consent of the Commission of Anatomy except that written consent is not required for an autopsy performed pursuant to Part 2 of this Article.

(e)   Due caution shall be taken to shield the unclaimed body from public view.

(f)   Notwithstanding anything contained in this section, an unclaimed body shall not mean a dead body for which the deceased has made a gift pursuant to Part 3A of this Article.

(g)   Nothing in this Part shall require the officers, employees or agents of a county to notify the Commission of Anatomy regarding the bodies of minors who were in the custody of the county at the time of death and whose final disposition will be arranged by the county. In the absence of notification, the expenses of the final disposition shall be a charge upon the county having custody.

(h)   The provisions of this Part shall not apply to bodies within the jurisdiction of the medical examiner under G.S. 130A-383 or 130A-384.

(i)   In addition to the other duties of the Commission of Anatomy, when the Commission of Anatomy is notified by the Lifeguardianship Council of the Association of Retarded Citizens of North Carolina, Inc., that the Council intends to claim a body, the Commission shall release the body to the Council. The Lifeguardianship Council shall notify the Commission of Anatomy within 24 hours after death of its intent to claim a body for burial or other humane and caring disposition. (1975, c. 694, s. 3; 1977, c. 458; 1983, c. 891, s. 2; 1987, c. 470; 1989, c. 222; c. 770, s. 75; 2008-153, s. 7.)

§ 130A-416. Commission of Anatomy rules.

The Commission of Anatomy is authorized to adopt rules necessary to implement the provisions of this Part. (1983, c. 891, s. 2.)

Part 6. Final Disposition or Transportation of Deceased Migrant Agricultural Workers and Their Dependents.

§ 130A-417. Definitions.

The following definitions shall apply throughout this Part:

(1)   "Dependent" means child, grandchild, spouse or parent of a migrant agricultural worker who moves with the migrant agricultural worker in response to the demand for seasonal agricultural labor.

(2)   "Migrant agricultural worker" means a worker who moves in response to the demand for seasonal agricultural labor. (1983, c. 891, s. 2.)

§ 130A-418. Deceased migrant agricultural workers and their dependents.

(a)   Notwithstanding any other provisions of law, a person having knowledge of the death of a migrant agricultural worker or a worker's dependent shall without delay report the death to the department of social services in the county in which the body is located together with any information regarding the deceased including identity, place of employment, permanent residence, and the name, address and telephone number of any relative and any interested person. The county department of social services shall, within a reasonable time of receiving this report, transmit to the Department notice of the death and information received upon notification. The Department shall make reasonable effort to inform the next-of-kin and any interested person of the death.

(b)   If the identity of the person cannot be determined within a reasonable period of time, or if the body is unclaimed 10 days after death, the body shall be offered to the Commission of Anatomy and, upon its request, shall be delivered to the Commission of Anatomy. If the Commission of Anatomy does not request an unclaimed body offered it or the estate, and if the relatives or other interested persons claiming the body are unable to provide for the final disposition of the migrant agricultural worker or dependent, the Department is authorized and directed to arrange for the final disposition of the decedent.

(c)   If the estate, relatives or interested persons are able to provide for final disposition but are unable to effect the transportation of the decedent to the decedent's legal residence or the legal residence of the relatives or interested persons, the Department is authorized and directed to allocate a sum of not more than two hundred dollars ($200.00) to defray the transportation expenses.

(d)   The Secretary is authorized to adopt rules necessary to implement this section. (1975, c. 891; 1977, c. 648; 1983, c. 891, s. 2.)

§ 130A-419. Reserved for future codification purposes.

Part 7. Disposition of Body or Body Parts.

§ 130A-420. Authority to dispose of body or body parts.

(a)   An individual at least 18 years of age may authorize the type, place, and method of disposition of the individual's own dead body by methods in the following order:

(1)   Pursuant to a preneed funeral contract executed pursuant to Article 13D of Chapter 90 of the General Statutes or pursuant to a cremation authorization form executed pursuant to Article 13C of Chapter 90 of the General Statutes.

(2)   Pursuant to a health care power of attorney to the extent provided in Article 3 of Chapter 32A of the General Statutes.

(3) Pursuant to a written will.

(4) Pursuant to a written statement other than a will signed by the individual and witnessed by two persons who are at least 18 years old.

(a1) An individual at least 18 years of age may delegate his or her right to dispose of his or her own dead human body to any person by one of the following methods:

(1) Any means authorized in subsection (a) of this section.

(2) By completing United States Department of Defense Record of Emergency Data, DD Form 93, or its successor form. A delegation made by filling out this form shall only be effective if the individual dies under the circumstances described in 10 U.S.C. § 1481(a)(1) through (8). A delegation under this subdivision takes precedence over any of the methods set forth in this section.

(b) If a decedent has left no written authorization for the disposal of the decedent's body as permitted under subsection (a) of this section, the following competent persons in the order listed may authorize the type, method, place, and disposition of the decedent's body:

(1) The surviving spouse.

(2) A majority of the surviving children over 18 years of age, who can be located after reasonable efforts.

(3) The surviving parents.

(4) A majority of the surviving siblings over 18 years of age, who can be located after reasonable efforts.

(5) A majority of the persons in the classes of the next degrees of kinship, in descending order, who, under State law, would inherit the decedent's estate if the decedent died intestate who are at least 18 years of age and can be located after reasonable efforts.

(6) A person who has exhibited special care and concern for the decedent and is willing and able to make decisions about the disposition.

(7) In the case of indigents or any other individuals whose final disposition is the responsibility of the State or any of its instrumentalities, a public administrator, medical examiner, coroner, State-appointed guardian, or any other public official charged with arranging the final disposition of the decedent.

(8) In the case of individuals who have donated their bodies to science or whose death occurred in a nursing home or private institution and in which the institution is charged with making arrangements for the final disposition of the decedent, a representative of the institution.

(9) In the absence of any of the persons described in subdivisions (1) through (8) of this subsection, any person willing to assume responsibility for the disposition of the body.

This subsection does not grant to any person the right to cancel a preneed funeral contract executed pursuant to Article 13D of Chapter 90 of the General Statutes, to prohibit the substitution of a preneed licensee as authorized under G.S. 90-210.63, or to permit modification of preneed contracts under G.S. 90-210.63A. If an individual is incompetent at the time of the decedent's death, the individual shall be treated as if he or she predeceased the decedent. An attending physician may certify the incompetence of an individual and the certification shall apply to the rights under this section only. Any individual under this section may waive his or her rights under this subsection by any written statement notarized by a notary public or signed by two witnesses.

(b1) A person who does not exercise his or her right to dispose of the decedent's body under subsection (b) of this section within five days of notification or 10 days from the date of death, whichever is earlier, shall be deemed to have waived his or her right to authorize disposition of the decedent's body or contest disposition in accordance with this section.

(c) An individual at least 18 years of age may, in a writing signed by the individual, authorize the disposition of one or more of the individual's body parts that has been or will be removed. If the individual does not authorize the disposition, a person listed in subsection (b) of this section may authorize the disposition as if the individual was deceased.

(d) This section does not apply to the disposition of dead human bodies as anatomical gifts under Part 3A of Article 16 of Chapter 130A of the General Statutes or the right to perform autopsies under Part 2 of Article 16 of Chapter

130A of the General Statutes. (1997-399, s. 34; 2007-531, s. 26; 2008-153, s. 8; 2010-191, s. 1.)

§ 130A-421. Reserved for future codification purposes.

Article 17.

Childhood Vaccine-Related Injury Compensation Program.

§ 130A-422. Definitions.

The following definitions apply throughout this Article, unless the context clearly implies otherwise:

(1) "Claimant" means any person who files a claim for compensation for a vaccine-related injury pursuant to G.S. 130A-425(b). In the case of a minor or incompetent, a claim may be filed by a guardian ad litem, parent, guardian, or other legal representative; and, in the case of a decedent, the claim may be filed by an administrator, executor, or other legal representative.

In the event that more than one person claims to have suffered compensable injuries as the result of the administration of a covered vaccine to a single individual, all these persons shall be treated for purposes of this Article as if they were a single claimant. A single joint claim shall be filed on behalf of all these persons, and the limitations on awards set forth in G.S. 130A-427(b) apply to that joint claim or subsequent joint action as if it were a claim filed on behalf of a single individual.

(2) "Commission" means the North Carolina Industrial Commission.

(3) "Covered vaccine" means a vaccine administered pursuant to the requirements of G.S. 130A-152.

(4) "Respondent" means the person or entity the claimant identifies in the claim as the agent of causality of the vaccine-related injury.

(5) "Vaccine-related injury", with respect to persons engaged in the manufacture, distribution, or sale, or administration of a covered vaccine, means any injury, disability, illness, death, or condition caused by the vaccine. "Vaccine-related injury" shall not mean any injury, disability, illness, death, or

condition caused by the method of injection of the vaccine into the body. (1985 (Reg. Sess., 1986), c. 1008, s. 1; 1987, c. 215, s. 8.)

§ 130A-423. North Carolina Childhood Vaccine-Related Injury Compensation Program; exclusive remedy; relationship to federal law; subrogation.

(a)   There is established the North Carolina Childhood Vaccine-Related Injury Compensation Program.

(b)   The rights and remedies granted the claimant, the claimant's parent, guardian ad litem, guardian, or personal representative shall exclude all other rights and remedies of the claimant, his parent, guardian ad litem, guardian, or personal representative against any respondent at common law or otherwise on account of injury, illness, disability, death, or condition. If an action is filed, it shall be dismissed, with prejudice, on the motion of any party under law.

(b1)   A claimant may file a petition pursuant to this Article only after the claimant has filed an election pursuant to Section 2121 of the Public Health Service Act, P.L. 99-660, permitting the claimant to file a civil action for damages for a vaccine-related injury or death or if the claimant is otherwise permitted by federal law to file an action against a vaccine manufacturer.

(c)   Nothing in this Article prohibits any individual from bringing a civil action against a vaccine manufacturer for damages for a vaccine-related injury or death if the action is not barred by federal law under subtitle 2 of Title XXI of the Public Health Service Act.

(d)   If any action is brought against a vaccine manufacturer as permitted by subtitle 2 of Title XXI of the Public Health Service Act and subsection (c) of this section, the plaintiff in the action may recover damages only to the extent permitted by subdivisions (1) through (3) of subsection (a) of G.S. 130A-427. The aggregate amount awarded in any action may not exceed the limitation established by subsection (b) of G.S. 130A-427. Regardless of whether an action is brought against a vaccine manufacturer, a claimant who has filed an election pursuant to Section 2121 of the Public Health Service Act, as enacted into federal law by Public Law 99-660, permitting a claimant to file a civil action for damages for a vaccine-related injury or death, or who is otherwise permitted by federal law to file an action against a vaccine manufacturer, may file a petition pursuant to G.S. 130A-425 to obtain services from the Department pursuant to subdivision (5) of subsection (a) of G.S. 130A-427 and, if no action has been brought against a vaccine manufacturer, to obtain other relief available pursuant to G.S. 130A-427.

(e) In order to prevent recovery of duplicate damages, or the imposition of duplicate liability, in the event that an individual seeks an award pursuant to G.S. 130A-427 and also files suit against the manufacturer as permitted by subtitle 2 of Title XXI of the Public Health Service Act and subsection (c) of this section, the following provisions shall apply:

(1) If, at the time an award is made pursuant to G.S. 130A-427, an individual has already recovered damages from a manufacturer pursuant to a judgment or settlement, the award shall consist only of a commitment to provide services pursuant to subdivision (5) of subsection (a) of G.S. 130A-427.

(2) If, at any time after an award is made to a claimant pursuant to G.S. 130A-427, an individual recovers damages for the same vaccine-related injury from a manufacturer pursuant to a judgment or settlement, the individual who recovers the damages shall reimburse the State for all amounts previously recovered from the State in the prior proceeding. Before a defendant in any action for a vaccine-related injury pays any amount to a plaintiff to discharge a judgment or settlement, he shall request from the Secretary a statement itemizing any reimbursement owed by the plaintiff pursuant to this subdivision, and, if any reimbursement is owed by the plaintiff to the Department, the defendant shall pay the reimbursable amounts, as determined by the Secretary, directly to the Department. This payment shall discharge the plaintiff's obligations to the State under this subdivision and any obligation the defendant may have to the plaintiff with respect to these amounts.

(3) If:

a. An award has been made to a claimant for an element of damages pursuant to G.S. 130A-427; and

b. An individual has recovered for the same element of damages pursuant to a judgment in, or settlement of, an action for the same vaccine-related injury brought against a manufacturer, and that amount has not been remitted to the State pursuant to subdivision (2) of this subsection; and

c. The State seeks to recover the amounts it paid in an action it brings against the manufacturer pursuant to G.S. 130A-430;

any judgment obtained by the State under G.S. 130A-430 shall be reduced by the amount necessary to prevent the double recovery of any element of damages from the manufacturer. Nothing in this subdivision limits the State's right to obtain reimbursement from a claimant under subdivision (2) of this subsection with respect to any double payment that might be received by the claimant.

(f)   Subrogation claims pursued under the National Childhood Vaccine Injury Act of 1986 shall be filed with the appropriate court, not with the Industrial Commission. (1985 (Reg. Sess., 1986), c. 1008, s. 1; 1987, c. 215, ss. 1, 2; 1989, c. 727, ss. 148, 149; 1991, c. 410, s. 1; 1997-443, s. 11A.85.)

§ 130A-424. Industrial Commission authorized to hear and determine claims; damages.

The North Carolina Industrial Commission is authorized to hear and pass upon all claims filed pursuant to this Article. The members of the Commission, or a deputy thereof, have power to issue subpoenas, administer oaths, conduct hearings, take evidence, enter orders, opinions, settlements, and awards, and punish for contempt. The Commission may appoint deputies and clerical assistants to carry out the purpose and intent of this Article, and this deputy or deputies are vested with the same power and authority to hear and determine claims filed pursuant to this Article as is by this Article vested in the members of the Commission. (1985 (Reg. Sess., 1986), c. 1008, s. 1.)

§ 130A-425. Filing of claims.

(a)   Notwithstanding any other provision of State law, no action for compensation for a vaccine-related injury may be filed against any person unless that person was named as a respondent in a claim filed pursuant to this section and unless the claim was filed within the applicable time period set forth in G.S. 130A-429.

(b)   In all claims filed pursuant to this Article, the claimant or the person in whose behalf the claim is made shall file with the Commission a verified petition in duplicate, setting forth the following information:

(1) The name and address of the claimant;

(2) The name and address of each respondent;

(3) The amount of compensation in money and services sought to be recovered;

(4) The time and place where the injury occurred;

(5) A brief statement of the facts and circumstances surrounding the injury and giving rise to the claim; and

(6) Supporting documentation and a statement of the claim that the claimant or the person in whose behalf the claim is made suffered a vaccine-related injury and has not previously collected an award or settlement of a civil action for damages for this injury. This supporting documentation shall include all available medical records pertaining to the alleged injury, including autopsy reports, if any, and if the injured person was under two years of age at the time of injury, all prenatal, obstetrical, and pediatric records of care preceding the injury, and an identification of any unavailable records known to the claimant or the person in whose behalf the claim is made.

(7) Documentation to show that the claimant has filed an election pursuant to Section 2121 of the Public Health Service Act, P.L. 99-660, permitting such claimant to file a civil action for damages for a vaccine-related injury or death or documentation to show that such claimant is otherwise permitted by federal law to file an action against a vaccine manufacturer.

(c) Upon receipt of this verified petition in duplicate, the Commission shall enter the case upon its hearing docket and shall determine the matter in the county where the injury occurred unless the parties agree or the Commission directs that the case may be heard in some other county. All parties shall be given reasonable notice of the date when and the place where the claim will be heard. Immediately upon receipt of the claim, the Commission shall serve a copy of the verified petition on each respondent by registered or certified mail. The Commission shall also send a copy of the verified petition to the Secretary, who shall be a party to all proceedings involving the claim, and to the Attorney General who shall represent the State's interest in all the proceedings involving the claim.

(d) The Commission shall adopt rules necessary to govern the proceedings required by this Article. The Rules of Civil Procedure as contained in G.S. 1A-1 et seq. and the General Rules of Practice for the Superior and District Courts as authorized by G.S. 7A-34 apply to claims filed with the Industrial Commission under this Article. The Commission shall keep a record of all proceedings conducted under this Article, and has the right to subpoena any persons and records it considers necessary in making its determinations. The Commission may require all persons called as witnesses to testify under oath or affirmation, and any member of the Commission may administer oaths. If any persons refuse to comply with any subpoena issued pursuant to this Article or to testify with respect to any matter relevant to proceedings conducted under this Article, the Superior Court of Wake County, on application of the Commission, may issue an order requiring the person to comply with the subpoena and to testify. Any failure to obey any such order may be punished by the court as for contempt. (1985 (Reg. Sess., 1986), c. 1008, s. 1; 1987, c. 215, s. 3; 1989, c. 727, s. 150; 1991, c. 410, s. 2.)

§ 130A-426. Determination of claims.

(a) The Commission shall determine, on the basis of the evidence presented to it, the following issues:

(1) Whether any injuries alleged in the claim are vaccine-related injuries; and

(2) How much compensation, if any, is awardable pursuant to G.S. 130A-427.

(b) If the Commission determines pursuant to subsection (a) of this section that the injuries alleged in the claim are not vaccine-related injuries, it shall render a decision denying any compensation. If the Commission decides that any of the injuries are vaccine-related injuries it shall make an award pursuant to guidelines it establishes specifically adopted to relate to vaccine-related injuries. (1985 (Reg. Sess., 1986), c. 1008, s. 1.)

§ 130A-427. Commission awards for vaccine-related injuries; duties of Secretary.

(a) Upon determining that a claimant has sustained a vaccine-related injury, the Commission shall make an award providing compensation or services for any or all of the following:

(1) Actual and projected reasonable expenses of medical care, developmental evaluation, special education, vocational training, physical, emotional or behavioral therapy, and residential and custodial care and service expenses, that cannot be provided by the Department pursuant to subdivision (5) of this subsection;

(2) Loss of earnings and projected earnings, determined in accordance with generally accepted actuarial principles;

(3) Noneconomic, general damages arising from pain, suffering, and emotional distress;

(4) Reasonable attorneys' fees;

(5) Needs that the Secretary determines on a case-by-case basis shall be met by medical, health, developmental evaluation, special education, vocational training, physical, emotional, or behavioral therapy, residential and custodial care, and other essential and necessary services, to be provided the injured party by the programs and services administered by the Department. The Secretary shall develop an itemized list of the service needs of the injured party upon review and evaluation of the injured party's medical record and shall present it to the Commission prior to the Commission's determination. In the event that the Commission's award includes the provision of any of these services, the Secretary shall develop a comprehensive, coordinated plan for the delivery of these services to the injured party. Notwithstanding any other provision of State law, the Secretary shall waive all eligibility criteria in determining eligibility for services provided by the Department under the plan of care developed pursuant to this subdivision. If the award includes any such services, these services shall be provided by the Department free of any cost to the injured party.

(b) The money compensation component of the award may not be made pursuant to this section in excess of an aggregate amount of the present day value amount of three hundred thousand dollars ($300,000) with respect to all injuries claimed to have resulted from the administration of a covered vaccine to a single individual. The value of all services to be provided by the Department, as part of this award is in addition to the total amount of money compensation, and is not included in the limitation prescribed by this subsection on the amount of money compensation that may be awarded. No damages may be awarded pursuant to subdivision (a)(3) on behalf of any person to whom the covered vaccine was not administered. (1985 (Reg. Sess., 1986), c. 1008, s. 1; 1989, c. 727, s. 151; 1997-443, s. 11A.86.)

§ 130A-428. Notice of determination of claim; appeal to full commission.

(a) Decisions of the Commission pursuant to G.S. 130A-427 shall be final and binding on the claimant and each respondent.

(b) Notwithstanding subsection (a), upon determination of the claim, the Commission shall notify all parties concerned in writing of its decision and any party shall have 15 days after receipt of such notice within which to file notice of appeal with the Commission. This appeal, when so taken, shall be heard by the Commission, sitting as a full commission, on the basis of the record in the matter and upon oral argument of the parties, and the full commission may amend, set aside, or strike out the decision of the hearing commissioner and may issue its own findings of fact and conclusions of law. Upon determination of the claim by the Commission, sitting as a full commission, the Commission shall notify all parties concerned in writing of its decision.

(c) The decision of the Commission, if not reviewed in due time, or an award of the Commission, shall be conclusive and binding as to all questions of fact; but any party to the proceedings may, within 30 days from the date of the decision or award, or within 30 days after receipt of notice to be sent by registered mail or certified mail of the award, but not thereafter, appeal from the decision or award of the Commission to the Court of Appeals for errors of law under the same terms and conditions as govern appeals from the Superior Court to the Court of Appeals in ordinary civil actions. The procedure for the appeal shall be provided by the Rules of Appellate Procedure. (1985 (Reg. Sess., 1986), c. 1008, s. 1.)

§ 130A-429. Limitation on claims.

(a) Except as provided in subsection (b) of this section, any claim under this Article that is filed more than six years after the administration of a vaccine alleged to have caused a vaccine-related injury is barred. Claims on behalf of minors or incompetent persons shall be filed by their parents, guardians ad litem, or guardians within the applicable limitations period established by this section.

(b) Claims that are filed in accordance with the procedures set forth in G.S. 130A-425(b) within six years after the date of the enactment of this Article shall not be barred unless, on the date the claim was filed, the claimant was barred by the applicable statute of limitations from filing an action for damages with respect to the subject matter of the claim.

(c) The period of limitation set forth in this section shall be stayed beginning on the date the claimant files a petition under Section 2111 of the Public Health Service Act, P.L. 99-660, and ending 120 days after the date final judgment is entered on the petition. (1985 (Reg. Sess., 1986), c. 1008, s. 1; 1991, c. 410, s. 3.)

§ 130A-430. Right of State to bring action against health care provider and manufacturer.

(a) If the Industrial Commission makes an award for a claimant who it determines has sustained a vaccine-related injury, the State may, within two years of the date the Commission renders its decision, bring an action against the health care provider who administered the vaccine on the ground that the health care provider was negligent in administering the vaccine. Damages in an action brought under this section are limited to the amount of the award made by the Commission plus the estimated present value of all the services to be provided to the claimant by the Department under G.S. 130A-427.

(b) Manufacturer. - If the Industrial Commission makes an award for a claimant who it determines has sustained a vaccine-related injury, the State may, within two years of the date the Commission renders its decision, bring an action against the manufacturer who made the vaccine on the ground that the vaccine was a defective product. Damages in an action brought under this section are limited to the amount of the award made by the Commission plus the estimated present value of all the services to be provided to the claimant by the Department under G.S. 130A-427, the reasonable costs of prosecuting the action, including, but not limited to, attorneys' fees, fees charged by witnesses, and costs of exhibits. For purposes of this subsection, a defective product is a covered vaccine that was manufactured, transported, or stored in a negligent manner, or was distributed after its expiration date, or that otherwise violated the applicable requirements of any license, approval, or permit, or any applicable standards or requirements issued under Section 351 of the Public Health Service Act, as amended, or the federal Food, Drug, and Cosmetic Act, as these standards or requirements were interpreted or applied by the federal agency charged with their enforcement. The negligence or other action in violation of applicable federal standards or requirements shall be demonstrated by the State, by a preponderance of the evidence, to be the proximate cause of the injury for which an award was rendered pursuant to G.S. 130A-427, in order to allow recovery by the State against the manufacturer pursuant to this subsection. (1985 (Reg. Sess., 1986), c. 1008, s. 1; 1987, c. 215, s. 4; 1989, c. 727, s. 152; 1997-443, s. 11A.87.)

§ 130A-431. Certain vaccine diversions made felony.

Any person who (i) receives a vaccine designated by the manufacturer for use in the State, (ii) directly or indirectly diverts the vaccine to a location outside the State, and (iii) directly or indirectly profits as a result of this diversion, is guilty of a Class I felony. The fine shall be twenty-five dollars ($25.00) per dose of the diverted vaccine or one hundred thousand dollars ($100,000), whichever is less. A health care professional convicted of a Class I felony pursuant to this section who is found by the court to have diverted more than 300 doses of covered vaccine shall have his license suspended for one year. (1985 (Reg. Sess., 1986), c. 1008, s. 1; 1987, c. 215, s. 5; 1993, c. 539, s. 1306; 1994, Ex. Sess., c. 24, s. 14(c).)

§ 130A-432. Scope.

This Article applies to all claims for vaccine-related injuries occurring on and after October 1, 1986 and, at the option of the claimant, to claims for vaccine-related injuries that occurred before October 1, 1986 if such claim has not been resolved by final judgment or by settlement agreement or is not barred by a statute of limitations.

This Article applies to all claims for vaccine-related injuries alleged to have been caused by covered vaccines administered within the State, regardless of where an action relating to the injuries is brought and regardless of where the injuries are alleged to have occurred. (1985 (Reg. Sess., 1986), c. 1008, s. 1; 1987, c. 215, s. 6.)

§ 130A-433. Contracts for purchase of vaccines; distribution; fee; rules.

(a) Notwithstanding any law to the contrary, the Secretary may enter into contracts with the manufacturers and suppliers of covered vaccines and with other public entities either within or without the State for the purchase of covered vaccines and may provide for the distribution or sale of the covered vaccines to health care providers. Local health departments shall distribute the covered vaccines at the request of the Department. The Secretary shall adopt rules to implement this Article except for subsection (b) of this section.

(b) Except as otherwise provided in G.S. 130A-153(a), a health care provider who receives vaccine from the State may charge no more than a reasonable fee established by the Commission for Public Health for the administration of the vaccine. (1985 (Reg. Sess., 1986), c. 1008, s. 2; 1987, c. 215, s. 7; 1989, c. 727, s. 153; 1993, c. 321, s. 281(b); 2007-182, s. 2; 2009-451, s. 10.29A(b).)

§ 130A-434. Child Vaccine Injury Compensation Fund established; payments from Fund; transfer of appropriations and receipts.

(a) There is established the Child Vaccine Injury Compensation Fund within the Department to finance the North Carolina Childhood Vaccine-Related Injury Compensation Program created by this article. The money compensation components of all awards made pursuant to Article 17 of Chapter 130A of the General Statutes shall be paid by the Department from the Fund.

(b) Should the Department find that the sum of appropriations and receipts is insufficient to meet financial obligations incurred in the administration of this article, appropriations and receipts in the Department which would otherwise revert to the General Fund may be transferred to the Child Vaccine Injury Compensation Fund in order to meet such obligations. The Department may also budget anticipated receipts as needed to implement this Article. (1985

(Reg. Sess., 1986), c. 1008, s. 3(a), 3(b); 1989, c. 727, s. 154; 1997-443, s. 11A.88.)

§§ 130A-435 through 130A-439. Reserved for future codification purposes.

Article 18.

Health Assessments for Kindergarten Children in the Public Schools.

§ 130A-440. Health assessment required.

(a) Every child in this State entering kindergarten in the public schools shall receive a health assessment. The health assessment shall be made no more than 12 months prior to the date of school entry. No child shall attend kindergarten unless a health assessment transmittal form, developed pursuant to G.S. 130A-441, indicating that the child has received the health assessment required by this section, is presented to the school principal. The medical provider, or the parent, guardian, or person in loco parentis, must present a completed health assessment transmittal form to the principal of the school on or before the child's first day of attendance. If a health assessment transmittal form is not presented on or before the first day, the principal shall present a notice of deficiency to the parent, guardian, or responsible person. The parent, guardian, or responsible person shall have 30 calendar days from the first day of attendance to present the required health assessment transmittal form for the child. Upon termination of 30 calendar days, the principal shall not permit the child to attend the school until the required health assessment transmittal form has been presented.

(b) A health assessment shall include a medical history and physical examination with screening for vision and hearing and, if appropriate, testing for anemia and tuberculosis. Vision screening shall be conducted in accordance with G.S. 130A-440.1. The health assessment may also include dental screening and developmental screening for cognition, language, and motor function. The developmental screening of cognition and language abilities may be conducted in accordance with G.S. 115C-83.5(a).

(c) The health assessment shall be conducted by a physician licensed to practice medicine, a physician's assistant as defined in G.S. 90-18.1(a), a certified nurse practitioner, or a public health nurse meeting the Department's Standards for Early Periodic Screening, Diagnosis, and Treatment Screening.

(d) This Article shall not apply to children entering kindergarten in private church schools, schools of religious charter, or qualified nonpublic schools, regulated by Article 39 of Chapter 115C of the General Statutes. (1985 (Reg. Sess., 1986), c. 1017, s. 1; 1987, c. 114, s. 1; 1989, c. 727, s. 155; 1993, c. 124, s. 1; 1995, c. 123, s. 10; 2006-240, s. 1(b); 2012-142, s. 7A.1(h).)

§ 130A-440.1. Early Childhood Vision Care.

(a) Vision Screening Required for Children Entering Kindergarten. - Every child in this State entering kindergarten in the public schools, beginning with the 2007-2008 school year, shall obtain vision screening in accordance with vision screening standards adopted by the Governor's Commission on Early Childhood Vision Care. Within 180 days of the start of the school year, the parent of the child shall present to the school principal or the principal's designee certification that the child has, within the past 12 months, obtained vision screening conducted by a licensed physician, optometrist, physician assistant, nurse practitioner, registered nurse, orthoptist, or a vision screener certified by Prevent Blindness North Carolina, or a comprehensive eye examination performed by an ophthalmologist or optometrist. The health assessment transmittal form required pursuant to G.S. 130A-440 qualifies as certification that the child has obtained the required vision screening. All providers conducting vision screening shall provide each parent in writing the results of the vision screening on forms bearing the signature of the provider supplied to the provider by the Governor's Commission on Early Childhood Vision Care. The provider shall also orally communicate this information to the parent and shall take reasonable steps to ensure that the parent understands the information communicated. In the instance where a child enters the first grade without having been enrolled in a kindergarten program requiring a vision screening, the requirements for vision screening under this subsection shall apply.

(a1) Comprehensive Eye Examination. - For children who receive and fail to pass a vision screening as required under subsection (a) of this section, a comprehensive eye examination is required. If a public school teacher, administrator, or other appropriate school personnel has reason to believe that a child enrolled in kindergarten through third grade is having problems with vision, the school personnel may recommend to the child's parent that the child have a comprehensive eye examination. Notification to the parent shall also inform the parent that funds may be available from the Governor's Commission on Early Childhood Vision Care to pay providers for the examination, including corrective lenses.

The comprehensive eye examination shall be conducted by a duly licensed optometrist or ophthalmologist. The comprehensive eye examination conducted pursuant to this section shall consist of a complete and thorough examination of the eye and shall include:

(1)	Measurement of visual acuity;

(2)	Ocular alignment and motility;

(3)	Depth perception - stereopsis;

(4)	Fusion;

(5)	Slit lamp examination of the lid margins, conjunctivae, cornea, anterior chamber, iris, and crystalline lens;

(6)	Examination of the ocular adnexa, the anterior segment, and pupils; and

(7)	Cycloplegic refraction and dilated fundus examination.

Health assessment vision screening under G.S. 130A-440 is not a comprehensive eye examination for purposes of this section.

(b)	Repealed by Session Laws 2006-240, s. 1(a), effective August 13, 2006.

(c)	The results of a comprehensive eye examination conducted under this section shall be included on the comprehensive eye examination transmittal form developed by the Commission pursuant to G.S. 143B-216.75 and shall contain a summary of the comprehensive eye examination performed by the optometrist or ophthalmologist. Any treatment recommendations by the optometrist or ophthalmologist, such as spectacles for schoolwork, shall appear in the summary and school health card. The provider shall present a signed transmittal form to the parent upon completion of the examination. The parent shall submit the transmittal form to the school in accordance with this section.

(d) Repealed by Session Laws 2006-240, s. 1(a), effective August 13, 2006.

(e) G.S. 130A-441, 130A-442, and 130A-443, pertaining to health assessments, apply to comprehensive eye examinations required under this section.

(f) No child shall be excluded from attending school for a parent's failure to obtain a comprehensive eye examination required under this section. If a parent fails or refuses to obtain a comprehensive eye examination or to provide the certification of a comprehensive eye examination, the school shall send a written reminder to the parent of required eye examinations and shall include information about funds that may be available from the Governor's Commission on Early Childhood Vision Care.

(g) In adopting standards for vision screening under this section and as required under G.S. 130A-440, the Commission shall take into account the resources necessary to comply with the standards and, if standards will require additional resources, shall mitigate the impact on resources without compromising vision screening effectiveness.

(h) As used in this section, the term "parent" means the parent, guardian, or person standing in loco parentis. (2005-276, s. 10.59F(g); 2005-345, s. 20(d); 2006-240, s. 1(a).)

§ 130A-441. Reporting.

(a) Health assessment results shall be submitted to the school principal by the medical provider on health assessment transmittal forms developed by the Department and the Department of Public Instruction.

(b) Each school having a kindergarten shall maintain on file the health assessment results. The files shall be open to inspection by the Department, the Department of Public Instruction, or their authorized representatives and persons inspecting the files shall maintain the confidentiality of the files. Upon transfer of a child to another kindergarten, a copy of the health assessment results shall be provided upon request and without charge to the new kindergarten.

(c)   Within 60 calendar days after the commencement of a new school year, the principal shall file a health assessment status report with the Department on forms developed by the Department and the Department of Public Instruction. The report shall document the number of children in compliance and not in compliance with G.S. 130A-440(a). (1985 (Reg. Sess., 1986), c. 1017, s. 1; 1987, c. 114, s. 2; 1989, c. 727, s. 156; 1993, c. 124, s. 2.)

§ 130A-442. Religious exemption.

If the bona fide religious beliefs of the parent, guardian or person in loco parentis of a child are contrary to the health assessment requirements contained in this Article, this Article shall not apply to the child. Upon submission of a written statement of the bona fide religious beliefs and opposition to the health assessment requirements, the child may attend kindergarten without submitting a health assessment report. (1985 (Reg. Sess., 1986), c. 1017, s. 1; 1987, c. 114, s. 2.)

§ 130A-443. Rules.

Rules governing the contents for health assessment reports, the procedure for reporting under this Article, and those persons authorized to inspect the files shall be developed jointly by the Department of Public Instruction and the Commission for Public Health and shall be adopted by the Commission for Public Health. (1985 (Reg. Sess., 1986), c. 1017, s. 1; 2007-182, s. 2.)

Article 19.

Asbestos Hazard Management.

§ 130A-444. Definitions.

Unless a different meaning is required by the context, the following definitions apply throughout this Article:

(1)   "AHERA" means Title II, Asbestos Hazard Emergency Response Act of the Toxic Substances Control Act, 15 U.S.C. § 2601, et seq., as amended by

the Asbestos School Hazard Abatement Reauthorization Act of 1990, P.L. 101-637, 104 Stat. 4589 ("ASHARA").

(2)　"Asbestos" means asbestiform varieties of chrysotile (serpentine), crocidolite (riebeckite), amosite (cummingtonite-grunerite), anthophyllite, tremolite and actinolite.

(3)　"Asbestos containing material" means material which contains more than one percent (1%) asbestos, including friable asbestos containing material and nonfriable asbestos containing material.

(3a)　"Asbestos NESHAP for demolition and renovation" means that portion of the National Emission Standards for Hazardous Air Pollutants for asbestos that governs demolition and renovation as set out in 40 CFR §§ 61.141, 61.145, 61.150, and 61.154 (1 July 1993 edition).

(4)　"Abatement" means work performed to repair, maintain, remove, isolate, or encapsulate asbestos containing material. The term does not include inspections, preparation of management plans, abatement project design, taking of samples, or project overview.

(5)　"Friable" means any material that when dry can be broken, crumbled, pulverized, or reduced to powder by hand pressure, and includes previously nonfriable material after such material becomes damaged to the extent that when dry it can be crumbled, pulverized, or reduced to powder by hand pressure.

(6)　"Management" means all activities related to asbestos containing material, including inspections, preparation of management plans, abatement project design, abatement, project overview, and taking of samples.

(6a)　"Person" means an individual, a corporation, a company, an association, a partnership, a unit of local government, a State or federal agency, or any other legal entity.

(7)　"Public area" means those areas in any building other than a residence that are not covered under the Occupational Safety and Health Act of 1970, Pub. L. 91-596, 84 Stat. 1590, 29 U.S.C. § 651, et seq., as amended.

(8) "Removal" means stripping, chipping, sanding, sawing, drilling, scraping, sucking, and other methods of separating material from its installed location in a building.

(9) "Residence" means any single family dwelling or any multi-family dwelling of fewer than 10 units. (1989, c. 724, s. 1; 1993 (Reg. Sess., 1994), c. 686, s. 2; 1995, c. 123, s. 7.)

§ 130A-445. Management of asbestos containing material in schools.

All school buildings subject to the provisions of AHERA shall be inspected for asbestos containing materials and shall prepare and submit management plans to the Department. The Commission shall adopt rules governing school management plans. These rules shall specify the content and format of plans, the plan review and approval process, schedules and methods for implementation of approved plans, and periodic inspection requirements. (1989, c. 724, s. 1.)

§ 130A-446. Asbestos exposure standard for public areas.

The Commission shall adopt rules to establish a maximum airborne asbestos exposure level for public areas. Such rules shall also specify sampling and analysis procedures. (1989, c. 724, s. 1.)

§ 130A-447. Accreditation of persons performing asbestos management and approval of training courses.

(a) No person shall commence or continue to perform asbestos management activities unless he has been accredited by the Department. No person shall commence or continue to provide asbestos related training courses unless the course has been approved by the Department. The Commission shall adopt rules governing the accreditation of persons performing asbestos management activities and the approval of training courses. Such rules shall include categories of accreditation and shall specify appropriate education, experience, and training requirements. The rules shall establish separate categories of accreditation for inspectors, management planners, abatement designers, supervisors, workers, air monitors, and supervising air monitors. These rules shall be at least as stringent as the accreditation plan required under AHERA and regulations adopted pursuant thereto.

(b) A person who applies for accreditation in the worker category may engage in asbestos containing material management activities as though he were accredited in the worker category for up to 90 days after the date he submits his application. No person whose application is rejected may continue to engage in asbestos containing material management activities under this subsection.

(c) The following persons are exempt from the accreditation requirements:

(1) The owner or operator of a building, other than school buildings subject to the provisions of AHERA, and his permanent employees when performing small-scale, short duration activities, as defined in 40 C.F.R. Pt. 763, Subpt. E, Appendix C (1994).

(2) A person performing asbestos containing material management activities in his personal residence.

(3) Governmental regulatory personnel performing inspections of asbestos containing material management activities solely for the purpose of determining compliance with applicable statutes or regulations.

(4) Persons licensed by the General Contractors Licensing Board, State Board of Examiners of Plumbing and Heating Contractors, State Board of Examiners of Electrical Contractors, or the State Board of Refrigeration Examiners when engaged in activities associated with their license when performing small-scale, short duration activities, as defined in 40 C.F.R. Pt. 763, Subpt. E, Appendix C (1994). (1989, c. 724, s. 1; 1993 (Reg. Sess., 1994), c. 686, s. 3; 1995, c. 123, s. 8.)

§ 130A-448. Asbestos management accreditation fees and course approval fees.

(a) The Department shall establish and collect asbestos containing material management accreditation and annual renewal fees to support the asbestos hazard management program. The fees shall not exceed one hundred dollars ($100.00) per accreditation category, except that the fee for the abatement worker category shall not exceed twenty-five dollars ($25.00). A person who is accredited in more than one category shall pay a fee for each category.

(b) The Department shall establish and collect fees for approving asbestos management training courses and fees for renewing course approval annually to support the asbestos hazard management program. The fees for approving a training course shall not exceed one thousand five hundred dollars ($1,500) for each course. The annual renewal fees shall not exceed five hundred dollars ($500.00) for each course. Each category of a training course shall be subject to a separate fee for its initial approval and a separate fee for its annual renewal. (1989, c. 724, s. 1; 1993 (Reg. Sess., 1994), c. 686, s. 4.)

§ 130A-449. Asbestos containing material removal permits.

No person shall engage in asbestos abatement involving more than 35 cubic feet, 160 square feet, or 260 linear feet per job of asbestos containing material without an asbestos containing material removal permit issued by the Department. The Commission shall adopt rules governing such permits. Such rules may provide for exemption from the requirements of this section. (1989, c. 724, s. 1.)

§ 130A-450. Asbestos containing material removal permit fees.

An applicant for an asbestos containing material removal permit is subject to a fee payable to the Department. The fee is a departmental receipt of the Department and must be used to offset the cost of the asbestos hazard management program. An applicant for a permit must indicate whether the asbestos is to be removed as part of a renovation or a demolition. If the asbestos is to be removed as part of a renovation, the fee is the amount set by the Department and may not exceed one percent (1%) of the contracted price or twenty cents ($.20) per square foot or linear foot of asbestos containing material to be removed, whichever is greater. If the asbestos is to be removed as part of a demolition, the fee is the greater of the following, not to exceed one thousand five hundred dollars ($1,500):

(1) One percent (1%) of the contracted price.

(2) An amount set by the Department not to exceed twenty cents ($.20) per square foot or linear foot of asbestos containing material to be removed. (1989, c. 724, s. 1; 2008-107, s. 29.6(a).)

§ 130A-451. Commission to adopt rules.

For the protection of the public health, the Commission shall adopt rules to implement this Article, AHERA, and the asbestos NESHAP for renovations and demolitions. (1989, c. 724, s. 1; 1993 (Reg. Sess., 1994), c. 686, s. 5.)

§ 130A-452. Local air pollution control programs.

(a) The Department may authorize any local air pollution control program to adopt and enforce the asbestos NESHAP for demolition and renovation if the local air pollution control program is certified by the North Carolina Environmental Management Commission pursuant to G.S. 143-215.112. The Department shall authorize any local air pollution control program to adopt and enforce the asbestos NESHAP for demolition and renovation if the local air pollution control program was certified by the North Carolina Environmental Management Commission pursuant to G.S. 143-215.112 prior to October 1, 1994. A local air pollution control program shall continue to be authorized by the Department to enforce the asbestos NESHAP for demolition and renovation so long as the local air pollution control program maintains its certification under G.S. 143-215.112 and complies with any rules adopted by the Commission for Public Health pursuant to subsection (b) of this section. Any local air pollution control program authorized to adopt and enforce the asbestos NESHAP for demolition and renovation shall have the authority to enforce the asbestos NESHAP for demolition and renovation under G.S. 130A-18, 130A-22(b1), 130A-22(b2), and 130A-25. Judicial review of an administrative penalty assessed under G.S. 130-22(b1) and G.S. 130A-22(b2) shall be as provided in G.S. 143-215.112(d2)(1) and Article 4 of Chapter 150B of the General Statutes.

(b) The Commission for Public Health shall adopt rules regarding the authorization of local air pollution control programs to enforce the asbestos

NESHAP for demolition and renovation. (1993 (Reg. Sess., 1994), c. 686, s. 7; 1995, c. 123, s. 6; 2007-182, s. 2.)

§ 130A-453. Reserved for future codification purposes.

Article 19A.

Lead-Based Paint Hazard Management Program.

§ 130A-453.01. Definitions.

Unless otherwise required by the context, the definitions set out in 40 Code of Federal Regulations § 745.223 (As set out in Vol. 61, No. 169, of the Federal Register, pages 45813 to 45815, 29 August 1996) apply throughout this Article. (1997-523, s. 1.)

§ 130A-453.02. Purpose of Article.

(a) This Article is enacted to establish an authorized State program under section 404 of the Toxic Substances Control Act (15 U.S.C. § 2684), as enacted by Subtitle B, section 1021 of the Residential Lead-Based Paint Hazard Reduction Act of 1992 (Pub. L. 102-550, 106 Stat. 3916), that will apply in this State in lieu of the corresponding federal program administered by the federal Environmental Protection Agency. This Article requires a person who performs an inspection, risk assessment, or abatement of a child-occupied facility or target housing to be certified and establishes the procedure and requirements for certification. It also requires a person who conducts an abatement of a child-occupied facility or target housing to obtain a permit for the abatement.

(b) This Article does not require the inspection, risk assessment, or abatement of a child-occupied facility or target housing under any circumstance. G.S. 130A-131.5 and the rules adopted to implement that section authorize the Department to order an abatement to eliminate a lead poisoning hazard. This Article does not expand or otherwise change that authority. (1997-523, s. 1.)

§ 130A-453.03. Certification of individuals who perform inspections, risk assessments, or abatements.

(a) Requirement. - An individual shall not perform or offer to perform an inspection, risk assessment, or abatement of target housing or a child-occupied facility unless the individual is certified by the Department to perform the activity. Performance of an inspection, risk assessment, or abatement encompasses a range of activities. To ensure proper performance of all aspects of an inspection, risk assessment, or abatement, the certification requirement imposed on an individual applies to each activity. The categories of individual certification are inspector, risk-assessor, designer, supervisor, worker, and any other category required by federal law. The category of risk-assessor includes the category of inspector. Thus, a person who is certified as a risk-assessor is not required to be certified as an inspector. Otherwise, an individual who performs or offers to perform activities within the scope of more than one category must be certified in each category.

(b) Exemption. - The certification requirement imposed by this section does not apply to an individual who performs an abatement of a residential dwelling the person owns and occupies as a residence, unless the residential dwelling is occupied by a person or persons other than the owner or the owner's immediate family while an abatement is being performed, or a child residing in the dwelling has been identified as having an elevated blood lead level. (1997-523, s. 1.)

§ 130A-453.04. Certification and other requirements of firms that perform inspections, risk assessments, or abatements.

A firm or other entity shall not perform or offer to perform an inspection, risk assessment, or abatement of target housing or a child-occupied facility unless the entity is certified by the Department as a firm that is qualified to perform the activity. An entity that performs an inspection, risk assessment, or abatement of target housing or a child-occupied facility shall not use an individual to perform the inspection, risk assessment, or abatement unless the individual is certified by the Department to perform the activity. (1997-523, s. 1.)

§ 130A-453.05. Qualifications for certification of individuals and firms.

To be certified under this Article, a person must meet the qualification requirements set by the Commission. Qualification requirements include education, training, experience, the successful completion of an examination, and payment of any applicable fee. (1997-523, s. 1.)

§ 130A-453.06. Renewal of certification.

A certification of an individual or a firm issued under this Article expires on the last day of the 12th month after the certification is issued. A certification may be renewed by paying the renewal fee and meeting any standards for renewal, such as refresher training, established by the Commission. (1997-523, s. 1.)

§ 130A-453.07. Accreditation of training courses and training providers.

Completion of a training course on inspection, risk assessment, or abatement does not satisfy a training requirement that is a condition for certification under this Article unless both the course provider and the course have been accredited by the Department. The Commission shall establish the procedure and standards for a course provider and a course to be accredited. (1997-523, s. 1.)

§ 130A-453.08. Certification and accreditation fee schedule.

(a) The Commission shall establish fees for the items listed in the table below. A fee for an item may not exceed the maximum amount set in the table. The fees for examination and certification apply to each category in which a person is examined for certification or is certified.

Item
Maximum Fee

Examination for certification
$75

Certification as worker
50

Certification in any category other

than worker
150

Course provider accreditation
150

Initial course accreditation
2,000

Renewal course accreditation
750.

(b) Use. - The fees imposed under this section are departmental receipts and shall be used by the Department to administer this Article.

(c) Exemptions. - The examination and certification fees imposed under this section do not apply to governmental regulatory personnel who perform inspections, risk assessments, or abatements solely for the purpose of determining compliance with applicable statutes or rules. The course provider fees imposed under this section do not apply to the State, a unit of local government, or a nonprofit entity. The course accreditation fees imposed under this section do not apply to a course offered by the State, a unit of local government, or a nonprofit entity. (1997-523, s. 1.)

§ 130A-453.09. Abatement permits.

(a) Requirement. - No person shall conduct an abatement of target housing or a child-occupied facility unless the person has obtained a permit for the abatement from the Department. The Commission shall establish the procedure for obtaining a permit.

(b) Permit Fee. - An applicant for an abatement permit must pay an application fee to the Department. The fee is two percent (2%) of the contracted price for the corrective action to be performed in the abatement, not to exceed five hundred dollars ($500.00). The fee imposed under this section is a departmental receipt and shall be used by the Department to administer this Article.

(c) Exemption. - An individual who owns a single-family dwelling, conducts an abatement on the dwelling, and will reside in the dwelling after the abatement is completed is not required to obtain a permit to conduct the abatement, unless the dwelling is occupied by a person or persons other than the owner or the owner's immediate family while the abatement is being performed, or a child residing in the building has been identified as having an elevated blood lead level. If a permit is required, an individual who performs an abatement of a residential dwelling that the individual owns and occupies as a residence is not required to pay a fee for the permit. (1997-523, s. 1.)

§ 130A-453.10. Standards to ensure elimination of hazards; consumer information.

(a) Standards. - The Commission shall establish standards to ensure that inspections, risk assessments, and abatements performed under this Article result in the elimination of lead-based paint hazards. An inspection, risk assessment, or abatement performed under this Article must be performed in accordance with these standards.

(b) Information. - The Department shall prepare a fact sheet on abatement for distribution to consumers. The sheet shall list the various measures for abatement of a child-occupied facility or target housing and give the relative cost of each measure. A person who is certified under this Article shall give a copy of the sheet to a person for whom the certified person performs an abatement. (1997-523, s. 1.)

§ 130A-453.11. Commission to adopt rules.

The Commission shall adopt rules to implement this Article. (1997-523, s. 1.)

§ 130A-453.12: Reserved for future codification purposes.

§ 130A-453.13: Reserved for future codification purposes.

§ 130A-453.14: Reserved for future codification purposes.

§ 130A-453.15: Reserved for future codification purposes.

§ 130A-453.16: Reserved for future codification purposes.

§ 130A-453.17: Reserved for future codification purposes.

§ 130A-453.18: Reserved for future codification purposes.

§ 130A-453.19: Reserved for future codification purposes.

§ 130A-453.20: Reserved for future codification purposes.

§ 130A-453.21: Reserved for future codification purposes.

Article 19B.

Certification and Accreditation of Lead-Based Paint Renovation Activities.

§ 130A-453.22. Definitions.

(a)   Except as provided in subsection (b) of this section and in any rules adopted under this Article, the definitions set out in 40 C.F.R. §§ 745.83 and 745.223, as amended, apply throughout this Article.

(b)   Unless otherwise required by the context, the following definitions apply throughout this Article:

(1)   Certified dust sampling technician. - An individual who (i) is employed by a certified renovation firm, (ii) has successfully completed a dust sampling technician training course accredited by the Department, and (iii) is certified by the Department to perform dust clearance sampling after the completion of renovation activities, if the person contracting for the renovation activity requests dust clearance sampling.

(2) Certified renovation firm. - A company, partnership, corporation, sole proprietorship, association, or other business entity or individual doing business in the State, or a federal, State, tribal, or local government agency, or a nonprofit organization that has been certified by the Department to perform renovation activities covered by this Article.

(3) Certified renovator. - An individual who (i) is employed by a certified renovation firm, (ii) either performs or directs trained workers who perform renovation activities, (iii) has successfully completed a renovation training course accredited by the Department or the United States Environmental Protection Agency, and (iv) is certified with the Department to perform renovation activities.

(4) Child-occupied facility. - A building, or portion of a building, constructed prior to 1978, visited regularly by the same child under 6 years of age, on at least two different days within any week (Sunday through Saturday period), provided that each day's visit lasts at least three hours and the combined weekly visits last at least six hours, and the combined annual visits last at least 60 hours. Child-occupied facilities may include, but are not limited to, day care centers, preschools, and kindergarten classrooms. Child-occupied facilities may be located in target housing or in public or commercial buildings. With respect to common areas in public or commercial buildings, the child-occupied facility encompasses those common areas, both interior and exterior, routinely used by children under age 6.

(5) Renovation activities. - The activities relative to lead-based paint renovations including the use of recognized lead test kits, information distribution, work practices such as cleaning verification and dust clearance sampling, as well as the activities performed by a certified firm, certified renovator, or certified dust sampling technician. Renovation activities include all activities included in the definition of the term "renovation" in 40 C.F.R. § 745.83.

(6) Target housing - Any housing constructed prior to 1978, except housing for the elderly or persons with disabilities, unless one or more children age 6 years or under resides or is expected to reside in such housing for the elderly or persons with disabilities, or any zero-bedroom dwelling. For purposes of this Article, a zero-bedroom dwelling is any residential dwelling in which the living areas are not separated from the sleeping area. The term includes efficiencies, studio apartments, dormitory housing, military barracks, and rentals of individual rooms in residential dwellings.

(7) Trained renovation worker. - An individual who (i) receives on-the-job training and direction pertaining to the individual's assigned tasks in renovation work in target housing or child-occupied facilities from a certified renovator and (ii) is employed by a certified renovation firm. (2009-488, s. 1.)

§ 130A-453.23. Purpose.

(a) This Article is enacted to establish an authorized State program under sections 402 and 406 of the Toxic Substance Control Act, 15 U.S.C. §§ 2682 and 2686, as enacted by Subtitle B of the Residential Lead-Based Paint Hazard Reduction Act of 1992, 42 U.S.C. § 4852(d), that will apply in this State in lieu of the corresponding federal program administered by the United States Environmental Protection Agency (EPA). This Article requires that renovations for compensation in target housing and child-occupied facilities be performed or directed by certified renovators and certified firms; establishes procedures and requirements for certification of individuals and firms that perform renovation activities for compensation; and establishes renovation work practice standards. This Article also requires the accreditation of renovation training providers and courses and establishes record-keeping requirements.

(b) Certified renovation firms are required to distribute EPA-approved pamphlets. (2009-488, s. 1.)

§ 130A-453.24. Certification of individuals and firms that perform renovations, cleaning verification, and dust clearance sampling.

(a) No firm shall perform, offer, or claim to perform renovation activities for compensation in target housing or child-occupied facilities unless the firm is a certified renovation firm.

(b) No individual shall:

(1) Perform, offer, or claim to perform renovation activities for compensation in target housing or child-occupied facilities unless the individual is a certified renovator.

(2) Perform as a trained renovation worker for compensation in target housing or child-occupied facilities unless the individual is employed by a certified renovation firm and is trained and supervised in his or her assigned tasks by a certified renovator.

(3) Conduct dust clearance sampling for compensation in target housing or child-occupied facilities unless the individual is a certified dust sampling technician, risk assessor, or lead-based paint inspector. For purposes of this Article, the terms "risk assessor" and "lead-based paint inspector" shall have the same meaning as provided in Article 19A of this Chapter.

(4) Conduct cleaning verification for compensation in target housing or child-occupied facilities unless the individual is a certified renovator.

(c) The Commission shall adopt rules governing the certification of individuals and firms performing renovation, cleaning verification, or dust clearance sampling. The rules adopted shall include, but not be limited to, requirements for qualifications, training, and experience, and the payment of fees pursuant to G.S. 130A-453.27. (2009-488, s. 1.)

§ 130A-453.25. Renewals of certification.

(a) Certification as a renovation firm under this Article expires on the last day of the 12th month after the certification is issued and shall be renewed annually. A firm may renew its certification by paying the renewal fees and meeting the standards for renewal established by the Commission.

(b) Certification as a dust sampling technician expires on the last day of the month of the year after certification training is completed and shall be renewed annually. A certified dust sampling technician may renew his or her certification by paying the renewal fees and meeting the standards for renewal established by the Commission.

(c) A certified renovator shall renew his or her certification every five years by meeting the standards for renewal established by the Commission. (2009-488, s. 1.)

§ 130A-453.26. Accreditation of training courses and training providers.

(a) No training provider shall provide, offer, or claim to provide:

(1) Training or refresher courses in renovation unless the training or courses have been accredited by the Department.

(2) Dust sampling technician courses or refresher courses unless the courses have been accredited by the Department.

(b) The Commission shall adopt rules governing the annual accreditation of training providers and the annual accreditation of initial and refresher training courses.

(c) Accreditation as a training provider expires on the last day of the calendar year following the year the accreditation was issued. Accreditation of a training course or refresher course expires on the last day of the calendar year following the year the accreditation was issued. The accreditation of a training provider and the accreditation of a training or refresher course may be renewed by complying with this Article and any standards established by the Commission.

(d) Training providers and training courses accredited by the EPA are granted reciprocity, but providers and courses must be registered with the Department and comply with this Article. (2009-488, s. 1.)

§ 130A-453.27. Certification and accreditation fee schedule.

(a) The Department shall collect annual accreditation and certification fees authorized under this Article, including initial and renewal fees. The fees collected shall be used for the ongoing administration of this Article and shall not revert to the General Fund at the end of the fiscal year. The fees shall not exceed the following:

Maximum Fee

(1)	Accreditation of a training provider	$150.00
(2)	Reaccreditation of a training provider	$150.00

(3)   Accreditation or reaccreditation of initial courses

(Per course per language) $2,000

(4)   Accreditation or reaccreditation of refresher courses

(Per course per language) $2,000

(5)   Certification or recertification of a firm $300.00

(6)   Certification or recertification of a dust sampling

technician $150.00

(b)   The accreditation fees imposed under this section do not apply to local or State governmental regulatory agency personnel, Indian tribes, or nonprofit training providers. (2009-488, s. 1.)

§ 130A-453.28. Work practices and responsibilities of renovation firms, renovators, and dust sampling technicians.

The Commission shall establish standards for work practices and define the responsibilities of certified renovators and certified renovation firms and individuals. (2009-488, s. 1.)

§ 130A-453.29. Record retention, information distribution, and reporting requirements.

The Commission shall establish standards for record keeping, record retention, and information distribution; and reporting requirements for training providers, certified renovators, and certified renovation firms and individuals. (2009-488, s. 1.)

§ 130A-453.30. Exemptions from renovation, repair, and painting requirements.

The Commission shall adopt rules exempting certain renovation activities from this Article. (2009-488, s. 1.)

§ 130A-453.31. Commission to adopt rules.

The Commission shall adopt rules to implement this Article. (2009-488, s. 1.)

§ 130A-454. Reserved for future codification purposes

Article 20.

Occupational Health.

§ 130A-455. Reportable diseases, illnesses, and injuries.

The Commission shall adopt rules establishing a list of serious and preventable occupational injuries that occur while working on a farm, and serious and preventable occupational diseases and illnesses to be reported to the Department. Occupational diseases and illnesses are defined as those diseases and illnesses which result from exposure to a health hazard in the workplace. The Commission shall adopt rules establishing the specific information to be submitted when making a report required by this Article, time limits for reporting, and the form of the report. The rules adopted by the Commission shall avoid duplication of reporting and minimize the cost to the physicians, medical facilities, laboratories, or other persons reporting under this act. (1993, c. 486.)

§ 130A-456. Physicians to report.

A physician licensed to practice medicine in this State who treats a person for an occupational injury that occurred while working on a farm or an occupational disease, illness, declared by the Commission to be reportable, shall report the information required by the Commission to the Department. (1993, c. 486.)

§ 130A-457. Medical facilities to report.

A medical facility in which there is a patient who has an occupational injury that occurred while working on a farm, or an occupational disease, illness, declared by the Commission to be reportable, may report information specified by the Commission to the Department. (1993, c. 486.)

§ 130A-458. Persons in charge of laboratories to report.

A person in charge of a laboratory providing diagnostic service in this State shall report to the Department laboratory findings related to occupational diseases and illnesses for which laboratory reporting is required by the Commission. (1993, c. 486, s. 1; 2001-28, s. 3.)

§ 130A-459. Immunity of persons who report.

A person who in good faith makes a report pursuant to the provisions of this Article shall be immune from any civil liability that might otherwise be incurred or imposed as a result of making the report. (1993, c. 486.)

§ 130A-460. Report to Department of Labor.

(a) Each report to the Department pursuant to the Article shall be evaluated for its potential indication of an exposure to a health hazard. If an on-site visit is deemed necessary, a copy of the report for work sites for which the Department of Labor has jurisdiction for the enforcement of occupational health laws shall be forwarded to the Department of Labor. The Department of Labor and the Department may exchange information regarding specific workplaces and conditions and such information shall retain the same confidentiality provided by the originating agency.

(b) If the Department of Labor determines that an on-site visit is necessary for enforcement purposes, the Department of Labor shall inform the Department within 30 days of the receipt of the report, and a representative of the Department may participate in the visit. The Department shall not contact or otherwise notify any employer of a pending investigation prior to the determination by the Department of Labor regarding the necessity of an on-site visit and shall not give advance notice of a visit if one is necessary.

(c) Subsection (b) shall not apply to inspections conducted for the Industrial Commission pursuant to G.S. 97-76 and shall not affect the allocation of responsibilities set forth in G.S. 74-24.4(c). (1993, c. 486.)

§§ 130A-461 through 130A-464. Reserved for future codification purposes.

Article 21.

Advance Health Care Directive Registry.

§ 130A-465. Advance Health Care Directive Registry establishment.

The Secretary of State shall establish and maintain a statewide, on-line, central registry for advance health care directives. The registry shall be accessible over the Internet through a site maintained by the Secretary of State. (2001-455, s. 1; 2001-513, s. 30(b).)

§ 130A-466. Filing requirements.

(a) A person may submit any of the following documents and the revocations of these documents to the Secretary of State for filing in the Advance Health Care Directive Registry established pursuant to this Article:

(1) A health care power of attorney under Article 3 of Chapter 32A of the General Statutes.

(2) A declaration of a desire for a natural death under Article 23 of Chapter 90 of the General Statutes.

(3) An advance instruction for mental health treatment under Part 2 of Article 3 of Chapter 122C of the General Statutes.

(4) A declaration of an anatomical gift under Part 3A of Article 16 of Chapter 130A of the General Statutes.

(b) Any document and any revocation of a document submitted for filing in the registry shall be notarized regardless of whether notarization is required for its validity. This subsection does not apply to a declaration of an anatomical gift described in subdivision (a)(4) of this section.

(c) The document may be submitted for filing only by the person who executed the document.

(d) The person who submits the document shall supply a return address.

(e) The document shall be accompanied by any fee required by this Article. (2001-455, s. 1; 2001-513, s. 30(b); 2003-70, s. 1; 2007-538, s. 10.)

§ 130A-467. Validity of unregistered documents.

Failure to register a document with the registry maintained by the Secretary of State pursuant to this Article shall not affect the document's validity. Failure to notify the Secretary of State of the revocation of a document filed with the registry shall not affect the validity of a revocation that meets the statutory requirements for the revocation to be valid. (2001-455, s. 1; 2001-513, s. 30(b).)

§ 130A-468. Filing of documents with the registry.

(a) When the Secretary of State receives a document that may be filed with the registry pursuant to this Article, the Secretary shall create a digital reproduction of that document and enter the reproduced document into the registry database. The Secretary is not required to review a document to ensure that it complies with the particular statutory requirements applicable to the document. Each document entered into the registry database shall be assigned a unique file number and password.

(b) Upon entering the reproduced document into the registry database, the Secretary shall return the original document and a wallet-size card containing the document's file number and password to the person who submitted the document.

(c)   When the Secretary of State receives a revocation of a document that is filed with the registry and that document's file number and password, or a request to remove that document from the registry without its revocation, the Secretary shall delete that document from the registry database.

(d)   The Secretary of State's entry of a document into, or removal of a document from, the registry database does not do any of the following:

(1)   Affect the validity of the document in whole or in part.

(2)   Relate to the accuracy of information contained in the document.

(3)   Create a presumption regarding the validity of the document, regarding the accuracy of information contained in the document, or that the statutory requirements for the document have been met. (2001-455, s. 1; 2001-513, s. 30(b); 2007-502, s. 16.)

§ 130A-469. Disclosure of information contained in the registry.

The registry shall be accessible only over the Internet. A document filed in the registry shall be accessible only if a person attempting to access the document enters both the file number and password of the document. Documents filed in the registry, file numbers, passwords, and any other information maintained by the Secretary of State under this Article shall not be subject to disclosure pursuant to Chapter 132 of the General Statutes. (2001-455, s. 1; 2001-513, s. 30(b).)

§ 130A-470. Fees for using the registry; other funds for the registry.

(a)   The Secretary of State shall charge a fee of ten dollars ($10.00) for filing a document, other than a revocation, with the registry. The Secretary of State shall not charge a fee for filing a revocation with the registry. The fee shall be applied to the cost of maintaining the registry and to promoting public education and awareness of the registry.

(b) The Secretary of State, on behalf of the State, may accept gifts, donations, devises, and other forms of voluntary contributions; may apply for grants from public and private sources; and may expend funds received under this subsection for the purpose of promoting public education and awareness of the registry.

(c) All fees, funds, and gifts received pursuant to this section shall be subject to audit by the State Auditor and shall be expended in conformity with Chapter 143C of the General Statutes. (2001-455, s. 1; 2001-513, s. 30(b); 2006-203, s. 70; 2011-284, s. 89.)

§ 130A-471. Limitation of liability.

The State of North Carolina, the Secretary of State, and any agent or person employed by the Secretary of State shall not be liable for any claims or demands arising out of the administration or operation of the registry authorized by this Article, except for acts of gross negligence, willful misconduct, or intentional wrongdoing. (2001-455, s. 1; 2001-513, s. 30(b).)

§§ 130A-472 through 130A-474: Reserved for future codification purposes.

Article 22.

A Terrorist Incident Using Nuclear, Biological, or Chemical Agents.

§ 130A-475. Suspected terrorist attack.

(a) If the State Health Director reasonably suspects that a public health threat may exist and that the threat may have been caused by a terrorist incident using nuclear, biological, or chemical agents, the State Health Director is authorized to order any of the following:

(1) Require any person or animal to submit to examinations and tests to determine possible exposure to the nuclear, biological, or chemical agents.

(2) Test any real or personal property necessary to determine the presence of nuclear, biological, or chemical agents.

(3) Evacuate or close any real property, including any building, structure, or land when necessary to investigate suspected contamination of the property. The period of closure during an investigation shall not exceed 10 calendar days. If the State Health Director determines that a longer period of closure is necessary to complete the investigation, the Director may institute an action in superior court to order the property to remain closed until the investigation is completed.

(4) Limit the freedom of movement or action of a person or animal that is contaminated with, or reasonably suspected of being contaminated with, a biological, chemical or nuclear agent that may be conveyed to other persons or animals.

(5) Limit access by any person or animal to an area or facility that is housing persons or animals whose movement or action has been limited under subdivision (4) of this subsection or to an area or facility that is contaminated with, or reasonably suspected of being contaminated with, a biological, chemical or nuclear agent that may be conveyed to other persons or animals. Nothing in this subdivision shall be construed to restrict the access of authorized health care, law enforcement, or emergency medical services personnel to quarantine or isolation premises as necessary in conducting their duties.

(b) The authority under subsection (a) of this section shall be exercised only when and so long as a public health threat may exist, all other reasonable means for correcting the problem have been exhausted, and no less restrictive alternative exists. Before applying the authority under subdivision (4) or (5) of subsection (a) of this section to livestock or poultry for the purpose of preventing the direct or indirect conveyance of a biological, chemical or nuclear agent to persons, the State Health Director shall consult with the State Veterinarian in the Department of Agriculture and Consumer Services.

The period of limited freedom of movement or access under subdivisions (4) and (5) of subsection (a) of this section shall not exceed 30 calendar days. Any person substantially affected by that limitation may institute, in superior court in Wake County or in the county in which the limitation is imposed, an action to review the limitation. The State Health Director shall give the persons known by the State Health Director to be substantially affected by the limitation reasonable notice under the circumstances of the right to institute an action to review the limitation. If a person or a person's representative requests a hearing, the hearing shall be held within 72 hours of the filing of the request, excluding Saturdays and Sundays. The person substantially affected by that limitation is entitled to be represented by counsel of the person's own choice or if the person is indigent, the person shall be represented by counsel appointed in accordance with Article 36 of Chapter 7A of the General Statutes and the rules adopted by the Office of Indigent Defense Services. The court shall reduce or terminate the limitation unless it determines, by the preponderance of the evidence, that the limitation is reasonably necessary to prevent or limit the conveyance of biological, chemical or nuclear agents to others, and may apply such conditions to the limitation as the court deems reasonable and necessary.

If the State Health Director determines that a 30-calendar-day limitation on freedom of movement or access is not adequate to protect the public health, the State Health Director must institute in superior court in the county in which the limitation is imposed, an action to obtain an order extending the period limiting the freedom of movement or access. If the person substantially affected by the limitation has already instituted an action in superior court in Wake County, the State Health Director must institute the action in superior court in Wake County or as a counterclaim in the pending case. The court shall continue the limitation for a period not to exceed 30 days, subject to conditions it deems reasonable and necessary, if it determines by the preponderance of the evidence, that additional limitation is reasonably necessary to prevent or limit the conveyance of biological, chemical, or nuclear agents to others. The court order shall specify the period of time the limitation is to be continued and shall provide for automatic termination of the order upon written determination by the State Health Director or local health director that the limitation on freedom of movement or access is no longer necessary to protect the public health. In addition, where the petitioner can prove by a preponderance of the evidence that the limitation on freedom of movement or access was not or is no longer needed for protection of the public health, the person so limited may move the trial court to reconsider its order extending the limitation on freedom of movement or access before the time for the order otherwise expires and may seek immediate or expedited termination of the order. Before the expiration of an order issued under this section, the State Health Director may move to continue the order for additional periods not to exceed 30 days each.

(c)   If the State Health Director reasonably suspects that there exists a public health threat that may have been caused by a terrorist incident using nuclear, biological, or chemical agents, the State Health Director shall notify the Governor and the Secretary of Public Safety. If the Secretary of Public Safety reasonably suspects that a public health threat may exist and that the threat may have been caused by a terrorist incident using nuclear, biological, or chemical agents, the Secretary shall notify the Governor and the State Health Director.

(d) For the purpose of this Article, the term "public health threat" means a situation that is likely to cause an immediate risk to human life, an immediate risk of serious physical injury or illness, or an immediate risk of serious adverse health effects.

(e) Nothing in this section shall limit any authority otherwise granted to local or State public health officials under this Chapter. (2002-179, s. 1; 2004-80, s. 3; 2004-199, s. 33; 2011-145, s. 19.1(g).)

§ 130A-476. Access to health information.

(a) Notwithstanding any other provision of law, a health care provider, a person in charge of a health care facility, or a unit of State or local government may report to the State Health Director or a local health director any events that may indicate the existence of a case or outbreak of an illness, condition, or health hazard that may have been caused by a terrorist incident using nuclear, biological, or chemical agents. Events that may be reported include unusual types or numbers of symptoms or illnesses presented to the provider, unusual trends in health care visits, or unusual trends in prescriptions or purchases of over-the-counter pharmaceuticals. To the extent practicable, a person who makes a report under this subsection shall not disclose personally identifiable information. A person disclosing or not disclosing information pursuant to this subsection is immune from any civil or criminal liability that might otherwise be incurred or imposed based on the disclosure or lack of disclosure provided that the health care provider was acting in good faith and without malice. In any proceeding involving liability, good faith and lack of malice are presumed. Notwithstanding the foregoing, if a health care provider or unit of State or local government willfully does not disclose information pursuant to this subsection, the immunity from civil or criminal liability provided under this subsection shall not be available if the person had actual knowledge that a condition or illness was caused by use of a nuclear, biological, or chemical weapon of mass destruction as defined in G.S. 14-288.21(c).

(b) The State Health Director may issue a temporary order requiring health care providers to report symptoms, diseases, conditions, trends in use of health care services, or other health-related information when necessary to conduct a public health investigation or surveillance of an illness, condition, or health hazard that may have been caused by a terrorist incident using nuclear, biological, or chemical agents. The order shall specify which health care providers must report, what information is to be reported, and the period of time for which reporting is required. The period of time for which reporting is required pursuant to a temporary order shall not exceed 90 days. The Commission may adopt rules to continue the reporting requirement when necessary to protect the public health.

(c) Health care providers and persons in charge of health care facilities or laboratories shall, upon request and proper identification, permit the State Health Director or a local health director to examine, review, and obtain a copy of records containing confidential or protected health information, or a summary of pertinent portions of those records, (i) that pertain to a report authorized by subsection (a) or required by subsection (b) of this section, or (ii) that, in the opinion of the State Health Director or local health director, are necessary for an investigation of a case or outbreak of an illness, condition, or health hazard that may have been caused by a terrorist incident using nuclear, biological, or chemical agents.

(d) A person who makes a report pursuant to subsection (b) of this section or permits examination, review, or copying of medical records pursuant to subsection (c) of this section is immune from any civil or criminal liability that otherwise might be incurred or imposed as a result of complying with those subsections.

(e) Confidential or protected health information received by the State Health Director or a local health director pursuant to this section shall be confidential and shall not be released, except when the release is:

(1) Made pursuant to any other provision of law;

(2) To another federal, state, or local public health agency for the purpose of preventing or controlling a public health threat; or

(3) To a court or law enforcement official or law enforcement officer for the purpose of enforcing the provisions of this Chapter or for the purpose of investigating a terrorist incident using nuclear, biological, or chemical agents. A

court or law enforcement official or law enforcement officer who receives the information shall not disclose it further, except (i) when necessary to conduct an investigation of a terrorist incident using nuclear, biological, or chemical agents, or (ii) when the State Health Director or a local health director seeks the assistance of the court or law enforcement official or law enforcement officer in preventing or controlling the public health threat and expressly authorizes the disclosure as necessary for that purpose.

(f) Repealed by Session Laws 2004-124, s. 10.34(a), effective January 1, 2005.

(g) In this section the following terms shall include:

(1) "Health care provider" includes a physician licensed to practice medicine in North Carolina or a person who is licensed, certified, or credentialed to practice or provide health care services, including, but not limited to, pharmacists, dentists, physician assistants, registered nurses, licensed practical nurses, advanced practice nurses, chiropractors, respiratory care therapists, and emergency medical technicians; and

(2) "Health care facility" includes hospitals, skilled nursing facilities, intermediate care facilities, psychiatric facilities, rehabilitation facilities, home health agencies, ambulatory surgical facilities, or any other health care related facility, whether publicly or privately owned. (2002-179, s. 1; 2004-80, s. 7; 2004-124, s. 10.34(a).)

§ 130A-477. Abatement of public health threat.

If it is determined that a public health threat may exist because of the contamination of property caused by a terrorist incident using nuclear, biological, or chemical agents, the State Health Director may order any action to abate that public health threat. To the extent that any owner, lessee, operator, or other person in control of the property is innocent of culpability in the creation of the public health threat, that person shall not be responsible for the costs of abating the public health threat. (2002-179, s. 1.)

§ 130A-478. Tort liability.

Article 31 of Chapter 143 applies to negligent acts committed by any officer, employee, involuntary servant or agent of the State acting pursuant to this Article. (2002-179, s. 1.)

§ 130A-479. Biological agents registry; rules; penalties.

(a) The Department shall establish and administer a program for the registration of biological agents. The biological agents registry shall identify the biological agents possessed and maintained by any person in this State and shall contain other information required under rules adopted by the Commission.

(b) The following definitions apply in this section:

(1) "Biological agent" means:

a. Any select agent that is a microorganism, virus, bacterium, fungus, rickettsia, or toxin listed in Appendix A of Part 72 of Title 42 of the Code of Federal Regulations.

b. Any genetically modified microorganisms or genetic elements from an organism on Appendix A of Part 72 of Title 42 of the Code of Federal Regulations, shown to produce or encode for a factor associated with a disease.

c. Any genetically modified microorganisms or genetic elements that contain nucleic acid sequences coding for any of the toxins listed on Appendix A of Part 72 of Title 42 of the Code of Federal Regulations, or their toxic submits.

(2) "Person" means any association, business, corporation, facility, firm, individual, institution of higher education, organization, partnership, society, State agency, or other legal entity.

(c) The Commission shall adopt rules for the implementation of the registry program, as follows:

(1) Determining and listing the biological agents required to be reported under this section.

(2) Designating persons required to make reports and specific information required to be reported including time limits for reporting, form of reports, and to whom reports shall be submitted.

(3) Providing for the release of information in the registry to State and federal law enforcement agencies and the United States Centers for Disease Control and Prevention pursuant to a communicable disease investigation commenced or conducted by the Department, the Commission, or other state or federal law enforcement agency having investigatory authority, or in connection with any investigation involving release, theft, or loss of biological agents.

(4) Establishing a system of safeguards that requires persons possessing and maintaining biological agents subject to this section to comply with the same federal standards that apply to persons registered to possess the same agents under federal law.

(5) Establishing a process for persons that possess and maintain biological agents to alert appropriate authorities of unauthorized possession or attempted possession of biological agents. The rules shall designate appropriate authorities for receipt of alerts from these persons.

(d) Any person that possesses and maintains any biological agent required to be reported under this section shall report to the Department the information required by the Commission for inclusion in the biological agent registry.

(e) Except as otherwise provided in this section, information prepared for or maintained in the registry under this section shall be confidential and shall not be a public record under G.S. 132-1. The Department may, in accordance with rules adopted by the Commission, release information contained in the biological agent registry for the purpose of conducting or aiding in a communicable disease investigation. The Department shall cooperate with and may share information contained in the biological agent registry with the United States Centers for Disease Control and Prevention, and state and federal law enforcement agencies in any investigation involving the release, theft, or loss of a biological agent required to be reported under this section. Release of information from the registry as authorized under this subsection shall not render the information released a public record under G.S. 132-1. Release of information from the registry as authorized under this subsection also shall not render the information prepared for or maintained in the registry a public record under G.S. 132-1.

(f)   The Department shall impose a civil penalty for a willful or knowing violation of this section in the amount of up to one thousand dollars ($1,000). Each day of a continuing violation shall be a separate offense. Any person wishing to contest a penalty shall be entitled to an administrative hearing in accordance with Chapter 150B of the General Statutes. (2001-469, s. 1; 2002-179, s. 2(a).)

§ 130A-480. Emergency department data reporting.

(a)   For the purpose of ensuring the protection of the public health, the State Health Director shall develop a syndromic surveillance program for hospital emergency departments in order to detect and investigate public health threats that may result from (i) a terrorist incident using nuclear, biological, or chemical agents or (ii) an epidemic or infectious, communicable, or other disease. The State Health Director shall specify the data to be reported by hospitals pursuant to this program, subject to the following:

(1)   Each hospital shall submit electronically available emergency department data as specified by rule by the Commission. The Commission, in consultation with hospitals, shall establish by rule a schedule for the implementation of full electronic reporting capability of all data elements by all hospitals. The schedule shall take into consideration the number of data elements already reported by the hospital, the hospital's capacity to electronically maintain the remaining elements, available funding, and other relevant factors.

(2)   None of the following data for patients or their relatives, employers, or household members may be collected by the State Health Director: names; postal or street address information, other than town or city, county, state, and the first five digits of the zip code; geocode information; telephone numbers; fax numbers; electronic mail addresses; social security numbers; health plan beneficiary numbers; account numbers; certificate or license numbers; vehicle identifiers and serial numbers, including license plate numbers; device identifiers and serial numbers; web universal resource locators (URLs); Internet protocol (IP) address numbers; biometric identifiers, including finger and voice prints; and full face photographic images and any comparable images.

(b)   The following are not public records under Chapter 132 of the General Statutes and are privileged and confidential:

(1) Data reported to the State Health Director pursuant to this section.

(2) Data collected or maintained by any entity with whom the State Health Director contracts for the reporting, collection, or analysis of data pursuant to this section.

The State Health Director shall maintain the confidentiality of the data reported pursuant to this section and shall ensure that adequate measures are taken to provide system security for all data and information. The State Health Director may share data with local health departments and the Centers for Disease Control and Prevention (CDC) for public health purposes. Local health departments are bound by the confidentiality provisions of this section. The Department shall enter into an agreement with the CDC to ensure that the CDC complies with the confidentiality provisions of this section. The State Health Director shall not allow information that it receives pursuant to this section to be used for commercial purposes and shall not release data except as authorized by other provisions of law.

(c) A person is immune from liability for actions arising from the required submission of data under this Article.

(d) For purposes of this section, "hospital" means a hospital, as defined in G.S. 131E-214.1(3), that operates an emergency room on a 24-hour basis. The term does not include a psychiatric hospital that operates an emergency room.

(e) Administrative emergency department data shall be reported by hospitals under Article 11A of Chapter 131E of the General Statutes. (2004-124, s. 10.34(b); 2006-264, s. 64(a); 2007-8, s. 1.)

§ 130A-481. Food defense.

The Department of Agriculture and Consumer Services, Department of Environment and Natural Resources, and Department of Health and Human Services shall jointly develop a plan to protect the food supply from intentional contamination. The plan shall address protection of the food supply from production to consumption, including, but not limited to, the protection of plants, crops, and livestock. (2006-80, s. 2.)

§ 130A-482. Reserved for future codification purposes.

§ 130A-483. Reserved for future codification purposes.

§ 130A-484. Reserved for future codification purposes.

§ 130A-485. Vaccination program established; definitions.

(a) The Department and local health departments shall offer a vaccination program for first responders who may be exposed to infectious diseases when deployed to disaster locations. The vaccinations shall include, but are not limited to, hepatitis A vaccination, hepatitis B vaccination, diphtheria-tetanus vaccination, influenza vaccination, pneumococcal vaccination, and other vaccinations when recommended by the United States Public Health Service and in accordance with Federal Emergency Management Directors Policy. Immune globulin will be made available when necessary, as determined by the State Health Director.

(b) Participation in the vaccination program is voluntary by the first responders, except for first responders who are classified as having "occupational exposure" to bloodborne pathogens as defined by the Occupational Safety and Health Administration Standard contained at 29 C.F.R. § 1910.10300 who shall be required to take the designated vaccinations or otherwise required by law.

(c) Nothing in this section shall require first responders, except first responders for whom the vaccination program is not voluntary as set forth in subsection (b) of this section, who present a written statement from a licensed physician indicating that a vaccine is medically contraindicated for the first responder or who sign a written statement that the administration of a vaccination conflicts with the first responder's religious tenets, to receive a vaccine.

(d) In the event of a vaccine shortage, the State Public Health Director, in consultation with the Centers for Disease Control and Prevention, shall give priority for vaccination to first responders deployed to a disaster location.

(e) The Department shall notify first responders of the availability of the vaccination program and shall provide educational materials on ways to prevent exposure to infectious diseases.

(f) As used in this section, unless the context clearly requires otherwise, the term:

(1) "Bioterrorism" means the intentional use of any microorganism, virus, infectious substance, biological product, or biological agent as defined in G.S. 130A-479 that may be engineered as a result of biotechnology or any naturally occurring or bioengineered component of any microorganism, virus, infectious substance, or biological product to cause or attempt to cause death, disease, or other biological malfunction in any living organism.

(2) "Disaster location" means any geographical location where a bioterrorism attack, terrorist incident, catastrophic or natural disaster, or emergency occurs.

(3) "First responders" means State and local law enforcement personnel, fire department personnel, and emergency medical personnel who will be deployed to bioterrorism attacks, terrorist attacks, catastrophic or natural disasters, or emergencies. (2003-227, s. 1.)

§§ 130A-486 through 130A-490. Reserved for future codification purposes.

Article 23.

Smoking Prohibited in Public Places and Places of Employment.

Part 1A. Findings and Intent.

§ 130A-491. Legislative findings and intent.

(a) Findings. - The General Assembly finds that secondhand smoke has been proven to cause cancer, heart disease, and asthma attacks in both smokers and nonsmokers. In 2006, a report issued by the United States Surgeon General stated that the scientific evidence indicates that there is no risk-free level of exposure to secondhand smoke.

(b) Intent. - It is the intent of the General Assembly to protect the health of individuals in public places and places of employment and riding in State government vehicles from the risks related to secondhand smoke. It is further the intent of the General Assembly to allow local governments to adopt local laws governing smoking within their jurisdictions that are more restrictive than the State law. (2007-193, s. 1; 2008-149, s. 1; 2009-27, s. 1.)

§ 130A-492. Definitions.

The following definitions apply in this Article:

(1) "Bar". - An establishment with a permit to sell alcoholic beverages pursuant to subdivision (1), (3), (5), or (10) of G.S. 18B-1001.

(2) "Cigar bar". - An establishment with a permit to sell alcoholic beverages pursuant to subdivision (1), (3), (5), or (10) of G.S. 18B-1001 that satisfies all of the following:

a. Generates sixty percent (60%) or more of its quarterly gross revenue from the sale of alcoholic beverages and twenty-five percent (25%) or more of its quarterly gross revenue from the sale of cigars;

b. Has a humidor on the premises; and

c. Does not allow individuals under the age of 21 to enter the premises.

Revenue generated from other tobacco sales, including cigarette vending machines, shall not be used to determine whether an establishment satisfies the definition of cigar bar.

(3) "Employee". - A person who is employed by an employer, or who contracts with an employer or third person to perform services for an employer, or who otherwise performs services for an employer with or without compensation.

(4) "Employer". - An individual person, business, association, political subdivision, or other public or private entity, including a nonprofit entity, that employs or contracts for or accepts the provision of services from one or more employees.

(5) "Enclosed area". - An area with a roof or other overhead covering of any kind and walls or side coverings of any kind, regardless of the presence of openings for ingress and egress, on all sides or on all sides but one.

(6) "Grounds". - An unenclosed area owned, leased, or occupied by State or local government.

(7) "Local government". - A local political subdivision of this State, an airport authority, or an authority or body created by an ordinance, joint resolution, or rules of any such entity.

(8) "Local government building". - A building owned, leased as lessor, or the area leased as lessee and occupied by a local government.

(9) "Local vehicle". - A passenger-carrying vehicle owned, leased, or otherwise controlled by local government and assigned permanently or temporarily by local government to local government employees, agencies, institutions, or facilities for official local government business.

(10) "Lodging establishment". - An establishment that provides lodging for pay to the public.

(11) "Private club". - A country club or an organization that maintains selective members, is operated by the membership, does not provide food or lodging for pay to anyone who is not a member or a member's guest, and is either incorporated as a nonprofit corporation in accordance with Chapter 55A of the General Statutes or is exempt from federal income tax under the Internal Revenue Code as defined in G.S. 105-130.2(1). For the purposes of this Article, private club includes country club.

(12) "Private residence". - A private dwelling that is not a child care facility, as defined in G.S. 110-86(3), and not a long-term care facility, as defined in G.S. 131E-14.3(a)(1).

(13) "Private vehicle". - A privately owned vehicle that is not used for commercial or employment purposes.

(14) "Public place". - An enclosed area to which the public is invited or in which the public is permitted.

(15) "Restaurant". - A food or lodging establishment that prepares and serves drink or food as regulated by the Commission pursuant to Part 6 of Article 8 of this Chapter.

(16) "Smoking". - The use or possession of a lighted cigarette, lighted cigar, lighted pipe, or any other lighted tobacco product.

(17) "State government". - The political unit for the State of North Carolina, including all agencies of the executive, judicial, and legislative branches of government.

(18) "State government building". - A building owned, leased as lessor, or the area leased as lessee and occupied by State government.

(19) "State vehicle". - A passenger-carrying vehicle owned, leased, or otherwise controlled by the State and assigned permanently or temporarily to a State employee or State agency or institution for official State business.

(20) "Tobacco shop". - A business establishment, the main purpose of which is the sale of tobacco, tobacco products, and accessories for such products, that receives no less than seventy-five percent (75%) of its total annual revenues from the sale of tobacco, tobacco products, and accessories for such products, and does not serve food or alcohol on its premises. (2007-193, s. 1; 2008-149, s. 2; 2009-27, s. 1; 2009-550, s. 6(a).)

§ 130A-493. Smoking prohibited in State government buildings and State vehicles.

(a) Notwithstanding Article 64 of Chapter 143 of the General Statutes pertaining to State-controlled buildings, smoking is prohibited inside State government buildings except as provided in subsection (b) of this section.

(b) Smoking is permitted inside State government buildings that are used for medical or scientific research to the extent that smoking is an integral part of the research. Smoking permitted under this subsection shall be confined to the area where the research is being conducted.

(c) The individual in charge of the State government building or the individual's designee shall post signs in conspicuous areas of the building. The signs shall state that "smoking is prohibited" and may include the international "No Smoking" symbol, which consists of a pictorial representation of a burning cigarette enclosed in a red circle with a red bar across it. In addition, the individual in charge of the building or the individual's designee shall:

(1)   Direct a person who is smoking inside the building to extinguish the lighted smoking product.

(2)   In a State psychiatric hospital, provide written notice to individuals upon admittance that smoking is prohibited inside the building and obtain the signature of the individual or the individual's representative acknowledging receipt of the notice.

(c1)   Smoking is prohibited inside State vehicles. The individual or the individual's designee in charge of assigning the vehicle shall place one or more signs in conspicuous areas of the vehicle. The signs shall state that "smoking is prohibited" and may include the international "No Smoking" symbol, which consists of a pictorial representation of a burning cigarette enclosed in a red circle with a red bar across it. If the vehicle is used for undercover law enforcement operations, a sign is not required to be placed in the vehicle as provided in this subsection.

(d)   Notwithstanding G.S. 130A-25, a violation of Article 23 of this Chapter shall not be punishable as a criminal violation. (2007-193, s. 1; 2007-459, s. 4.1; 2008-149, s. 3; 2009-27, s. 1.)

§ 130A-494. Other prohibitions.

Nothing in this Article repeals any other law prohibiting smoking, nor does it limit any law allowing regulation or prohibition of smoking on walkways or on the grounds of buildings. (2007-193, ss. 1, 3.2.)

§ 130A-495. Rules.

The Commission shall adopt rules to implement this Part. (2007-193, s. 1.)

Part 1C. Smoking Prohibited in Restaurants and Bars.

§ 130A-496. Smoking prohibited in restaurants and bars.

(a) Notwithstanding Article 64 of Chapter 143 of the General Statutes, smoking is prohibited in all enclosed areas of restaurants and bars, except as provided in subsection (b) of this section.

(b) Smoking may be permitted in the following places:

(1) A designated smoking guest room in a lodging establishment. No greater than twenty percent (20%) of a lodging establishment's guest rooms may be designated smoking guest rooms.

(2) A cigar bar if smoke from the cigar bar does not migrate into an enclosed area where smoking is prohibited pursuant to this Article. A cigar bar that begins operation after July 1, 2009, may only allow smoking if it is located in a freestanding structure occupied solely by the cigar bar and smoke from the cigar bar does not migrate into an enclosed area where smoking is prohibited pursuant to this Article. To qualify under this subsection, the cigar bar must satisfactorily report on a quarterly basis to the Department, on a form prescribed by the Department, the revenue generated from the sale of alcoholic beverages and cigars as a percentage of quarterly gross revenue. The Department shall determine whether any additional documentation is required of the cigar bar to authenticate or verify revenue data submitted by the cigar bar. This subdivision shall not apply to any business that is established for the purpose of avoiding compliance with this Article.

(3) A private club. (2009-27, s. 1.)

§ 130A-497. Implementation and enforcement.

(a) A person who manages, operates, or controls a restaurant or bar in which smoking is prohibited shall:

(1) Conspicuously post signs clearly stating that smoking is prohibited. The signs may include the international "No Smoking" symbol, which consists of a pictorial representation of a burning cigarette enclosed in a red circle with a red bar across it.

(2) Remove all indoor ashtrays and other smoking receptacles.

(3) Direct a person who is smoking to extinguish the lighted tobacco product.

(b) Continuing to smoke in a nonsmoking area described in this Part following oral or written notice by the person in charge of the area or the person's designee constitutes an infraction, and the person committing the infraction may be punished by a fine of not more than fifty dollars ($50.00).

(c) Conviction of an infraction under this section has no consequence other than payment of a penalty. A person found responsible for a violation of this section may not be assessed court costs.

(d) Notwithstanding G.S. 130A-25, a violation of this Part shall not be punishable as a misdemeanor.

(e) Administrative penalties imposed under G.S. 130A-22(h1) against a person who manages, operates, or controls a restaurant or bar and fails to comply with the provisions of this Article and the rules adopted by the Commission to implement the provisions of this Article shall only be enforced by a local health director.

(f) The Commission shall adopt rules to implement the provisions of this Article. (2009-27, s. 1.)

Part 2. Local Government Regulation of Smoking.

§ 130A-498. Local governments may restrict smoking in public places.

(a) Except as otherwise provided in subsection (b1) of this section, and notwithstanding any other provision of Article 64 of Chapter 143 of the General Statutes to the contrary, a local government may adopt and enforce ordinances, board of health rules, and policies restricting or prohibiting smoking that are more restrictive than State law and that apply in local government buildings, on local government grounds, in local vehicles, or in public places. A rule or policy adopted on and after July 1, 2009 pursuant to this subsection by a local board of health or an entity exercising the powers of a local board of health must be approved by an ordinance adopted by the Board of County Commissioners of the county to which the rule applies. The definitions set forth in G.S. 130A-492 in Part 1A of this Article apply to this section and shall apply to any local ordinance, rule, or law adopted by a local government under this section.

(b)   Repealed by Session Laws 2009-27, s. 1, effective January 2, 2010.

(b1)   A local ordinance or other rules, laws, or policies adopted under this section may not restrict or prohibit smoking in the following places:

(1)   A private residence.

(2)   A private vehicle.

(3)   A tobacco shop if smoke from the business does not migrate into an enclosed area where smoking is prohibited pursuant to this Article. A tobacco shop that begins operation after July 1, 2009, may only allow smoking if it is located in a freestanding structure occupied solely by the tobacco shop and smoke from the shop does not migrate into an enclosed area where smoking is prohibited pursuant to this Article.

(4)   All of the premises, facilities, and vehicles owned, operated, or leased by any tobacco products processor or manufacturer, or any tobacco leaf grower, processor, or dealer.

(5)   A designated smoking guest room in a lodging establishment. No greater than twenty percent (20%) of a lodging establishment's guest rooms may be designated smoking guest rooms.

(6)   A cigar bar if smoke from the cigar bar does not migrate into an enclosed area where smoking is prohibited pursuant to this Article. A cigar bar that begins operation after July 1, 2009, may only allow smoking if it is located in a freestanding structure occupied solely by the cigar bar and smoke from the cigar bar does not migrate into an enclosed area where smoking is prohibited pursuant to this Article. To qualify under this subsection, the cigar bar must satisfactorily report on a quarterly basis to the Department, on a form prescribed by the Department, the revenue generated from the sale of alcoholic beverages and cigars as a percentage of quarterly gross revenue. The Department shall determine whether any additional documentation is required of the cigar bar to authenticate or verify revenue data submitted by the cigar bar. This subdivision shall not apply to any business that is established for the purpose of avoiding compliance with this Article.

(7) A private club.

(8) A motion picture, television, theater, or other live production set. This exemption applies only to the actor or performer portraying the use of tobacco products during the production.

(c) Repealed by Session Laws 2009-27, s. 1, effective January 2, 2010.

(c1) Continuing to smoke in violation of a local ordinance or other rules, laws, or policies adopted under this section constitutes an infraction, and the person committing the infraction may be punished by a fine of not more than fifty dollars ($50.00). Conviction of an infraction under this section has no consequence other than payment of a penalty. A person smoking in violation of a local ordinance or other rules, laws, or policies adopted under this section may not be assessed court costs.

(d) Repealed by Session Laws 2009-27, s. 1, effective January 2, 2010.

(d1) Notwithstanding G.S. 130A-25 or any other provision of law, a violation of a local ordinance, rule, law, or policy adopted under this section shall not be punishable as a misdemeanor.

(d2) A local government may enforce an ordinance, rule, law, or policy under this section against a person who manages, operates, or controls a public place only as provided in G.S. 130A-22(h1).

(e) A county ordinance adopted under this section is subject to the provisions of G.S. 153A-122. (2007-193, ss. 2, 3.1; 2007-484, s. 31.7; 2008-95, s. 1; 2008-149, s. 4; 2009-27, s. 1.)

§ 130A-499: Reserved for future codification purposes.

§ 130A-500: Reserved for future codification purposes.

§ 130A-501: Reserved for future codification purposes.

§ 130A-502: Reserved for future codification purposes.

§ 130A-503: Reserved for future codification purposes.

§ 130A-504: Reserved for future codification purposes.

§ 130A-505: Reserved for future codification purposes.

§ 130A-506: Reserved for future codification purposes.

§ 130A-507: Reserved for future codification purposes.

§ 130A-508: Reserved for future codification purposes.

§ 130A-509: Reserved for future codification purposes.

§ 130A-510: Reserved for future codification purposes.

Chapter 130B.

Hazardous Waste Management Commission.

§§ 130B-1 through 130B-24: Repealed by Session Laws 2001-474, s. 1, effective November 29, 2001.

§§ 131-1 through 131-188: Repealed by Session Laws 1983, c. 775, s. 1.

Chapter 131A.

Health Care Facilities Finance Act.

§131A-1. Short title.

This Chapter shall be known, and may be cited, as the "Health Care Facilities Finance Act." (1975, c. 766, s. 1.)

§ 131A-2. Legislative findings.

It is hereby declared to be the policy of the State of North Carolina to promote the public health and welfare by providing means for financing, refinancing, acquiring, constructing, equipping and providing of health care facilities to serve the people of the State and to make accessible to them modern and efficient health care facilities.

The General Assembly hereby finds and declares that:

(1) There is a need to overcome existing and anticipated physical and technical obsolescence of existing health care facilities and to provide additional modern and efficient health care facilities in the State; and

(2) Unless measures are adopted to alleviate such need, the shortage of such facilities will become increasingly more urgent and serious; and

(3) In order to meet such shortage and thereby promote the public health and welfare of the people of the State, it is necessary for the State to assist in the providing of adequate modern and efficient health care facilities in the State so that health and hospital care and services may be expanded, improved and fostered to the fullest extent practicable.

The General Assembly hereby further finds and declares that the financing, refinancing, acquiring, constructing, equipping and providing of health care facilities are public uses and public purposes and that enactment of this Chapter is necessary and proper for effectuating the purposes hereof. (1975, c. 766, s. 1; 1993, c. 553, s. 42.)

§ 131A-3. Definitions.

As used or referred to in this Chapter, the following words and terms shall have the following meanings, unless the context clearly indicates otherwise:

(1) "Bonds" or "notes" means the revenue bonds or bond anticipation notes, respectively, authorized to be issued by the Commission under this Chapter;

(2) "Commission" means the North Carolina Medical Care Commission, created by Part 10 of Article 3 of Chapter 143B of the General Statutes, or, should said Commission be abolished or otherwise divested of its functions under this Chapter, the public body succeeding it in its principal functions, or upon which are conferred by law the rights, powers and duties given by this Chapter to the Commission;

(3) "Cost" as applied to any health care facilities means the cost of construction or acquisition; the cost of acquisition of property, including rights in land and other property, both real and personal and improved and unimproved; the cost of demolishing, removing or relocating any buildings or structures on land so acquired, including the cost of acquiring any land to which such buildings or structures may be moved or relocated; the cost of all machinery, fixed and movable equipment and furnishings; financing charges, interest prior to and during construction and, if deemed advisable by the Commission, for a period not exceeding two years after the estimated date of completion of construction, the cost of engineering and architectural surveys, plans and specifications; the cost of consulting and legal services and other expenses necessary or incident to determining the feasibility or practicability of constructing or acquiring such health care facilities; the cost of administrative and other expenses necessary or incident to the construction or acquisition of such health care facilities, and the financing of the construction or acquisition thereof, including reasonable provision for working capital and a reserve for debt service; the cost of reimbursing any public or nonprofit agency for any payments made for any cost described above or the refinancing of any cost described above, provided that no payment shall be reimbursed or any cost be refinanced if such payment was made or such cost was incurred earlier than two years prior to the effective date of this Chapter; provided further, that it is the intent that any costs described above shall be payable solely from the revenues of the health care facilities;

(4) "Health care facilities" means any one or more buildings, structures, additions, extensions, improvements or other facilities, whether or not located on the same site or sites, machinery, equipment, furnishings or other real or personal property suitable for health care or medical care; and includes, without limitation: general hospitals, chronic diseases, maternity, mental, tuberculosis and other specialized hospitals; facilities for intensive care and self-care; nursing homes, including skilled nursing facilities and intermediate care facilities; facilities for continuing care of the elderly and infirm; clinics and outpatient facilities; clinical, pathological and other laboratories; health care research facilities; laundries; training facilities for nurses, interns, physicians and other staff members; food preparation and food service facilities; administration buildings, central service and other administrative facilities; communication, computer; and other electronic facilities, fire-fighting facilities, pharmaceutical facilities and recreational facilities; storage space, X-ray, laser, radiotherapy and other apparatus and equipment; dispensaries; utilities; vehicular parking lots and garages; office facilities for health care facilities staff members and physicians; and such other health care facilities customarily under the

jurisdiction of or provided by hospitals, or any combination of the foregoing, with all necessary, convenient or related interests in land, machinery, apparatus, appliances, equipment, furnishings, appurtenances, site preparation, landscaping and physical amenities;

(5) "Non-profit agency" means any nonprofit corporation existing or hereafter created and empowered to acquire, by lease or otherwise, operate or maintain health care facilities;

(6) "Public agency" means any county, city, town, hospital district or other political subdivision of the State existing or hereafter created pursuant to the laws of the State authorized to acquire, by lease or otherwise, operate or maintain health care facilities;

(7) "State" means the State of North Carolina;

(8) "Federally guaranteed security" means any security, investment or evidence of indebtedness issued pursuant to any provision of federal law for the purpose of financing or refinancing the cost of any health care facilities which is insured or guaranteed, directly or indirectly, in whole or in part as to the repayment of principal or interest by the United States of America or any instrumentality thereof;

(9) "Federally insured mortgage note" means any loan secured by a mortgage or deed of trust on any health care facilities owned or leased by any public or nonprofit agency which is insured or guaranteed, directly or indirectly, in whole or in part as to the repayment of principal and interest by the United States of America or any instrumentality thereof, or any commitment by the United States of America or any instrumentality thereof to so insure or guarantee such a loan secured by a mortgage or a deed of trust.

(10) "Continuing care" means the furnishing, pursuant to a continuing care agreement, of shelter, food, and nursing care to an individual not related by consanguinity or affinity to the provider furnishing such care. Other personal services provided shall be designated in the continuing care agreement. Continuing care shall include only life care, care for life, or care for a term of years;

(11) "Life care" or "care for life" means a life lease, life membership, life estate, or similar agreement between an individual and a provider by which the

individual pays a fee for the right to occupy a space in the continuing care facility and to receive continuing care for life; and

(12)   "Care for a term of years" means an agreement between an individual and a provider whereby the individual pays a fee for the right to occupy space in a continuing care facility, and to receive continuing care, for at least one year, but for less than the life of the member. (1975, c. 766, s. 1; 1979, c. 54, s. 1; 1981, c. 64; c. 867, ss. 1, 2; 2005-238, s. 13.)

§ 131A-4. Additional powers.

The Commission shall have all of the powers necessary or convenient to carry out and effectuate the purposes and provisions of this Chapter, including, but without limiting the generality of the foregoing, the power:

(1)   To make and execute contracts and agreements necessary or incidental to the exercise of its powers and duties under this Chapter, including loan agreements and agreements of sale or leases with and mortgages and conveyances to public and nonprofit agencies, persons, firms, corporations, governmental agencies and others;

(2)   To acquire by purchase, the exercise of the power of eminent domain but only in connection with a financing for a public agency, lease, gift or otherwise, or to obtain options for the acquisition of, any property, real or personal, improved or unimproved, including interests in land in fee or less than fee for any health care facilities, upon such terms and at such cost as shall be agreed upon by the owner and the Commission;

(3)   To arrange or contract with any county, city, town or other political subdivision or instrumentality of the State for the opening or closing of streets or for the furnishing of utility or other services to any health care facilities;

(4)   To sell, convey, lease as lessor, mortgage, exchange, transfer, or otherwise dispose of, or to grant options for any such purposes with respect to, any real or personal property or interest therein;

(5)   To pledge or assign any money, purchase price payments, rents, loan repayments, charges, fees or other revenues, including any federally guaranteed security and moneys received therefrom whether such securities

are initially acquired by the Commission or a public or nonprofit agency, and any proceeds derived by the Commission from sales of property, insurance, condemnation awards or other sources;

(6) To pledge or assign the revenues and receipts from any health care facilities and any agreement of sale or lease or the purchase price payments, rent and income received thereunder;

(7) To borrow money as herein provided to carry out and effectuate its corporate purposes and to issue in evidence thereof bonds and notes for the purpose of providing funds to pay all or any part of the cost of any health care facilities, to lend money to any public or nonprofit agency to pay all or any part of the cost of health care facilities, to acquire any federally guaranteed security or any federally insured mortgage note, to lend money to any public or nonprofit agency for the acquisition of any federally guaranteed security and to issue revenue refunding bonds;

(8) To finance, acquire, construct, equip, provide, operate, own, repair, maintain, extend, improve, rehabilitate, renovate and furnish any health care facilities and to pay all or any part of the cost thereof from the proceeds of bonds or notes or from any contribution, gift or donation or other funds available to the Commission for such purpose;

(9) To fix, revise, charge and collect or cause to be fixed, revised, charged and collected purchase price payments, rents, loan repayments, fees, professional contracts and charges for the use of, or services rendered by, any health care facilities;

(10) To employ fiscal consultants, consulting engineers, architects, attorneys, health care consultants, appraisers and such other consultants and employees as may be required in the judgment of the Commission and to fix and pay their compensation from funds available to the Commission therefor and to select and retain subject to approval of the Local Government Commission the financial consultants, underwriters and bond attorneys to be associated with the issuance of any bonds and to pay for services rendered by underwriters, financial consultants or bond attorneys out of the proceeds of any such issue with regard to which the services were performed;

(11) To conduct studies and surveys respecting the need for health care facilities and their location, financing and construction;

(12) To apply for, accept, receive and agree to and comply with the terms and conditions governing grants, loans, advances, contributions, interest subsidies and other aid with respect to health care facilities from federal and State agencies or instrumentalities and to accept, receive and agree to and comply with the terms and conditions governing payments under any health insurance programs;

(13) To sue and be sued in its own name, plead and be impleaded;

(14) To acquire and enter into commitments to acquire any federally guaranteed security or federally insured mortgage note and to pledge or otherwise use any such federally guaranteed security or federally insured mortgage note in such manner as the Commission deems in its best interest to secure or otherwise provide a source of repayment on any of its bonds or notes issued on behalf of any public or nonprofit agency to finance or refinance the cost of any health care facilities.

Any power granted to the Commission under the provisions of this Chapter may be exercised by the executive committee of the Commission when the Commission is not in session, except that the executive committee may not overrule, reverse or disregard any action of the full Commission. The chairman of the Commission may call meetings of the executive committee at any time. (1975, c. 766, s. 1; 1977, c. 267; 1979, c. 54, ss. 2-6; 1985, c. 723, s. 4.)

§ 131A-5. Criteria and requirements.

In undertaking any health care facilities pursuant to this Chapter, the Commission shall be guided by and shall observe the following criteria and requirements; provided that the determination of the Commission as to its compliance with such criteria and requirements shall be final and conclusive:

(1) There is a need for the health care facilities in the area in which the health care facilities are to be located;

(2) No health care facilities shall be sold or leased nor any loan made to any public or nonprofit agency which is not financially responsible and capable of fulfilling its obligations, including its obligations under an agreement of sale or lease or a loan agreement to make purchase price payments, to pay rent, to operate, repair and maintain at its own expense the health care facilities and to

discharge such other responsibilities as may be imposed under the agreement of sale or lease or loan agreement;

(3) Adequate provision shall be made for the payment of the principal of and the interest on the bonds and any necessary reserves therefor and for the operation, repair and maintenance of the health care facilities at the expense of the public or nonprofit agency; and

(4) The public facilities, including utilities, and public services necessary for the health care facilities will be made available. (1975, c. 766, s. 1; 1979, c. 54, s. 7.)

§ 131A-6. Additional powers of public agencies.

For the purposes of this Chapter, public agencies are authorized and empowered to enter into contracts and agreements, including loan agreements and agreements of sale or lease, with the Commission to facilitate the financing or refinancing, acquiring, constructing, equipping, providing, operating and maintaining of health care facilities and pursuant to any such loan agreement or agreement of sale or lease to operate, repair and maintain any health care facilities and, subject to the provisions of G.S. 131A-8, to pay the cost thereof and the loan repayments, purchase price payments or rent therefor from any funds available for such purposes. In addition, public agencies may mortgage, pledge, assign, grant a security interest in, or otherwise encumber a health care facility, whether owned or leased, to secure obligations under a loan agreement or similar debt instrument in connection with the issuance of bonds or notes by the Commission under this Chapter. Property subject to a mortgage, deed of trust, security interest, or similar lien pursuant to this section may be sold at foreclosure in any manner permitted by the instrument creating the encumbrance, without compliance with any other provision of law regarding the disposition of publicly owned property. The granting of a lien on, or security interest in, a health care facility and the conveyance of this property pursuant to the provisions of the lien or security interest are not subject to the provisions of G.S. 131E-8, 131E-13, or 131E-14. (1975, c. 766, s. 1; 1979, c. 54, s. 8; 2005-238, s. 14.)

§ 131A-7. Procedural requirements.

In addition to health care facilities initiated by the Commission, any public or nonprofit agency may submit to the Commission, and the Commission may consider, a proposal for financing health care facilities using such forms and following such instructions as may be prescribed by the Commission. Such proposal shall set forth the type and location of the health care facilities and may include other information and data available to the public or nonprofit agency respecting the health care facilities and the extent to which such health care facilities conform to the criteria and requirements set forth in this Chapter. The Commission may request the public or nonprofit agency to provide additional information and data respecting the health care facilities. The Commission is authorized to make or cause to be made such investigations, surveys, studies, reports and reviews as in its judgment are necessary and desirable to determine the feasibility and desirability of the health care facilities, the extent to which the health care facilities will contribute to the health and welfare of the area in which they will be located, the powers, experience, background, financial condition, record of service and capability of the management of the public or nonprofit agency, the extent to which the health care facilities otherwise conform to the criteria and requirements of this Chapter, and such other factors as may be deemed relevant or convenient in carrying out the purposes of this Chapter. (1975, c. 766, s. 1.)

§ 131A-8. Operation of health care facilities; loan agreements; agreements of sale or lease; conveyance of interest in health care facilities.

All health care facilities shall be operated to serve and benefit the public and there shall be no discrimination against any person based on race, creed, color or national origin.

The Commission may sell or lease any health care facilities to a public or nonprofit agency for operation and maintenance or lend money to any public or nonprofit agency in such manner as shall effectuate the purposes of this Chapter, under a loan agreement or an agreement of sale or lease in form and substance not inconsistent herewith. Any such loan agreement or agreement of sale or lease may include provisions that:

(1)   The public or nonprofit agency shall, at its own expense, operate, repair and maintain the health care facilities covered by such agreement;

(2) The purchase price payments to be made under the agreement of sale, the rent payable under the agreement of lease or the loan repayments under the loan agreement shall in the aggregate be not less than an amount sufficient to pay all of the interest, principal and any redemption premium on the bonds or notes issued by the Commission to pay the cost of the health care facilities sold or leased thereunder or to make the loan with respect thereto;

(3) The public or nonprofit agency shall pay all other costs incurred by the Commission in connection with the providing of the health care facilities covered by any such agreement, except such costs as may be paid out of the proceeds of bonds or notes or otherwise, including, but without limitation, insurance costs, the cost of administering the resolution authorizing the issuance of, or any trust agreement securing, such bonds or notes and the fees and expenses of trustees, paying agents, attorneys, consultants and others;

(4) The loan agreement or the agreement of sale or lease shall terminate not earlier than the date on which all such bonds and all other obligations incurred by the Commission in connection with the health care facilities covered by any such agreement shall be retired or provision for such retirement shall be made; and

(5) The obligation of the public or nonprofit agency to make loan repayments or purchase price payments or to pay rent shall not be subject to cancellation, termination or abatement by the public or nonprofit agency until the bonds have been retired or provision has been made for such retirement.

All obligations payable by a public agency under a loan agreement or an agreement of sale or lease, including the obligation to make loan repayments or purchase price payments or to pay rent and to pay the costs of operating, repairing and maintaining health care facilities, shall be payable solely from the revenues of the health care facilities being purchased or leased or with respect to which a loan is made or other health care facilities of the health care facilities of the public agency or from any federally guaranteed security and moneys received therefrom and shall not be payable from or charged upon any funds of the public agency other than the revenues pledged to such payment; provided, however, that nothing herein shall restrict the power of any county, city, town or other political subdivision of the State or any hospital district created pursuant to Article 13C of Chapter 131 of the General Statutes to submit to its qualified voters a health care facility maintenance tax under Article 13B of said Chapter 131 for the purposes of financing the cost of operation, equipment and maintenance of any health care facility financed for any public agency under this

Chapter and all health care facilities authorized to be financed under this Chapter and leased to public agencies are hereby declared to be included within the definition "hospital facility" as used in said Article 13B.

Where the Commission has acquired a possessory or ownership interest in any health care facilities which it has undertaken on behalf of a public or nonprofit agency it shall promptly convey, without the payment of any consideration, all its right, title and interest in such health care facilities to such public or nonprofit agency upon the retirement or provision for the retirement of all bonds or notes issued and obligations incurred by the Commission in connection with such health care facilities. (1975, c. 766, s. 1; 1979, c. 54, s. 9.)

§ 131A-9. Construction contracts.

Contracts for the construction of any health care facilities on behalf of a public agency shall be awarded by the Commission in accordance with Article 8 of Chapter 143 of the General Statutes. If the Commission shall determine that the purposes of this Chapter will be more effectively served, the Commission in its discretion may award or cause to be awarded contracts for the construction of any health care facilities on behalf of a nonprofit agency upon a negotiated basis as determined by the Commission. The Commission shall prescribe such bid security requirements and other procedures in connection with the award of such contracts as in its judgment shall protect the public interest. The Commission may by written contract engage the services of the public or nonprofit agency in the construction of such health care facilities and may provide in such contract that such public or nonprofit agency, subject to such conditions and requirements consistent with the provisions of this Chapter as shall be prescribed in such contract, may act as an agent of, or an independent contractor for, the Commission for the performance of the functions described therein, including the acquisition of the site and other real property for such health care facilities, the preparation of plans, specifications and contract documents, the award of construction and other contracts upon a competitive or negotiated basis, the construction of such health care facilities directly by such public or nonprofit agency, the inspection and supervision of construction, the employment of engineers, architects, builders and other contractors and the provision of money to pay the cost thereof pending reimbursement by the Commission. Any such contract may provide that the Commission may, out of proceeds of bonds or notes, make advances to or reimburse the public or nonprofit agency for its costs incurred in the performance of such functions, and shall set forth the supporting documents required to be submitted to the Commission and the reviews, examinations and audits that shall be required in connection therewith to assure compliance with the provisions of this Chapter and such contract. (1975, c. 766, s. 1.)

§ 131A-10. Credit of State not pledged.

Bonds or notes issued under the provisions of this Chapter shall not be secured by a pledge of the faith and credit of the State or of any political subdivision thereof or be deemed to create an indebtedness of the State, or of any such political subdivision thereof, requiring any voter approval, but shall be payable solely from the revenues and other funds provided therefor. Each bond or note issued under this Chapter shall contain on the face thereof a statement to the effect that the Commission shall not be obligated to pay the same nor the interest thereon except from the revenues and other funds pledged therefor and that neither the faith and credit nor the taxing power of the State or of any political subdivision thereof is pledged as security for the payment of the principal of or the interest on such bond or note.

Expenses incurred by the Commission in carrying out the provisions of this Chapter may be made payable from funds provided pursuant to, or made available for use under, this Chapter and no liability shall be incurred by the Commission hereunder beyond the extent to which moneys shall have been so provided. (1975, c. 766, s. 1.)

§ 131A-11. Bonds and notes.

The Commission is hereby authorized to provide for the issuance, at one time or from time to time, of bonds, or notes in anticipation of the issuance of bonds, of the Commission to carry out and effectuate its corporate purposes. The principal of and the interest on such bonds or notes shall be payable solely from funds provided under this Chapter for such payment. Any such notes may be made payable from the proceeds of bonds or renewal notes or, in the event bond or renewal note proceeds are not available, such notes may be paid from any available revenues or other funds provided therefor. The bonds or notes of each issue shall be dated and may be made redeemable before maturity at the option of the Commission at such price or prices and upon such terms and conditions as may be determined by the Commission. Any such bonds or notes shall bear interest at such rate or rates as may be determined by the Local Government Commission of North Carolina with the approval of the Commission. Notes shall mature at such time or times not exceeding 10 years from their date or dates and bonds shall mature at such time or times not exceeding 40 years from their date or dates, as may be determined by the Commission. The Commission shall determine the form and manner of execution of the bonds or notes, including any interest coupons to be attached thereto, and shall fix the denomination or denominations and the place or places of payment of principal and interest, which may be any bank or trust company within or without the State. In case any officer whose signature or a facsimile of whose signature shall appear on any bonds or notes or coupons attached thereto shall cease to be such officer before the delivery thereof, such signature or such facsimile shall nevertheless be valid and sufficient for all purposes the same as if he had remained in office until such delivery. The Commission may also provide for the authentication of the bonds or notes by a trustee or fiscal agent. The bonds or notes may be issued in coupon or in registered form, or both, as the Commission may determine, and provision may be made for the registration of any coupon bonds or notes as to principal alone and also as to both principal and interest, and for the reconversion into coupon bonds or notes of any bonds or notes registered as to both principal and interest, and for the interchange of registered and coupon bonds or notes. No bonds or notes may be issued by the Commission under this Chapter unless the issuance thereof is approved by the Local Government Commission of North Carolina.

The Commission shall file with the Secretary of the Local Government Commission an application requesting approval of the issuance of such bonds or notes which shall contain such information and have attached to it such documents concerning the proposed financing and prospective borrower, vendee or lessee as the Secretary may require.

In determining whether a proposed bond or note issue should be approved, the Local Government Commission may consider, in addition to the criteria and requirements mentioned in G.S. 131A-5, the effect of the proposed financing upon any scheduled or proposed sale of tax-exempt obligations by the State or any of its agencies or departments or by any unit of local government in the State.

The Local Government Commission shall approve the issuance of such bonds or notes if, upon the information and evidence it receives, it finds and determines that the proposed financing will effectuate the purposes of this Chapter.

Upon the filing with the Local Government Commission of a resolution of the Commission requesting that its bonds or notes be sold, such bonds or notes may be sold in such manner, either at public or private sale, and for such price as the Local Government Commission shall determine to be for the best interests of the Commission and effectuate best the purposes of this Chapter, provided that such sale shall be approved by the Commission.

The proceeds of any bonds or notes shall be used solely for the purposes for which issued and shall be disbursed in such manner and under such restrictions, if any, as the Commission may provide in the resolution authorizing the issuance of, or any trust agreement securing, such bonds or notes.

Prior to the preparation of definitive bonds, the Commission may, under like restrictions, issue interim receipts or temporary bonds, with or without coupons, exchangeable for definitive bonds, when such bonds shall have been executed and are available for delivery. The Commission may also provide for the replacement of any bonds or notes which shall become mutilated or shall be destroyed or lost.

Bonds or notes may be issued under the provisions of this Chapter without obtaining, except as otherwise expressly provided in this Chapter, the consent of any department, division, commission, board, body, bureau or agency of the State, and without any other proceedings or the happening of any conditions or things other than those proceedings, conditions or things which are specifically required by this Chapter and the provisions of the resolution authorizing the issuance of, or any trust agreement securing, such bonds or notes. (1975, c. 766, s. 1; 1979, c. 54, s. 10.)

§ 131A-12. Trust agreement or resolution.

In the discretion of the Commission any bonds or notes issued under the provisions of this Chapter may be secured by a trust agreement by and between the Commission and a corporate trustee, which may be any trust company or bank having the powers of a trust company within or without the State. Such trust agreement or the resolution authorizing the issuance of such bonds or notes may pledge or assign all or any part of the revenues of the Commission received pursuant to this Chapter, including, without limitation, fees, loan repayments, purchase price payments, rents, charges, insurance proceeds, condemnation awards and any other revenues and funds received in connection with any health care facilities and may mortgage any health care facilities. Such trust agreement or resolution may contain such provisions for protecting and enforcing the rights and remedies of the holders of any such bonds or notes as may be reasonable and proper and not in violation of law, including covenants setting forth the duties of the Commission in relation to the purposes to which bond or note proceeds may be applied, the disposition or pledging of the revenues of the Commission, including any payments in respect of any federally guaranteed security or any federally insured mortgage note, the duties of the Commission with respect to the acquisition, construction, maintenance, repair and operation of any health care facilities, the fees, loan repayments, purchase price payments, rents and charges to be fixed and collected in connection therewith, the terms and conditions for the issuance of additional bonds or notes, and the custody, safeguarding and application of all moneys. All bonds issued under this Chapter shall be equally and ratably secured by a pledge, charge, and lien upon revenues provided for in such trust agreement or resolution, without priority by reason of number, or of dates of bonds, execution, or delivery, in accordance with the provisions of this Chapter and of such trust agreement or resolution; except that the Commission may provide in such trust agreement or resolution that bonds issued pursuant thereto shall to the extent and in the manner prescribed in such trust agreement or resolution be subordinated and junior in standing, with respect to the payment of principal and interest and the security thereof, to any other bonds. It shall be lawful for any bank or trust company incorporated under the laws of the State which may act as depositary of the proceeds of bonds or notes, revenues or other money hereunder to furnish such indemnifying bonds or to pledge such securities as may be required by the Commission. Any such trust agreement or resolution may set off the rights and remedies, including foreclosure of any mortgage, of the holders of any bonds or notes and of the trustee, and may restrict the individual right of action by any such holders. In addition to the foregoing, any such trust agreement or resolution may contain such other provisions as the Commission may deem reasonable and proper for the security of the holders of any bonds or notes. Expenses incurred in carrying out the provisions of such trust agreement or resolution may be treated as a part of the cost of any health care facilities or paid from the revenues pledged or assigned to the payment of the principal of and the interest on bonds or notes or from any other funds available to the Commission. (1975, c. 766, s. 1; 1979, c. 54, s. 11.)

§ 131A-13. Revenues; pledges of revenues.

(a) The Commission is hereby authorized to fix and to collect fees, loan repayments, purchase price payments, rents and charges for the use of any health care facilities, and any part or section thereof, and to contract with any public or nonprofit agency for the use thereof. The Commission may require that the public or nonprofit agency shall operate, repair or maintain such facilities and shall bear the cost thereof and other costs of the Commission in connection therewith, subject to the provisions of G.S. 131A-8 with respect to a public agency, as may be provided in the agreement of sale or lease or other contract with the Commission, in addition to other obligations imposed under such agreement or contract.

(b) The fees, purchase price payments, rents and charges shall be fixed so as to provide a fund sufficient, with such other funds as may be made available therefor, (i) to pay the costs of operating, repairing and maintaining the health care facilities, to the extent that adequate provision for the payment of such costs has not otherwise been provided for, (ii) to pay the principal of and the interest on all bonds or notes as the same shall become due and payable and (iii) to create and maintain any reserves provided for in the resolution authorizing the issuance of, or any trust agreement securing, such bonds; and such fees, purchase price payments, rents and charges may be applied or pledged to the payment of debt service on the bonds prior to the payment of the costs of operating, repairing and maintaining the health care facilities.

(c) All pledges of fees, loan repayments, purchase price payments, rents, charges and other revenues under the provisions of this Chapter shall be valid and binding from the time when such pledges are made. All such revenues so pledged and thereafter received by the Commission shall immediately be subject to the lien of such pledge without any physical delivery thereof or further act, and the lien of any such pledge shall be valid and binding as against all parties having claims of any kind in tort, contract or otherwise against the Commission, irrespective of whether such parties have notice thereof. The resolution or any trust agreement by which a pledge is created or any loan agreement, agreement of sale or lease need not be filed or recorded except in the records of the Commission.

(d) The State of North Carolina does pledge to and agree with the holders of any bonds or notes issued by the Commission that so long as any of such bonds or notes are outstanding and unpaid the State will not limit or alter the rights vested in the Commission at the time of issuance of the bonds or notes to fix, revise, charge, and collect or cause to be fixed, revised, charged and collected loan repayments, purchase price payments, rents, fees and charges for the use of or services rendered by any health care facilities in connection with which the bonds or notes were issued, so as to provide a fund sufficient, with such other funds as may be made available therefor, to pay the costs of operating, repairing and maintaining the health care facilities, to pay the principal of and the interest on all bonds and notes as the same shall become due and payable and to create and maintain any reserves provided therefor and to fulfill the terms of any agreements made with the bondholders or noteholders, nor will the State in any way impair the rights and remedies of the bondholders or noteholders until the bonds or notes and all costs and expenses in connection with any action or proceedings by or on behalf of the bondholders or noteholders, are fully paid, met and discharged. (1975, c. 766, s. 1; 1979, c. 54, s. 12.)

§ 131A-14. Trust funds.

Notwithstanding any other provisions of law to the contrary, all moneys received pursuant to the authority of this Chapter, including, without limitation, fees, loan repayments, purchase price payments, rents, charges, insurance proceeds, condemnation awards and any other revenues and funds received in connection with any health care facilities, shall be deemed to be trust funds to be held and applied solely as provided in this Chapter. The resolution authorizing the issuance of, or any trust agreement securing, any bonds or notes may provide that any of such moneys may be temporarily invested pending the disbursement thereof and shall provide that any officer with whom, or any bank or trust company with which, such moneys shall be deposited shall act as trustee of such moneys and shall hold and apply the same for the purposes of this Chapter, subject to such regulations as this Chapter and such resolution or trust agreement may provide. Any such moneys may be invested as provided in G.S. 159-30, as it may be amended from time to time. (1975, c. 766, s. 1; 1979, c. 54, s. 13.)

§ 131A-15. Remedies.

Any holder of bonds or notes issued under the provisions of this Chapter or any coupons appertaining thereto, and the trustee under any trust agreement or resolution authorizing the issuance of such bonds or notes, except to the extent the rights herein given may be restricted by such trust agreement or resolution, may, either at law or in equity, by suit, action, mandamus or other proceeding, protect and enforce any and all rights under the laws of the State or granted hereunder or under such trust agreement or resolution, or under any other contract executed by the Commission pursuant to this Chapter, and may enforce and compel the performance of all duties required by this Chapter or by such trust agreement or resolution to be performed by the Commission or by any officer thereof. (1975, c. 766, s. 1.)

§ 131A-16. Negotiable instruments.

All bonds and interest coupons appertaining thereto issued under this Chapter are hereby made investment securities within the meaning of and for all the purposes of Article 8 of the Uniform Commercial Code as enacted in this State, whether or not they are of such form and character as to be investment securities under said Article 8, subject only to the provisions of the bonds pertaining to registration. (1975, c. 766, s. 1.)

§ 131A-17. Bonds or notes eligible for investment.

Bonds or notes issued under the provisions of this Chapter are hereby made securities in which all public officers and public bodies of the State and its political subdivisions, all insurance companies, trust companies, banking associations, investment companies, executors, administrators, trustees and other fiduciaries may properly and legally invest funds, including capital in their control or belonging to them. Such bonds or notes are hereby made securities which may properly and legally be deposited with and received by any State or municipal officer or any agency or political subdivision of the State for any purpose for which the deposit of bonds, notes or obligations of the State is now or may hereafter be authorized by law. (1975, c. 766, s. 1.)

§ 131A-18. Refunding bonds or notes.

The Commission is hereby authorized to provide for the issuance of refunding bonds or notes for the purpose of refunding any bonds or notes then outstanding which shall have been issued under the provisions of this Chapter, including the payment of any redemption premium thereon and any interest accrued or to accrue to the date of redemption of such bonds or notes and, if deemed advisable by the Commission, for any corporate purpose of the Commission, including, without limitation:

(1) Constructing improvements, additions, extensions or enlargements of the health care facilities in connection with which the bonds or notes to be refunded shall have been issued, and

(2) Paying all or any part of the cost of any additional health care facilities.

The issuance of such bonds or notes, the maturities and other details thereof, the rights of the holders thereof, and the rights, duties and obligations of the Commission in respect of the same shall be governed by the provisions of this Chapter which relate to the issuance of bonds or notes, insofar as such provisions may be appropriate therefor.

Refunding bonds or notes may be sold or exchanged for outstanding bonds or notes issued under this Chapter and, if sold, the proceeds thereof may be applied, in addition to any other authorized purposes, to the purchase, redemption or payment of such refunding bonds or notes, with any other available funds, to the payment of the principal, accrued interest and any redemption premium on the bonds or notes being refunded, and, if so provided or permitted in the resolution authorizing the issuance of, or in the trust agreement securing, such bonds or notes, to the payment of any interest on such refunding bonds or notes and any expenses in connection with such refunding, such proceeds may be invested in direct obligations of, or obligations the principal of and the interest on which are unconditionally guaranteed by, the United States of America which shall mature or which shall be subject to redemption by the holders thereof, at the option of such holders, not later than the respective dates when the proceeds, together with the interest accruing thereon, will be required for the purposes intended. (1975, c. 766, s. 1.)

§ 131A-19. Annual report.

The Commission shall, promptly following the close of each fiscal year, submit an annual report of its activities under this Chapter for the preceding year to the Governor, the State Auditor, the Secretary of Health and Human Services, the General Assembly, and the Local Government Commission. The Commission shall cause an audit of its books and accounts relating to its activities under this Chapter to be made at least once in each year by an independent certified public accountant and the cost thereof may be paid from any available moneys of the Commission. (1975, c. 766, s. 1; 1997-443, s. 11A.118(a); 2006-203, s. 71.)

§ 131A-20. Officers not liable.

No member or officer of the Commission shall be subject to any personal liability or accountability by reason of his execution of any bonds or notes or the issuance thereof. (1975, c. 766, s. 1.)

§ 131A-21. Tax exemption.

The exercise of the powers granted by this Chapter will be in all respects for the benefit of the people of the State and will promote their health and welfare. If bonds or notes are issued by the Commission to provide or improve a health care facility, then until the bonds or notes are retired, the facility for which bonds or notes are issued is exempt from property taxes to the extent provided in this section. If refunding bonds or notes are issued to refund bonds or notes issued to provide or improve a health care facility, the facility will continue to be exempt from property taxes as provided in this section until such time as the refunding bonds or notes are retired, provided that the final maturity of the refunding bonds or notes does not extend beyond the final maturity of the original bonds or notes.

Property may be exempt from property taxes as provided in this section if a timely application for the exemption is filed with the assessor of the county in which the property is located as required under G.S. 105-282.1. The property tax exemption under this section shall not exceed the lesser of the original principal amount of the bonds or notes or the assessed value for ad valorem tax purposes of the facility. If bonds or notes are issued to finance more than one health care facility, only that portion of the principal amount of the bonds or notes used to provide or improve the particular facility, including any allocable reserves and financing costs, may be considered for the purpose of determining the amount of the exemption allowable under this section. The exemption authorized by this section shall begin with the first full tax year of the taxpayer following the issuance of the bonds and notes. This section does not affect a health care facility's eligibility for a property tax exemption under Subchapter II of Chapter 105 of the General Statutes.

Any bonds or notes issued by the Commission under the provisions of this Chapter shall at all times be free from taxation by the State or any local unit or political subdivision or other instrumentality of the State, excepting inheritance, estate, or gift taxes, income taxes on the gain from the transfer of the bonds and notes, and franchise taxes. The interest on the bonds and notes is not subject to taxation as income. (1975, c. 766, s. 1; 1995, c. 46, s. 12; 2000-20, s. 1; 2001-139, s. 10.)

§ 131A-22. Conflict of interest.

If any member, officer or employee of the Commission shall be interested either directly or indirectly, or shall be an officer or employee of or have an ownership interest in any firm or corporation interested directly or indirectly, in any contract with the Commission, such interest shall be disclosed to the Commission and shall be set forth in the minutes of the Commission, and the member, officer or employee having such interest therein shall not participate on behalf of the Commission in the authorization of any such contract. (1975, c. 766, s. 1.)

§ 131A-23. Additional method.

The foregoing sections of this Chapter shall be deemed to provide an additional and alternative method for the doing of the things authorized thereby and shall be regarded as supplemental and additional to powers conferred by other laws, and shall not be regarded as in derogation of any powers now existing; provided, however, that the issuance of bonds or notes under the provisions of this Chapter need not comply with the requirements of any other law applicable to the issuance of bonds or notes. (1975, c. 766, s. 1.)

§ 131A-24. Liberal construction.

This Chapter, being necessary for the health and welfare of the people of the State, shall be liberally construed to effect the purposes thereof. (1975, c. 766, s. 1.)

§ 131A-25. Inconsistent laws inapplicable.

Insofar as the provisions of this Chapter are inconsistent with the provisions of any general or special laws, or parts thereof, the provisions of this Chapter shall be controlling. (1975, c. 766, s. 1.)

§§ 131B-1 through 131B-9: Repealed by Session Laws 1983, c. 775, s. 1.

Chapter 131C.

Charitable Solicitation Licensure Act.

§§ 131C-1 through 131C-22: Repealed by Session Laws 1993 (Reg. Sess., 1994), c. 759, s. 1.

Chapter 131D.

Inspection and Licensing of Facilities.

Article 1.

Adult Care Homes.

Part 1. Licensing.

§ 131D-1: Recodified as G. S. 131D-10.10 by Session Laws 2009-462, s. 1(b), effective October 1, 2009.

§ 131D-2: Repealed by Session Laws 2009-462, s. 1, effective October 1, 2009.

§ 131D-2.1. Definitions.

As used in this Article:

(1) Abuse. - The willful or grossly negligent infliction of physical pain, injury, or mental anguish, unreasonable confinement, or the willful or grossly negligent deprivation by the administrator or staff of an adult care home of services which are necessary to maintain mental and physical health.

(2) Administrator. - A person approved by the Department of Health and Human Services who has the responsibility for the total operation of a licensed adult care home.

(3) Adult care home. - An assisted living residence in which the housing management provides 24-hour scheduled and unscheduled personal care services to two or more residents, either directly or for scheduled needs, through formal written agreement with licensed home care or hospice agencies. Some licensed adult care homes provide supervision to persons with cognitive impairments whose decisions, if made independently, may jeopardize the safety or well-being of themselves or others and therefore require supervision. Medication in an adult care home may be administered by designated trained staff. Adult care homes that provide care to two to six unrelated residents are commonly called family care homes.

(3a) Adult care home resident discharge team. - A team consisting of one member from the department of social services and one member from the local management entity responsible for assisting in finding an appropriate placement for discharged residents, as established by the county department of social services in every county which contains an adult care home licensed under this Chapter.

(4) Amenities. - Services such as meals, housekeeping, transportation, and grocery shopping that do not involve hands-on personal care.

(5) Assisted living residence. - Any group housing and services program for two or more unrelated adults, by whatever name it is called, that makes available, at a minimum, one meal a day and housekeeping services and provides personal care services directly or through a formal written agreement with one or more licensed home care or hospice agencies. The Department may allow nursing service exceptions on a case-by-case basis. Settings in which services are delivered may include self-contained apartment units or single or

shared room units with private or area baths. Assisted living residences are to be distinguished from nursing homes subject to provisions of G.S. 131E-102. There are three types of assisted living residences: adult care homes, adult care homes that serve only elderly persons, and multiunit assisted housing with services. As used in this section, "elderly person" means:

a. Any person who has attained the age of 55 years or older and requires assistance with activities of daily living, housing, and services, or

b. Any adult who has a primary diagnosis of Alzheimer's disease or other form of dementia who requires assistance with activities of daily living, housing, and services provided by a licensed Alzheimer's and dementia care unit.

(6) Compensatory agent. - A spouse, relative, or other caretaker who lives with a resident and provides care to a resident.

(7) Department. - The Department of Health and Human Services unless some other meaning is clearly indicated from the context.

(8) Exploitation. - The illegal or improper use of an aged or disabled resident or the aged or disabled resident's resources for another's profit or advantage.

(9) Family care home. - An adult care home having two to six residents. The structure of a family care home may be no more than two stories high, and none of the aged or physically disabled persons being served there may be housed in the upper story without provision for two direct exterior ground-level accesses to the upper story.

(9a) Hearing Unit. - The chief hearing officer within the Division of Medical Assistance designated to preside over hearings regarding the transfer and discharge of adult care home residents, and the chief hearing officer's staff.

(10) Multiunit assisted housing with services. - An assisted living residence in which hands-on personal care services and nursing services which are arranged by housing management are provided by a licensed home care or hospice agency through an individualized written care plan. The housing management has a financial interest or financial affiliation or formal written agreement which makes personal care services accessible and available through at least one licensed home care or hospice agency. The resident has a choice of any provider, and the housing management may not combine charges

for housing and personal care services. All residents, or their compensatory agents, must be capable, through informed consent, of entering into a contract and must not be in need of 24-hour supervision. Assistance with self-administration of medications may be provided by appropriately trained staff when delegated by a licensed nurse according to the home care agency's established plan of care. Multiunit assisted housing with services programs are required to register annually with the Division of Health Service Regulation. Multiunit assisted housing with services programs are required to provide a disclosure statement to the Division of Health Service Regulation. The disclosure statement is required to be a part of the annual rental contract that includes a description of the following requirements:

a. Emergency response system;

b. Charges for services offered;

c. Limitations of tenancy;

d. Limitations of services;

e. Resident responsibilities;

f. Financial/legal relationship between housing management and home care or hospice agencies;

g. A listing of all home care or hospice agencies and other community services in the area;

h. An appeals process; and

i. Procedures for required initial and annual resident screening and referrals for services.

Continuing care retirement communities, subject to regulation by the Department of Insurance under Chapter 58 of the General Statutes, are exempt from the regulatory requirements for multiunit assisted housing with services programs.

(11) Neglect. - The failure to provide the services necessary to maintain a resident's physical or mental health.

(12) Personal care services. - Any hands-on services allowed to be performed by In-Home Aides II or III as outlined in Department rules.

(13) Registration. - The submission by a multiunit assisted housing with services provider of a disclosure statement containing all the information as outlined in subdivision (10) of this section.

(14) Resident. - A person living in an assisted living residence for the purpose of obtaining access to housing and services provided or made available by housing management.

(15) Secretary. - The Secretary of Health and Human Services unless some other meaning is clearly indicated from the context. (2009-462, ss. 1(e), 3(a); 2011-272, s. 1.)

§ 131D-2.2. Persons not to be cared for in adult care homes and multiunit assisted housing with services; hospice care; obtaining services.

(a) Adult Care Homes. - Except when a physician certifies that appropriate care can be provided on a temporary basis to meet the resident's needs and prevent unnecessary relocation, adult care homes shall not care for individuals with any of the following conditions or care needs:

(1) Ventilator dependency;

(2) Individuals requiring continuous licensed nursing care;

(3) Individuals whose physician certifies that placement is no longer appropriate;

(4) Individuals whose health needs cannot be met in the specific adult care home as determined by the residence; and

(5) Such other medical and functional care needs as the Medical Care Commission determines cannot be properly met in an adult care home.

(b) Multiunit Assisted Housing With Services. - Except when a physician certifies that appropriate care can be provided on a temporary basis to meet the resident's needs and prevent unnecessary relocation, multiunit assisted housing with services shall not care for individuals with any of the following conditions or care needs:

(1)   Ventilator dependency;

(2)   Dermal ulcers III and IV, except those stage III ulcers which are determined by an independent physician to be healing;

(3)   Intravenous therapy or injections directly into the vein, except for intermittent intravenous therapy managed by a home care or hospice agency licensed in this State;

(4)   Airborne infectious disease in a communicable state that requires isolation of the individual or requires special precautions by the caretaker to prevent transmission of the disease, including diseases such as tuberculosis and excluding infections such as the common cold;

(5)   Psychotropic medications without appropriate diagnosis and treatment plans;

(6)   Nasogastric tubes;

(7)   Gastric tubes, except when the individual is capable of independently feeding himself or herself and caring for the tube, or as managed by a home care or hospice agency licensed in this State;

(8)   Individuals requiring continuous licensed nursing care;

(9)   Individuals whose physician certifies that placement is no longer appropriate;

(10)   Unless the individual's independent physician determines otherwise, individuals who require maximum physical assistance as documented by a uniform assessment instrument and who meet Medicaid nursing facility level-of-care criteria as defined in the State Plan for Medical Assistance. Maximum physical assistance means that an individual has a rating of total dependence in four or more of the seven activities of daily living as documented on a uniform assessment instrument;

(11)   Individuals whose health needs cannot be met in the specific multiunit assisted housing with services as determined by the residence; and

(12) Such other medical and functional care needs as the Medical Care Commission determines cannot be properly met in multiunit assisted housing with services.

(c) Hospice Care. - At the request of the resident, hospice care may be provided in an assisted living residence under the same requirements for hospice programs as described in Article 10 of Chapter 131E of the General Statutes.

(d) Obtaining Services. - The resident of an assisted living facility has the right to obtain services at the resident's own expense from providers other than the housing management. This subsection shall not be construed to relieve the resident of the resident's contractual obligation to pay the housing management for any services covered by the contract between the resident and housing management. (2009-462, s. 1(e).)

§ 131D-2.3. Exemptions from licensure.

The following are excluded from this Article and are not required to be registered or obtain licensure under this Article:

(1) Facilities licensed under Chapter 122C or Chapter 131E of the General Statutes;

(2) Persons subject to rules of the Division of Vocational Rehabilitation Services;

(3) Facilities that care for no more than four persons, all of whom are under the supervision of the United States Veterans Administration;

(4) Facilities that make no charges for housing, amenities, or personal care service, either directly or indirectly; and

(5) Institutions that are maintained or operated by a unit of government and that were established, maintained, or operated by a unit of government and exempt from licensure by the Department on September 30, 1995. (2009-462, s. 1(e).)

§ 131D-2.4. Licensure of adult care homes for aged and disabled individuals; impact of prior violations on licensure; compliance history review; license renewal.

(a)   Licensure. - Except for those facilities exempt under G.S. 131D-2.3, the Department of Health and Human Services shall inspect and license all adult care homes. The Department shall issue a license for a facility not currently licensed as an adult care home for a period of six months. If the licensee demonstrates substantial compliance with Articles 1 and 3 of this Chapter and rules adopted thereunder, the Department shall issue a license for the balance of the calendar year.

(b)   Compliance History Review. - Prior to issuing a new license or renewing an existing license, the Department shall conduct a compliance history review of the facility and its principals and affiliates. The Department may refuse to license a facility when the compliance history review shows a pattern of noncompliance with State law by the facility or its principals or affiliates, or otherwise demonstrates disregard for the health, safety, and welfare of residents in current or past facilities. The Department shall require compliance history information and make its determination according to rules adopted by the Medical Care Commission.

(c)   Prior Violations. - No new license shall be issued for any adult care home to an applicant for licensure who:

(1)   Was the owner, principal, or affiliate of a licensable facility under this Chapter, Chapter 122C, or Article 7 of Chapter 110 of the General Statutes that had its license revoked until one full year after the date of revocation;

(2)   Is the owner, principal, or affiliate of an adult care home that was assessed a penalty for a Type A or Type B violation until the earlier of one year from the date the penalty was assessed or until the home has substantially complied with the correction plan established pursuant to G.S. 131D-34 and substantial compliance has been certified by the Department;

(3)   Is the owner, principal, or affiliate of an adult care home that had its license summarily suspended or downgraded to provisional status as a result of Type A or Type B violations until six months from the date of reinstatement of the license, restoration from provisional to full licensure, or termination of the provisional license, as applicable; or

(4) Is the owner, principal, or affiliate of a licensable facility that had its license summarily suspended or downgraded to provisional status as a result of violations under this Article or Chapter 122C of the General Statutes or had its license summarily suspended or denied under Article 7 of Chapter 110 of the General Statutes until six months from the date of the reinstatement of the license, restoration from provisional to full licensure, or termination of the provisional license, as applicable.

An applicant for new licensure may appeal a denial of certification of substantial compliance under subdivision (2) of this subsection by filing with the Department a request for review by the Secretary within 10 days of the date of denial of the certification. Within 10 days of receipt of the request for review, the Secretary shall issue to the applicant a written determination that either denies certification of substantial compliance or certifies substantial compliance. The decision of the Secretary is final.

(d) License Renewals. - License renewals shall be valid for one year from the date of renewal unless revoked earlier by the Secretary for failure to comply with any part of this section or any rules adopted hereunder. Licenses shall be renewed annually upon filing and the Department's approval of the renewal application. The Department shall not renew a license if outstanding fees, fines, and penalties imposed by the State against the home have not been paid. Fines and penalties for which an appeal is pending are exempt from consideration. The renewal application shall contain all necessary and reasonable information that the Department may require.

(e) In order for an adult care home to maintain its license, it shall not hinder or interfere with the proper performance of duty of a lawfully appointed community advisory committee, as defined by G.S. 131D-31 and G.S. 131D-32.

(f) The Department shall not issue a new license for a change of ownership of an adult care home if outstanding fees, fines, and penalties imposed by the State against the home have not been paid. Fines and penalties for which an appeal is pending are exempt from consideration. (2009-462, s. 1(e).)

§ 131D-2.5. License and registration fees.

(a) The Department shall charge each adult care home with six or fewer beds a nonrefundable annual license fee in the amount of three hundred fifteen dollars ($315.00). The Department shall charge each adult care home with more than six beds a nonrefundable annual license fee in the amount of three hundred sixty dollars ($360.00) plus a nonrefundable annual per-bed fee of seventeen dollars and fifty cents ($17.50).

(b) The Department shall charge each registered multiunit assisted housing with services program a nonrefundable annual registration fee of three hundred fifty dollars ($350.00). Any individual or corporation that establishes, conducts, manages, or operates a multiunit housing with services program, subject to registration under this section, that fails to register is guilty of a Class 3 misdemeanor and, upon conviction shall be punishable only by a fine of not more than fifty dollars ($50.00) for the first offense and not more than five hundred dollars ($500.00) for each subsequent offense. Each day of a continuing violation after conviction shall be considered a separate offense. (2009-451, s. 10.76(a1); 2009-462, ss. 1(e), 3(b).)

§ 131D-2.6. Legal action by Department.

(a) Notwithstanding the existence or pursuit of any other remedy, the Department may, in the manner provided by law, maintain an action in the name of the State for injunction or other process against any person to restrain or prevent the establishment, conduct, management, or operation of an adult care home without a license. Such action shall be instituted in the superior court of the county in which any unlicensed activity has occurred or is occurring.

(b) Any individual or corporation that establishes, conducts, manages, or operates a facility subject to licensure under this section without a license is guilty of a Class 3 misdemeanor and, upon conviction, shall be punishable only by a fine of not more than fifty dollars ($50.00) for the first offense and not more than five hundred dollars ($500.00) for each subsequent offense. Each day of a continuing violation after conviction shall be considered a separate offense.

(c) If any person shall hinder the proper performance of duty of the Secretary or the Secretary's representative in carrying out this section, the Secretary may institute an action in the superior court of the county in which the hindrance has occurred for injunctive relief against the continued hindrance, irrespective of all other remedies at law.

(d) Actions under this section shall be in accordance with Article 37 of Chapter 1 of the General Statutes and Rule 65 of the Rules of Civil Procedure. (2009-462, s. 1(e).)

§ 131D-2.7. Provisional license; license revocation; summary suspension of license; suspension of admission.

(a) Provisional License. - Except as otherwise provided in this section, the Department may amend a license by reducing it from a full license to a provisional license for a period of not more than 90 days whenever the Department finds that:

(1) The licensee has substantially failed to comply with the provisions of Articles 1 and 3 of this Chapter and the rules adopted pursuant to these Articles;

(2) There is a reasonable probability that the licensee can remedy the licensure deficiencies within a reasonable length of time; and

(3) There is a reasonable probability that the licensee will be able thereafter to remain in compliance with the licensure rules for the foreseeable future.

The Department may extend a provisional license for not more than one additional 90-day period upon finding that the licensee has made substantial progress toward remedying the licensure deficiencies that caused the license to be reduced to provisional status.

The Department also may issue a provisional license to a facility, pursuant to rules adopted by the Medical Care Commission, for substantial failure to comply with the provisions of this section or rules adopted pursuant to this section. Any facility wishing to contest the issuance of a provisional license shall be entitled to an administrative hearing as provided in the Administrative Procedure Act, Chapter 150B of the General Statutes. A petition for a contested case shall be filed within 30 days after the Department mails written notice of the issuance of the provisional license.

(b) License Revocation. - The Department may revoke a license whenever:

(1) The Department finds that:

a. The licensee has substantially failed to comply with the provisions of Articles 1 and 3 of this Chapter and the rules adopted pursuant to these Articles; and

b. It is not reasonably probable that the licensee can remedy the licensure deficiencies within a reasonable length of time; or

(2) The Department finds that:

a. The licensee has substantially failed to comply with the provisions of Articles 1 and 3 of this Chapter and the rules adopted pursuant to these Articles; and

b. Although the licensee may be able to remedy the deficiencies within a reasonable time, it is not reasonably probable that the licensee will be able to remain in compliance with licensure rules for the foreseeable future; or

c. The licensee has failed to comply with the provisions of Articles 1 and 3 of this Chapter and the rules adopted pursuant to these Articles, and the failure to comply endangered the health, safety, or welfare of the patients in the facility.

(c) Summary Suspension. - The Department may summarily suspend a license pursuant to G.S. 150B-3(c) whenever it finds substantial evidence of abuse, neglect, exploitation, or any condition which presents an imminent danger to the health and safety of any resident of the home. Any facility wishing to contest summary suspension of a license shall be entitled to an administrative hearing as provided in the Administrative Procedure Act, Chapter 150B of the General Statutes. A petition for a contested case shall be filed within 20 days after the Department mails a notice of summary suspension to the licensee.

(d) Suspension of Admissions.

(1) In addition to the administrative penalties described in this Article, the Secretary may suspend the admission of any new residents to an adult care home where the conditions of the adult care home are detrimental to the health or safety of the residents. This suspension shall be for the period determined by the Secretary and shall remain in effect until the Secretary is satisfied that conditions or circumstances merit removing the suspension.

(2) In imposing a suspension under this section, the Secretary shall consider the following factors:

a. The degree of sanctions necessary to ensure compliance with this section and rules adopted hereunder; and

b. The character and degree of impact of the conditions at the home on the health or safety of its residents.

(3) The Secretary of Health and Human Services shall adopt rules to implement this section.

(4) Any facility wishing to contest a suspension of admissions shall be entitled to an administrative hearing as provided in the Administrative Procedure Act, Chapter 150B of the General Statutes. A petition for a contested case shall be filed within 20 days after the Department mails a notice of suspension of admissions to the licensee. (2009-462, s. 1(e).)

§ 131D-2.8: Reserved for future codification purposes.

§ 131D-2.9: Reserved for future codification purposes.

§ 131D-2.10: Reserved for future codification purposes.

Part 2. Other Laws Pertaining to the Inspection and Operation of Adult Care Homes.

§ 131D-2.11. Inspections, monitoring, and review by State agency and county departments of social services.

(a) State Inspection and Monitoring. - The Department shall ensure that adult care homes required to be licensed by this Article are monitored for licensure compliance on a regular basis. All facilities licensed under this Article and adult care units in nursing homes are subject to inspections at all times by the Secretary. Except as provided in subsection (a1) of this section, the Division of Health Service Regulation shall inspect all adult care homes and adult care units in nursing homes on an annual basis. Beginning July 1, 2012, the Division of Health Service Regulation shall include as part of its inspection of all adult care homes a review of the facility's compliance with G.S. 131D-4.4A(b) and safe practices for injections and any other procedures during which bleeding typically occurs. In addition, the Department shall ensure that adult care homes are inspected every two years to determine compliance with physical plant and life-safety requirements.

(a1)   Waiver of Annual State Inspection. - The Division of Health Service Regulation may waive the annual inspection requirement under subsection (a) of this section for any adult care home that has achieved the highest rating in accordance with rules adopted by the North Carolina Medical Care Commission pursuant to G.S. 131D-10. However, at least once every two years the Division of Health Service Regulation shall inspect any adult care home for which the annual inspection requirement was waived.

(a2)   Informal Dispute Resolution. -

(1)   The Division of Health Service Regulation shall offer each adult care home an opportunity, at the facility's request and upon the facility's receipt of the official statement of deficiencies, to informally resolve disputed findings from inspections conducted by the Division of Health Service Regulation in accordance with this section.

(2)   Failure of the Division of Health Service Regulation to complete informal dispute resolution timely does not delay the effective date of any enforcement action taken by the Division of Health Service Regulation against an adult care home.

(3)   An adult care home is not entitled to seek a delay of any enforcement action against it on the grounds that the Division of Health Service Regulation has not completed informal dispute resolution prior to the effective date of the enforcement action.

(4)   If an adult care home successfully demonstrates during informal dispute resolution that any of the deficiencies cited in the official statement of deficiencies should not have been cited, the Division of Health Service Regulation shall remove the incorrectly cited deficiencies from the official statement of deficiencies and rescind any enforcement actions imposed on the adult care home solely as a result of the incorrectly cited deficiencies.

(5)   Upon request, the Division of Health Service Regulation shall provide an adult care home with written notification of these informal dispute resolution procedures.

(b) Monitoring by County. - The Department shall work with county departments of social services to do the routine monitoring in adult care homes to ensure compliance with State and federal laws, rules, and regulations in accordance with policy and procedures established by the Division of Health Service Regulation and to have the Division of Health Service Regulation oversee this monitoring. The county departments of social services shall document in a written report all on site visits, including monitoring visits, revisits, and complaint investigations. The county departments of social services shall submit to the Division of Health Service Regulation written reports of each facility visit within 20 working days of the visit.

(c) State Review of County Compliance. - The Division of Health Service Regulation shall conduct and document annual reviews of the county departments of social services' performance. When monitoring is not done timely or there is failure to identify or document noncompliance, the Department may intervene in the particular service in question. Department intervention shall include one or more of the following activities:

(1) Sending staff of the Department to the county departments of social services to provide technical assistance and to monitor the services being provided by the facility.

(2) Advising county personnel as to appropriate policies and procedures.

(3) Establishing a plan of action to correct county performance.

The Secretary may determine that the Department shall assume the county's regulatory responsibility for the county's adult care homes. (2009-462, s. 1(e); 2009-232, s. 3; 2011-99, s. 4; 2011-258, ss. 1, 2.)

§ 131D-2.12. Training requirements; county departments of social services.

(a) The county departments of social services' adult home specialists and their supervisors shall complete:

(1) Eight hours of prebasic training within 60 days of employment;

(2) Thirty-two hours of basic training within six months of employment;

(3)   Twenty-four hours of postbasic training within six months of the basic training program;

(4)   A minimum of eight hours of complaint investigation training within six months of employment; and

(5)   A minimum of 16 hours of statewide training annually by the Division of Health Service Regulation.

(b)   The joint training requirements by the Department shall be as provided in G.S. 143B-139.5B. (2009-462, s. 1(e).)

§ 131D-2.13. Departmental duties.

(a)   Enforcement of Room Ventilation and Temperature. - The Department shall monitor regularly the enforcement of rules pertaining to air circulation, ventilation, and room temperature in resident living quarters. These rules shall include the requirement that air conditioning or at least one fan per resident bedroom and living and dining areas be provided when the temperature in the main center corridor exceeds 80 degrees Fahrenheit.

(b)   Administrator Directory. - The Department shall keep an up-to-date directory of all persons who are administrators as defined in G.S. 131D-2.1.

(c)   Departmental Complaint Hotline. - Adult care homes shall post the Division of Health Service Regulation's complaint hotline number conspicuously in a public place in the facility.

(d)   Provider File. - The Department of Health and Human Services shall establish and maintain a provider file to record and monitor compliance histories of facilities, owners, operators, and affiliates of nursing homes and adult care homes.

(e)   Report on Use of Restraint. - The Department shall report annually on October 1 to the Joint Legislative Oversight Committee on Health and Human Services the following for the immediately preceding fiscal year:

(1)   The level of compliance of each adult care home with applicable State law and rules governing the use of physical restraint and physical hold of

residents. The information shall indicate areas of highest and lowest levels of compliance.

(2) The total number of adult care homes that reported deaths under G.S. 131D-34.1, the number of deaths reported by each facility, the number of deaths investigated pursuant to G.S. 131D-34.1, and the number found by the investigation to be related to the adult care home's use of physical restraint or physical hold. (2009-462, s. 1(e); 2011-291, s. 2.47.)

§ 131D-2.14. Confidentiality.

Notwithstanding G.S. 8-53 or any other law relating to confidentiality of communications between physician and patient, in the course of an inspection conducted under G.S. 131D-2.11:

(1) Department representatives may review any writing or other record concerning the admission, discharge, medication, care, medical condition, or history of any person who is or has been a resident of the facility being inspected.

(2) Any person involved in giving care or treatment at or through the facility may disclose information to Department representatives unless the resident objects in writing to review of the resident's records or disclosure of such information.

(3) The facility, its employees, and any other person interviewed in the course of an inspection shall be immune from liability for damages resulting from disclosure of any information to the Department. The Department shall not disclose:

a. Any confidential or privileged information obtained under this section unless the resident or the resident's legal representative authorizes disclosure in writing or unless a court of competent jurisdiction orders disclosure, or

b. The name of anyone who has furnished information concerning a facility without that person's consent.

The Department shall institute appropriate policies and procedures to ensure that unauthorized disclosure does not occur. All confidential or privileged information obtained under this section and the names of persons providing such information shall be exempt from Chapter 132 of the General Statutes.

(4) Notwithstanding any law to the contrary, Chapter 132 of the General Statutes, the Public Records Law, applies to all records of the State Division of Social Services of the Department of Health and Human Services and of any county department of social services regarding inspections of adult care facilities except for information in the records that is confidential or privileged, including medical records, or that contains the names of residents or complainants. (2009-462, s. 1(e).)

§ 131D-2.15. Resident assessments.

(a) The Department shall ensure that facilities conduct and complete an assessment of each resident within 72 hours of admitting the resident and annually thereafter. In conducting the assessment, the facility shall use an assessment instrument approved by the Secretary upon the advice of the Director of the Division of Aging and Adult Services. The Department shall provide ongoing training for facility personnel in the use of the approved assessment instrument.

The facility shall use the assessment to develop appropriate and comprehensive service plans and care plans and to determine the level and type of facility staff that is needed to meet the needs of residents. The assessment shall determine a resident's level of functioning and shall include, but not be limited to, cognitive status and physical functioning in activities of daily living. Activities of daily living are personal functions essential for the health and well-being of the resident. The assessment shall not serve as the basis for medical care. The assessment shall indicate if the resident requires referral to the resident's physician or other appropriate licensed health care professional or community resource.

(b) The Department, as part of its inspection and licensing of adult care homes, shall review assessments and related service plans and care plans for a selected number of residents. In conducting this review, the Department shall determine:

(1) Whether the appropriate assessment instrument was administered and interpreted correctly;

(2) Whether the facility is capable of providing the necessary services;

(3) Whether the service plan or care plan conforms to the results of an appropriately administered and interpreted assessment; and

(4) Whether the service plans or care plans are being implemented fully and in accordance with an appropriately administered and interpreted assessment.

(c) If the Department finds that the facility is not carrying out its assessment responsibilities in accordance with this section, the Department shall notify the facility and require the facility to implement a corrective action plan. The Department shall also notify the resident of the results of its review of the assessment, service plans, and care plans developed for the resident. In addition to administrative penalties, the Secretary may suspend the admission of any new residents to the facility. The suspension shall be for the period determined by the Secretary and shall remain in effect until the Secretary is satisfied that conditions or circumstances merit removing the suspension. (2009-462, s. 1(e).)

§ 131D-2.16. Rules.

Except as otherwise provided in this Article, the Medical Care Commission shall adopt rules necessary to carry out this Article. The Commission has the authority, in adopting rules, to specify the limitation of nursing services provided by assisted living residences. In developing rules, the Commission shall consider the need to ensure comparable quality of services provided to residents, whether these services are provided directly by a licensed assisted living provider, licensed home care agency, or hospice. In adult care homes, living arrangements where residents require supervision due to cognitive impairments, rules shall be adopted to ensure that supervision is appropriate and adequate to meet the special needs of these residents. Rule-making authority under this section is in addition to that conferred under G.S. 131D-4.3 and G.S. 131D-4.5. (2009-462, s. 1(e).)

§ 131D-2.17. Impact on other laws; severability.

(a) Nothing in this section shall be construed to supersede any federal or State antitrust, antikickback, or safe harbor laws or regulations.

(b) If any provisions of this section or the application of it to any person or circumstance is held invalid, the invalidity does not affect other provisions or applications of the section which can be given effect without the invalid provision or application, and to this end the provisions of this section are severable. (2009-462, s. 1(e).)

§ 131D-2.18. Application of other laws.

(a) Certification of assisted living administrators shall be as provided under Article 20A of Chapter 90 of the General Statutes.

(b) Compliance with the Health Care Personnel Registry shall be as provided under G.S. 131E-256.

(c) Rules for the operation of the adult care portion of a combination home, as defined in G.S. 131E-101, shall be as provided in G.S. 131E-104. (2009-462, s. 1(e).)

§ 131D-3: Repealed by Session Laws 1995, c. 449, s. 1.

§ 131D-4: Repealed by Session Laws 1995, c. 449, s. 2.

§ 131D-4.1. Adult care homes; legislative intent.

The General Assembly finds and declares that the ability to exercise personal control over one's life is fundamental to human dignity and quality of life and that dependence on others for some assistance with daily life activities should not require surrendering personal control of informed decision making or risk taking in all areas of one's life.

The General Assembly intends to ensure that adult care homes provide services that assist the residents in such a way as to assure quality of life and maximum flexibility in meeting individual needs and preserving individual autonomy. (1995, c. 449, s. 3; c. 535, s. 9.)

§ 131D-4.2. Adult care homes; family care homes; annual cost reports; exemptions; enforcement.

(a) Except for family care homes, adult care homes with a licensed capacity of seven to twenty beds, which are licensed pursuant to this Chapter, to Chapter 122C of the General Statutes, and to Chapter 131E of the General Statutes, shall submit audited reports of actual costs to the Department at least every two years in accordance with rules adopted by the Department under G.S. 143B-10. For years in which an audited report of actual costs is not required, an annual cost report shall be submitted to the Department in accordance with rules adopted by the Department under G.S. 143B-10. Adult care homes licensed under Chapter 131D of the General Statutes that have special care units shall include in reports required under this subsection cost reports specific to the special care unit and shall not average special care costs with other costs of the adult care home.

(b) Except for family care homes, adult care homes with a licensed capacity of twenty-one beds or more, which are licensed pursuant to this Chapter, to Chapter 122C of the General Statutes, and to Chapter 131E of the General Statutes, shall submit annual audited reports of actual costs to the Department of Health and Human Services, in accordance with rules adopted by the Department under G.S. 143B-10. Adult care homes licensed under Chapter 131D of the General Statutes that have special care units shall include in the reports required under this subsection cost reports specific to the special care unit and shall not average special care costs with other costs of the adult care home.

(c) Repealed by Session Laws 1999-334, s. 3.1.

(d) Facilities that do not receive State/County Special Assistance or Medicaid personal care are exempt from the reporting requirements of this section.

(e) Except as otherwise provided in this subsection, the annual reporting period for facilities licensed pursuant to this Chapter or Chapter 131E of the General Statutes shall be October 1 through September 30, with the annual report due by the following December 31, unless the Department determines there is good cause for delay. The annual report for combination facilities and free-standing adult care home facilities owned and operated by a hospital shall be due 15 days after the hospital's Medicare cost report is due. The annual report for combination facilities not owned and operated by a hospital shall be due 15 days after the nursing facility's Medicaid cost report is due. The annual reporting period for facilities licensed pursuant to Chapter 122C of the General Statutes shall be July 1 through June 30, with the annual report due by the following December 31, unless the Department determines there is good cause for delay. Under this subsection, good cause is an action that is uncontrollable by the provider. If the Department finds good cause for delay, it may extend the deadline for filing a report for up to an additional 30 days.

(f) The Department shall have the authority to conduct audits and review audits submitted pursuant to subsections (a), (b), and (c) above.

(g) The Department shall suspend admissions to facilities that fail to submit annual reports by December 31, or by the date established by the Department when good cause for delay is found pursuant to G.S. 131D-4.2(e). Suspension of admissions shall remain in effect until reports are submitted or licenses are suspended or revoked under subdivision (2) of this subsection. The Department may take either or both of the following actions to enforce compliance by a facility with this section, or to punish noncompliance:

(1) Seek a court order to enforce compliance;

(2) Suspend or revoke the facility's license, subject to the provisions of Chapter 150B of the General Statutes.

(h) The report documentation shall be used to adjust the adult care home rate annually, an adjustment that is in addition to the annual standard adjustment for inflation as determined by the Office of State Budget and Management. Rates for family care homes shall be based on market rate data. The Secretary of Health and Human Services shall adopt rules for the rate-setting methodology and audited cost reports in accordance with G.S. 143B-10. (1995, c. 449, s. 3; c. 535, s. 10; 1997-73, ss. 1, 2; 1997-443, s. 11A.118(a); 1998-212, s. 12.1A; 1999-334, ss. 3.1, 3.2; 2000-140, s. 93.1(a); 2001-157, s. 1; 2001-424, s. 12.2(b).)

§ 131D-4.3. Adult care home rules.

(a) Pursuant to G.S. 143B-165, the North Carolina Medical Care Commission shall adopt rules to ensure at a minimum, but shall not be limited to, the provision of the following by adult care homes:

(1) Repealed by Session Laws 2000-111, s. 1.

(2) A minimum of 75 hours of training for personal care aides performing heavy care tasks and a minimum of 40 hours of training for all personal care aides. The training for aides providing heavy care tasks shall be comparable to State-approved Certified Nurse Aide I training. For those aides meeting the 40-hour requirement, at least 20 hours shall be classroom training to include at a minimum:

a. Basic nursing skills;

b. Personal care skills;

c. Cognitive, behavioral, and social care;

d. Basic restorative services;

e. Residents' rights.

A minimum of 20 hours of training shall be provided for aides in family care homes that do not have heavy care residents. Persons who either pass a competency examination developed by the Department of Health and Human Services, have been employed as personal care aides for a period of time as established by the Department, or meet minimum requirements of a combination of training, testing, and experience as established by the Department shall be exempt from the training requirements of this subdivision;

(3) Monitoring and supervision of residents;

(4) Oversight and quality of care as stated in G.S. 131D-4.1; and

(5) Adult care homes shall comply with all of the following staffing requirements:

a. First shift (morning): 0.4 hours of aide duty for each resident (licensed capacity or resident census), or 8.0 hours of aide duty per each 20 residents (licensed capacity or resident census) plus 3.0 hours for all other residents, whichever is greater;

b. Second shift (afternoon): 0.4 hours of aide duty for each resident (licensed capacity or resident census), or 8.0 hours of aide duty per each 20 residents plus 3.0 hours for all other residents (licensed capacity or resident census), whichever is greater;

c. Third shift (evening): 8.0 hours of aide duty per 30 or fewer residents (licensed capacity or resident census).

In addition to these requirements, the facility shall provide staff to meet the needs of the facility's heavy care residents equal to the amount of time reimbursed by Medicaid. As used in this subdivision, the term "heavy care resident" means an individual residing in an adult care home who is defined "heavy care" by Medicaid and for which the facility is receiving enhanced Medicaid payments for such needs. Each facility shall post in a conspicuous place information about required staffing that enables residents and their families to ascertain each day the number of direct care staff and supervisors that are required by law to be on duty for each shift for that day.

(b) Rules to implement this section shall be adopted as emergency rules in accordance with Chapter 150B of the General Statutes.

(c) The Department may suspend or revoke a facility's license, subject to the provisions of Chapter 150B, to enforce compliance by a facility with this section or to punish noncompliance. (1995, c. 449, s. 3; c. 535, s. 10; 1997-443, s. 11A.118(a); 1998-212, s. 12.16B(a); 2000-111, s. 1; 2001-85, s. 1; 2001-487, s. 85(a).)

§ 131D-4.4. Adult care home minimum safety requirements; smoking prohibited inside long-term care facilities; penalty.

(a) In addition to other requirements established by this Article or by rules adopted pursuant to this Article or other provisions of law, every adult care home shall provide to each resident the care, safety, and services necessary to enable the resident to attain and maintain the highest practicable level of physical, emotional, and social well-being in accordance with:

(1) The resident's individual assessment and plan of care; and

(2) Rules and standards relating to quality of care and safety adopted under this Chapter.

(b) Smoking is prohibited inside long-term care facilities. As used in this section:

(1) "Long-term care facilities" include adult care homes, nursing homes, skilled nursing facilities, facilities licensed under Chapter 122C of the General Statutes, and other licensed facilities that provide long-term care services.

(2) "Smoking" means the use or possession of any lighted cigar, cigarette, pipe, or other lighted smoking product.

(3) "Inside" means a fully enclosed area.

(c) The person who owns, manages, operates, or otherwise controls a long-term care facility where smoking is prohibited under this section shall:

(1) Conspicuously post signs clearly stating that smoking is prohibited inside the facility. The signs may include the international "No Smoking" symbol, which consists of a pictorial representation of a burning cigarette enclosed in a red circle with a red bar across it.

(2) Direct any person who is smoking inside the facility to extinguish the lighted smoking product.

(3) Provide written notice to individuals upon admittance that smoking is prohibited inside the facility and obtain the signature of the individual or the individual's representative acknowledging receipt of the notice.

(d) The Department may impose an administrative penalty not to exceed two hundred dollars ($200.00) for each violation on any person who owns, manages, operates, or otherwise controls the long-term care facility and fails to comply with subsection (c) of this section. A violation of this section constitutes a civil offense only and is not a crime. (1999-334, s. 1.1; 2007-459, s. 1.)

§ 131D-4.4A. Adult care home infection prevention requirements.

(a) As used in this section, "adult care home staff" means any employee of an adult care home involved in direct resident care.

(b) In order to prevent transmission of HIV, hepatitis B, hepatitis C, and other bloodborne pathogens, each adult care home shall do all of the following, beginning January 1, 2012:

(1) Implement a written infection control policy consistent with the federal Centers for Disease Control and Prevention guidelines on infection control that addresses at least all of the following:

a. Proper disposal of single-use equipment used to puncture skin, mucous membranes, and other tissues, and proper disinfection of reusable patient care items that are used for multiple residents.

b. Sanitation of rooms and equipment, including cleaning procedures, agents, and schedules.

c. Accessibility of infection control devices and supplies.

d. Blood and bodily fluid precautions.

e. Procedures to be followed when adult care home staff is exposed to blood or other body fluids of another person in a manner that poses a significant risk of transmission of HIV, hepatitis B, hepatitis C, or other bloodborne pathogens.

f. Procedures to prohibit adult care home staff with exudative lesions or weeping dermatitis from engaging in direct resident care that involves the potential for contact between the resident, equipment, or devices and the lesion or dermatitis until the condition resolves.

(2) Require and monitor compliance with the facility's infection control policy.

(3) Update the infection control policy as necessary to prevent the transmission of HIV, hepatitis B, hepatitis C, and other bloodborne pathogens.

(4) Designate one on-site staff member for each noncontiguous facility who is knowledgeable about the federal Centers for Disease Control and Prevention guidelines on infection control to direct the facility's infection control activities and ensure that all adult care staff is trained in the facility's infection control policy. Beginning October 1, 2013, any nonsupervisory staff member designated to direct the facility's infection control activities shall complete the infection

control course developed by the Department pursuant to G.S. 131D-4.5C. (2011-99, s. 3.)

§ 131D-4.4B. Guidelines for reporting suspected communicable disease outbreaks.

The Department shall develop guidelines prescribing the manner in which an adult care home is to report a suspected communicable disease outbreak within the facility to the local health department. (2011-99, s. 3.)

§ 131D-4.5. Rules adopted by Medical Care Commission.

The Medical Care Commission shall adopt rules as follows:

(1) Establishing minimum medication administration standards for adult care homes. The rules shall include the minimum staffing and training requirements for medication aides and standards for professional supervision of adult care homes' medication controls. The requirements shall (i) include compliance with G.S. 131D-4.5B and (ii) be designed to reduce the medication error rate in adult care homes to an acceptable level. The requirements shall include, but need not be limited to, all of the following:

a. Training for medication aides, including periodic refresher training.

b. Standards for management of complex medication regimens.

c. Oversight by licensed professionals.

d. Measures to ensure proper storage of medication.

(2) Establishing training requirements for adult care home staff in behavioral interventions. The training shall include appropriate responses to behavioral problems posed by adult care residents. The training shall emphasize safety and humane care and shall specifically include alternatives to the use of restraints.

(3) Establishing minimum training and education qualifications for supervisors in adult care homes and specifying the safety responsibilities of supervisors. The minimum training qualifications shall include compliance with G.S. 131D-4.5C.

(4) Specifying the qualifications of staff who shall be on duty in adult care homes during various portions of the day in order to assure safe and quality care for the residents. The rules shall take into account varied resident needs and population mixes.

(5) Implementing the due process and appeal rights for discharge and transfer of residents in adult care homes afforded by G.S. 131D-21. The rules shall offer protections to residents for safe and orderly transfer and discharge.

(6) Establishing procedures for determining the compliance history of adult care homes' principals and affiliates. The rules shall include criteria for refusing to license facilities which have a history of, or have principals or affiliates with a history of, noncompliance with State law, or disregard for the health, safety, and welfare of residents.

(7) For the licensure of special care units in accordance with G.S. 131D-4.6, and for disclosures required to be made under G.S. 131D-8.

(8) For time limited provisional licenses and for granting extensions for provisional licenses.

(9) For the issuance of certificates to adult care homes as authorized under G.S. 131D-10. (1999-334, s. 1.1; 2000-111, s. 2; 2007-544, s. 3(a); 2011-99, ss. 1, 2; 2011-272, s. 2.)

§ 131D-4.5A. Fees for medication aides.

The Department may impose a fee, not to exceed twenty-five dollars ($25.00), on an applicant seeking certification as an assisted living home medication aide to cover the costs of testing and materials in administering a certification examination. (2010-31, s. 10.36A(a).)

§ 131D-4.5B. Adult care home medication aides; training and competency evaluation requirements.

(a) By January 1, 2012, the Division of Health Service Regulation shall develop a mandatory, annual in-service training program for adult care home medication aides on infection control, safe practices for injections and any other procedures during which bleeding typically occurs, and glucose monitoring. Each medication aide who successfully completes the in-service training program shall receive partial credit, in an amount determined by the Department, toward the continuing education requirements for adult care home medication aides established by the Commission pursuant to G.S. 131D-4.5.

(b) Beginning October 1, 2013, an adult care home is prohibited from allowing staff to perform any unsupervised medication aide duties unless that individual has previously worked as a medication aide during the previous 24 months in an adult care home or successfully completed all of the following:

(1) A five-hour training program developed by the Department that includes training and instruction in all of the following:

a. The key principles of medication administration.

b. The federal Centers for Disease Control and Prevention guidelines on infection control and, if applicable, safe injection practices and procedures for monitoring or testing in which bleeding occurs or the potential for bleeding exists.

(2) A clinical skills evaluation consistent with 10A NCAC 13F .0503 and 10A NCAC 13G .0503.

(3) Within 60 days from the date of hire, the individual must have completed the following:

a. An additional 10-hour training program developed by the Department that includes training and instruction in all of the following:

1. The key principles of medication administration.

2. The federal Centers of Disease Control and Prevention guidelines on infection control and, if applicable, safe injection practices and procedures for

monitoring or testing in which bleeding occurs or the potential for bleeding exists.

b.   An examination developed and administered by the Division of Health Service Regulation in accordance with subsection (c) of this section.

(c)   By October 1, 2012, the Division of Health Service Regulation shall develop and administer an examination for individuals seeking employment as a medication aide in an adult care home. (2011-99, s. 5.)

§ 131D-4.5C. Adult care home supervisors; infection control training requirements.

By December 1, 2011, the Department shall develop a mandatory, annual course for adult care home supervisors on federal Centers for Disease Control and Prevention guidelines on infection control. Each supervisor that successfully completes the mandatory infection control course shall receive credit, in an amount determined by the Department, toward the continuing education requirements for adult care home supervisors established by the Commission pursuant to G.S. 131D-4.5. (2011-99, s. 5.)

§ 131D-4.6. Licensure of special care units.

(a)   As used in this section, the term "special care unit" means a wing or hallway within an adult care home, or a program provided by an adult care home, that is designated especially for residents with Alzheimer's disease or other dementias, a mental health disability, or other special needs disease or condition as determined by the Medical Care Commission.

(b)   An adult care home that holds itself out to the public as providing a special care unit shall be licensed as such and shall, in addition to other licensing requirements for adult care homes, meet the standards established under rules adopted by the Medical Care Commission.

(c)   An adult care home that holds itself out to the public as providing a special care unit without being licensed as a special care unit is subject to licensure actions and penalties provided under Part 1 of this Article, as well as any other action permitted by law. (1999-334, s. 1.1; 2009-462, s. 4(f).)

§ 131D-4.7. Adult care home specialist fund.

There is established the adult care home specialist fund. The fund shall be maintained in and by the Department for the purpose of assisting county departments of social services in paying salaries of adult care home specialists. (1999-334, s. 1.1.)

§ 131D-4.8. Discharge of residents; appeals.

(a) An adult care home may initiate discharge of a resident based on any of the following reasons:

(1) The discharge is necessary to protect the welfare of the resident and the adult care home cannot meet the needs of the resident, as documented by the resident's physician, physician assistant, or nurse practitioner.

(2) The health of the resident has improved sufficiently so that the resident is no longer in need of the services provided by the adult care home, as documented by the resident's physician, physician assistant, or nurse practitioner.

(3) The safety of the resident or other individuals in the adult care home is endangered.

(4) The health of the resident or other individuals in the adult care home is endangered, as documented by a physician, physician assistant, or nurse practitioner.

(5) The resident has failed to pay the costs of services and accommodations by the payment due date specified in the resident's contract with the adult care home, after receiving written notice of warning of discharge for failure to pay.

(6) The discharge is mandated under this Article, Article 3 of this Chapter, or rules adopted by the Medical Care Commission.

(b) Upon arrival at any adult care home, an individual must be identified to receive a discharge notice on behalf of the resident. An adult care home shall notify a resident, the resident's legal representative, and the individual identified to receive a discharge notice of its intent to initiate the discharge of the resident under subsection (a) of this section, in writing, at least 30 days before the resident is discharged. The written notice shall include (i) the reasons for the discharge, (ii) an appropriate discharge destination if known, (iii) personal medical care information relating to the resident, as required by the Department, (iv) a copy of the Adult Care Home Notice of Discharge, (v) a copy of the Adult Care Home Hearing Request Form, and (vi) other information, as required under rules adopted by the Medical Care Commission. If a discharge is initiated under subdivision (a)(1) of this section on the basis that a resident's physician requires a different level of care for the resident, the discharge is not subject to appeal for that specific reason unless there is a documented conflict between two or more of the resident's physicians regarding the resident's appropriate level of care but remains subject to appeal on all other available grounds.

(c) During any appeal of a discharge to the Hearing Unit, if the Hearing Unit determines that the discharge destination identified in the written notice required by subsection (b) of this section does not include an appropriate discharge destination, the Department shall not prohibit discharge solely for that reason, provided that any discharge shall comply with subsection (e) of this section.

(d) If an adult care home resident or the resident's legal representative elects to appeal a discharge initiated by the adult care home, the appeal shall be to the Hearing Unit. The Hearing Unit shall decide all appeals pertaining to the discharge of adult care home residents. The decision of the Hearing Unit is the final agency decision. Any person aggrieved by a decision of the Hearing Unit pertaining to an adult care home resident discharge is entitled to immediate judicial review of the decision in Wake County Superior Court or in the superior court of the county where the person resides. The appellant shall file a petition for judicial review not later than 30 days after the person is served with a written copy of the Hearing Unit decision. Within 10 days after the petition for judicial review is filed with the superior court, the appellant shall serve copies of the petition by personal service or certified mail upon all parties who were parties of record to the appeal to the Hearing Unit. Other parties to the appeal to the Hearing Unit may file a response to the petition within 30 days after service. The Department as the decision maker in the appeal to the Hearing Unit is not a party of record. Within 30 days after receipt of a petition for judicial review, the Department shall transmit to the superior court the original or a certified copy of the official record in the appeal to the Hearing Unit, together with the final agency decision. In reviewing the Department's final decision, the superior court shall review the official record, de novo, and make findings of fact and conclusions of law. The decision of the Department remains in effect during the pendency of review by the superior court and any further review in the appellate courts.

(e) The facility shall convene the adult care home resident discharge team to assist with finding a placement for a resident if, at the time of notice of discharge, the destination is unknown, or the destination is not appropriate for the resident. The facility is not solely responsible for securing an appropriate discharge destination. Local management entities shall take the lead role for the discharge destination for those residents whose primary unmet needs are related to mental health, developmental disabilities, or substance abuse and who meet the criteria for the target population established by the Division of Mental Health, Developmental Disabilities, and Substance Abuse Services. Local departments of social services shall take the lead role for those residents whose primary unmet needs are related to health, including Alzheimer's disease and other forms of dementia, welfare, abuse, or neglect. When the adult care home resident discharge team is convened at the request of a facility, the adult care home resident discharge team shall consult with that facility, as well as the resident receiving the discharge notice and that resident's legal representative. Upon the request of the resident or the resident's legal representative, the Regional Long-Term Care Ombudsman shall serve as a member of the adult care home resident discharge team. The facility requesting the adult care home resident discharge team to be convened shall notify the resident and the resident's legal representative of this right. The adult care home resident discharge team shall provide the Hearing Unit with the discharge location at or before the discharge hearing.

(f) Meetings of the adult care home resident discharge team are not subject to the provisions of Article 33C of Chapter 143 of the General Statutes. All information and records acquired by the adult care home resident discharge team in the exercise of its duties are confidential unless all parties give written consent to the release of that information.

(g) If a discharge is under appeal to the Hearing Unit, the resident shall remain in the facility and shall not be subject to discharge until issuance of the decision of the Hearing Unit with the following exceptions:

(1)   The discharge is necessary for the resident's welfare and the resident's needs cannot be met in the facility as documented by the resident's physician, physician assistant, or nurse practitioner;

(2)   The safety of other individuals in the facility is endangered;

(3)   The health of other individuals in the facility is endangered as documented by a physician, physician assistant, or nurse practitioner. (2011-272, s. 4.)

§ 131D-5: Repealed by Session Laws 1983, c. 637, s. 1.

§ 131D-6. Certification of adult day care programs; purpose; definition; penalty.

(a)   It is the policy of this State to enable people who would otherwise need full-time care away from their own residences to remain in their residences as long as possible and to enjoy as much independence as possible. One of the programs that permits adults to remain in their residences and with their families is adult day care.

(b)   As used in this section "adult day care program" means the provision of group care and supervision in a place other than their usual place of abode on a less than 24-hour basis to adults who may be physically or mentally disabled. The Department of Health and Human Services shall annually inspect and certify all adult day care programs, under rules adopted by the Social Services Commission. The Social Services Commission shall adopt rules to protect the health, safety, and welfare of persons in adult day care programs. These rules shall include minimum standards relating to management of the program, staffing requirements, building requirements, fire safety, sanitation, nutrition, and program activities. Adult day care programs are not required to provide transportation to participants; however, those programs that choose to provide transportation shall comply with rules adopted by the Commission for the health and safety of participants during transport.

The Department of Health and Human Services shall enforce the rules of the Social Services Commission.

(b1) An adult day care program that provides or that advertises, markets, or otherwise promotes itself as providing special care services for persons with Alzheimer's disease or other dementias, a mental health disability, or other special needs disease or condition shall provide the following written disclosures to the Department and to persons seeking adult day care program special care services:

(1) A statement of the overall philosophy and mission of the adult day care program and how it reflects the special needs of participants with dementia.

(2) The process and criteria for providing or discontinuing special care services.

(3) The process used for assessment and establishment of the plan of care and its implementation, including how the plan of care is responsive to changes in the participant's condition.

(4) Staffing ratios and how they meet the participant's need for increased special care and supervision.

(5) Staff training that is dementia-specific.

(6) Physical environment and design features that specifically address the needs of participants with Alzheimer's disease or other dementias.

(7) Frequency and type of participant activities provided.

(8) Involvement of families in special care and availability of family support programs.

(9) Additional costs and fees to the participant for special care.

(b2) As part of its certification renewal procedures and inspections, the Department shall examine for accuracy the written disclosure of each adult day care program subject to this section. Substantial changes to written disclosures shall be reported to the Department at the time the change is made.

(b3) Nothing in this section shall be construed as prohibiting an adult day care program that does not advertise, market, or otherwise promote itself as providing special care services for persons with Alzheimer's disease or other dementias from providing adult day care services to persons with Alzheimer's disease or other dementias, a mental health disability, or other special needs disease or condition.

(b4)   As used in this section, the term "special care service" means a program, service, or activity designed especially for participants with Alzheimer's disease or other dementias, a mental health disability, or other special needs disease or condition as determined by the Medical Care Commission.

(c)   The Secretary may impose a civil penalty not to exceed one hundred dollars ($100.00) for each violation on a person, firm, agency, or corporation who willfully violates any provision of this section or any rule adopted by the Social Services Commission pursuant to this section. Each day of a continuing violation constitutes a separate violation.

In determining the amount of the civil penalty, the Secretary shall consider the degree and extent of the harm or potential harm caused by the violation.

The Social Services Commission shall adopt rules concerning the imposition of civil penalties under this subsection.

The clear proceeds of civil penalties imposed pursuant to this subsection shall be remitted to the Civil Penalty and Forfeiture Fund in accordance with G.S. 115C-457.2.

(c1)   Any person, firm, agency, or corporation that harms or willfully neglects a person under its care is guilty of a Class 1 misdemeanor.

(d)   The following programs are exempted from the provisions of this section:

(1)   Those that care for three people or less;

(2)   Those that care for two or more persons, all of whom are related by blood or marriage to the operator of the facility;

(3)   Those that are required by other statutes to be licensed by the Department of Health and Human Services. (1985, c. 349, s. 1; 1993, c. 539, s. 954; 1994, Ex. Sess., c. 24, s. 14(c); 1997-443, s. 11A.118(a); 1998-215, s. 77; 1999-334, s. 2.2; 2001-90, s. 1.)

§ 131D-7. Waiver of rules for certain adult care homes providing shelter or services during disaster or emergency.

(a) The Division of Health Service Regulation may temporarily waive, during disasters or emergencies declared in accordance with Article 1A of Chapter 166A of the General Statutes, any rules of the Commission pertaining to adult care homes to the extent necessary to allow the adult care home to provide temporary shelter and temporary services requested by the emergency management agency. The Division may identify, in advance of a declared disaster or emergency, rules that may be waived, and the extent the rules may be waived, upon a disaster or emergency being declared in accordance with Article 1A of Chapter 166A of the General Statutes. The Division may also waive rules under this subsection during a declared disaster or emergency upon the request of an emergency management agency and may rescind the waiver if, after investigation, the Division determines the waiver poses an unreasonable risk to the health, safety, or welfare of any of the persons occupying the adult care home. The emergency management agency requesting temporary shelter or temporary services shall notify the Division within 72 hours of the time the preapproved waivers are deemed by the emergency management agency to apply.

(b) As used in this section, "emergency management agency" is as defined in G.S. 166A-19.3. (1999-307, s. 2; 2007-182, s. 1; 2012-12, s. 2(s).)

§ 131D-8. Adult care home special care units; disclosure of information required.

(a) An adult care home licensed under this Part that provides care for persons in special care units as defined in G.S. 131D-4.6 shall disclose the form of care or treatment provided that distinguishes the special care unit as being especially designed for residents with Alzheimer's disease or other dementias, a mental health disability, or other special needs disease or condition. The disclosure shall be in writing and shall be made to all of the following:

(1) The Department as part of its licensing procedures.

(2) Each person seeking placement within a special care unit, or the person's authorized representative, prior to entering into an agreement with the person to provide special care.

(3) The Office of State Long-Term Care Ombudsman, annually, or more often if requested.

(b) Information that must be disclosed in writing shall include, but is not limited to, all of the following:

(1) A statement of the overall philosophy and mission of the licensed facility and how it reflects the special needs of residents with Alzheimer's disease or other dementias, a mental health disability, or other special needs disease or condition.

(2) The process and criteria for placement, transfer, or discharge to or from the special care unit.

(3) The process used for assessment and establishment of the plan of care and its implementation, including how the plan of care is responsive to changes in the resident's condition.

(4) Staffing ratios and how they meet the resident's need for increased care and supervision.

(5) Staff training that is dementia-specific.

(6) Physical environment and design features that specifically address the needs of residents with Alzheimer's disease or other dementias.

(7) Frequency and type of programs and activities for residents of the special care unit.

(8) Involvement of families in resident care, and availability of family support programs.

(9) Additional costs and fees to the resident for special care.

(c) As part of its license renewal procedures and inspections, the Department shall examine for accuracy the written disclosure of each adult care home subject to this section. Substantial changes to written disclosures shall be reported to the Department at the time the change is made.

(d) Nothing in this section shall be construed as prohibiting an adult care home that does not offer a special care unit from admitting a person with

Alzheimer's disease or other dementias, a mental health disability, or other special needs disease or condition. The disclosures required under this section apply only to an adult care home that advertises, markets, or otherwise promotes itself as providing a special care unit for persons with Alzheimer's disease or other dementias.

(e) As used in this section, the term "special care unit" has the same meaning as applies under G.S. 131D-4.6. (1999-334, s. 2.1; 1999-456, s. 61(a).)

§ 131D-9. Immunization of employees and residents of adult care homes.

(a) Except as provided in subsection (e) of this section, an adult care home licensed under this Article shall require residents and employees to be immunized annually against influenza virus and shall require residents to also be immunized against pneumococcal disease.

(b) Upon admission, an adult care home shall notify the resident of the immunization requirements of this section and shall request that the resident agree to be immunized against influenza virus and pneumococcal disease.

(b1) An adult care home shall notify every employee of the immunization requirements of this section and shall request that the employee agree to be immunized against the influenza virus.

(c) An adult care home shall document the annual immunization against influenza virus and the immunization against pneumococcal disease for each resident and each employee, as required under this section. Upon finding that a resident is lacking one or both of these immunizations or that an employee has not been immunized against influenza virus, or if the adult care home is unable to verify that the individual has received the required immunization, the adult care home shall provide or arrange for immunization. The immunization and documentation required shall occur not later than November 30 of each year.

(d) For an individual who becomes a resident of or who is newly employed by the adult care home after November 30 but before March 30 of the following year, the adult care home shall determine the individual's status for the immunizations required under this section, and if found to be deficient, the adult care home shall provide the immunization.

(e) No individual shall be required to receive vaccine under this section if the vaccine is medically contraindicated, or if the vaccine is against the individual's religious beliefs, or if the individual refuses the vaccine after being fully informed of the health risks of not being immunized.

(f) Notwithstanding any other provision of law to the contrary, the Commission for Public Health shall have the authority to adopt rules to implement the immunization requirements of this section.

(g) As used in this section, "employee" means an individual who is a part-time or full-time employee of the adult care home. (2000-112, ss. 1, 2; 2007-182, s. 1.3.)

§ 131D-10. Adult care home rated certificates.

(a) Rules adopted by the North Carolina Medical Care Commission for issuance of certificates to adult care homes shall contain a rating based, at a minimum, on the following:

(1) Inspections and substantiated complaint investigations conducted by the Department to determine compliance with licensing statutes and rules. Specific areas to be reviewed include:

a. Admission and discharge procedures.

b. Medication management.

c. Physical plant.

d. Resident care and services, including food services, resident activities programs, and safety measures.

e. Residents' rights.

f. Sanitation grade.

g. Special Care Units.

h. Use of physical restraints and alternatives.

(b) The initial ratings awarded to a facility pursuant to the rules adopted under this section shall be based on inspections, penalties imposed, and investigations of substantiated complaints that revealed noncompliance with statutes and rules, that occurred on or after the act becomes law.

(c) Type A penalties shall affect the rating for 24 months from the date the penalty is assessed. Type B penalties shall affect the rating for 12 months from the date the penalty is assessed.

(d) Adult care homes shall display the rating certificate in a location visible to the public. Certificates shall include the Web site address for the Department of Health and Human Services, Division of Health Service Regulation, which can be accessed for specific information regarding the basis of the facility rating. For access by the public on request, adult care homes shall also maintain on-site a copy of information provided by the Department of Health and Human Services, Division of Health Service Regulation, regarding the basis of the facility rating. In addition to information on the basis of the rating, the Department of Health and Human Services, Division of Health Service Regulation, shall make information available via its Web site and in the materials available on-site at the facility regarding quality improvement efforts undertaken by the facility including:

(1) Participation in any quality improvement programs approved by the Department.

(2) The facility's attainment of the North Carolina New Organizational Vision Award special licensure designation authorized in Article 5, Chapter 131E of the General Statutes. (2007-544, s. 3(b).)

Article 1A.

Control over Child Placing and Child Care.

Part 1. In General.

§ 131D-10.1. Foster Care Children's Bill of Rights; purpose.

(a) It is the policy of this State to strengthen and preserve the family as a unit consistent with a high priority of protecting children's welfare. When a child requires care outside the family unit, it is the duty of the State to assure that the quality of substitute care is as close as possible to the care and nurturing that society expects of a family. However, the State recognizes there are instances when protecting a child's welfare outweighs reunifying the family unit, and as such, the care of residential care facilities providing high quality services that include meeting the children's educational needs as determined by the Department of Health and Human Services, Division of Social Services can satisfy the standard of protecting a child's welfare, regardless of the child's age, particularly when the sibling groups can be kept intact. To that end, the General Assembly promotes the following in the provision of foster care:

(1)   A safe foster home free of violence, abuse, neglect, and danger.

(2)   First priority regarding placement in a home with siblings.

(3)   The ability to communicate with the assigned social worker or case worker overseeing the child's case and have calls made to the social worker or case worker returned within a reasonable period of time.

(4)   Allowing the child to remain enrolled in the school the child attended before being placed in foster care, if at all possible.

(5)   Having a social worker, when a child is removed from the home, to immediately begin conducting an investigation to identify and locate all grandparents, adult siblings, and other adult relatives of the child to provide those persons with specific information and explanation of various options to participate in placement of a child.

(6)   Participation in school extracurricular activities, community events, and religious practices.

(7)   Communication with the biological parents if the child placed in foster care receives any immunizations and whether any additional immunizations are needed if the child will be transitioning back into a home with his or her biological parents.

(8)   Establishing and having access to a bank or savings account in accordance with State laws and federal regulations.

(9)   Obtaining identification and permanent documents, including a birth certificate, social security card, and health records by the age of 16, to the extent allowed by federal and State law.

(10) The use of appropriate communication measures to maintain contact with siblings if the child placed in foster care is separated from his or her siblings.

(11) Meaningful participation in a transition plan for those phasing out of foster care, including participation in family team, treatment team, court, and school meetings.

A violation of subdivisions (1) through (11) of this subsection shall not be construed to create a cause of action under this section against the State, the Department of Health and Human Services, or a person or entity providing foster care pursuant to this Article.

(b) The purpose of this Article is to assign the authority to protect the health, safety and well-being of children separated from or being cared for away from their families. (1983, c. 637, s. 2; 2009-408, s. 1; 2013-326, s. 1.)

§ 131D-10.2. Definitions.

For purposes of this Article, unless the context clearly implies otherwise:

(1) "Adoption" means the act of creating a legal relationship between parent and child where it did not exist genetically.

(2) "Adoptive Home" means a family home approved by a child placing agency to accept a child for adoption.

(3) "Child" means an individual less than 18 years of age, who has not been emancipated under the provisions of Article 35 of Chapter 7B of the General Statutes.

(4) "Child Placing Agency" means a person authorized by statute or license under this Article to receive children for purposes of placement in residential group care, family foster homes or adoptive homes.

(5) "Children's Camp" means a residential child-care facility which provides foster care at either a permanent camp site or in a wilderness setting.

(6a)   "Criminal History" means a county, State, or federal conviction of a felony by a court of competent jurisdiction or a pending felony indictment of a crime for child abuse or neglect, spousal abuse, a crime against a child, including child pornography, or for a crime involving violence, including rape, sexual assault, or homicide, other than physical assault or battery; a county, State, or federal conviction of a felony by a court of competent jurisdiction or a pending felony indictment for physical assault, battery, or a drug-related offense, if the offense was committed within the past five years; or similar crimes under federal law or under the laws of other states.

(7)   "Department" means the Department of Health and Human Services.

(8)   "Family Foster Home" means the private residence of one or more individuals who permanently reside as members of the household and who provide continuing full-time foster care for a child or children who are placed there by a child placing agency or who provide continuing full-time foster care for two or more children who are unrelated to the adult members of the household by blood, marriage, guardianship or adoption.

(9)   "Foster Care" means the continuing provision of the essentials of daily living on a 24-hour basis for dependent, neglected, abused, abandoned, destitute, orphaned, undisciplined or delinquent children or other children who, due to similar problems of behavior or family conditions, are living apart from their parents, relatives, or guardians in a family foster home or residential child-care facility. The essentials of daily living include but are not limited to shelter, meals, clothing, education, recreation, and individual attention and supervision.

(9a)   "Foster Parent" means any individual who is 18 years of age or older who is licensed by the State to provide foster care.

(10)   "Person" means an individual, partnership, joint-stock company, trust, voluntary association, corporation, agency, or other organization or enterprise doing business in this State, whether or not for profit.

(11)   "Primarily Educational Institution" means any institution which operates one or more scholastic or vocational and technical education programs that can be offered in satisfaction of compulsory school attendance laws, in which the primary purpose of the housing and care of children is to meet their educational needs, provided such institution has complied with Article 39 of Chapter 115C of the General Statutes.

(12) "Provisional License" means a type of license granted by the Department to a person who is temporarily unable to comply with a rule or rules adopted under this Article.

(13) "Residential Child-Care Facility" means a staffed premise with paid or volunteer staff where children receive continuing full-time foster care. Residential child-care facility includes child-caring institutions, group homes, and children's camps which provide foster care.

(14) "Therapeutic Foster Home" means a family foster home where, in addition to the provision of foster care, foster parents who receive appropriate training provide a child with behavioral health treatment services under the supervision of a county department of social services, an area mental health program, or a licensed private agency and in compliance with licensing rules adopted by the Commission. (1983, c. 637, s. 2; 1993, c. 180, s. 5; 1995, c. 507, s. 23.26(a); 1997-140, s. 1; 1997-443, s. 11A.118(a); 1998-202, s. 13(hh); 2001-487, s. 84(b); 2007-276, s. 11.)

§ 131D-10.3. Licensure required.

(a) No person shall operate, establish or provide foster care for children or receive and place children in residential care facilities, family foster homes, or adoptive homes without first applying for a license to the Department and submitting the required information on application forms provided by the Department.

(b) Persons licensed or seeking a license under this Article shall permit the Department access to premises and information required to determine whether the person is in compliance with licensing rules of the Commission.

(c) Persons licensed pursuant to this Article shall be periodically reviewed by the Department to determine whether they comply with Commission rules and whether licensure shall continue.

(d) This Article shall apply to all persons intending to organize, develop or provide foster care for children or receive and place children in residential child-care facilities, family foster homes or adoptive homes irrespective of such persons having applied for or obtained a certification, registration or permit to carry on work not controlled by this Article except persons exempted in G.S. 131D-10.4.

(e)   Unless revoked or modified to a provisional or suspended status, the terms of a license issued by the Department shall be in force for a period not to exceed 24 months from the date of issuance under rules adopted by the Commission.

(f)   Persons licensed or seeking a license who are temporarily unable to comply with a rule or rules may be granted a provisional license. The provisional license can be issued for a period not to exceed six months. The noncompliance with a rule or rules shall not present an immediate threat to the health and safety of the children, and the person shall have a plan approved by the Department to correct the area(s) of noncompliance within the provisional period. A provisional license for an additional period of time to meet the same area(s) of noncompliance shall not be issued.

(g)   In accordance with Commission rules, a person may submit to the Department documentation of compliance with the standards of a nationally recognized accrediting body, and the Department on the basis of such accreditation may deem the person in compliance with one or more Commission licensing rules.

(h)   Except as provided in subsection (i) of this section, the Secretary shall not enroll any new provider for Medicaid Home or Community Based services or other Medicaid services, as defined in 42 C.F.R. 440.90, 42 C.F.R. 440.130(d), and 42 C.F.R. 440.180, or issue a license for a new facility or a new service to any applicant meeting any of the following criteria:

(1)   The applicant was the owner, principal, or affiliate of a licensable facility under Chapter 122C, Chapter 131D, or Article 7 of Chapter 110 that had its license revoked until 60 months after the date of the revocation.

(2)   The applicant is the owner, principal, or affiliate of a licensable facility that was assessed a penalty for a Type A or Type B violation under Article 3 of Chapter 122C, or any combination thereof, and any one of the following conditions exist:

a.   A single violation has been assessed in the six months prior to the application.

b. Two violations have been assessed in the 18 months prior to the application and 18 months have not passed from the date of the most recent violation.

c. Three violations have been assessed in the 36 months prior to the application and 36 months have not passed from the date of the most recent violation.

d. Four or more violations have been assessed in the 60 months prior to application and 60 months have not passed from the date of the most recent violation.

(3) The applicant is the owner, principal, or affiliate of a licensable facility that had its license summarily suspended or downgraded to provisional status as a result of violations under G.S. 122C-24.1(a) until 60 months after the date of reinstatement or restoration of the license.

(4) The applicant is the owner, principal, or affiliate of a licensable facility that had its license summarily suspended or downgraded to provisional status as a result of violations under Article 1A of Chapter 131D, or had its license summarily suspended or denied under Article 7 of Chapter 110 until 60 months after the date of reinstatement or restoration of the license.

(i) The Secretary may enroll a provider described in subsection (h) of this section if any of the following circumstances apply:

(1) The applicant is an area program or county program providing services under G.S. 122C-141, and there is no other provider of the service in the catchment area.

(2) The Secretary finds that the area program or county program has shown good cause by clear and convincing evidence why the enrollment should be allowed.

(j) For purposes of subdivision (h)(2) of this section, fines assessed prior to October 23, 2002, are not applicable to this provision. However, licensure or enrollment shall be denied if an applicant's history as a provider under Chapter 131D, Chapter 122C, or Article 7 of Chapter 110 is such that the Secretary has concluded the applicant will likely be unable to comply with licensing or enrollment statutes, rules, or regulations. In the event the Secretary denies licensure or enrollment under this subsection, the reasons for the denial and appeal rights pursuant to Article 3 of Chapter 150B shall be given to the provider in writing. (1983, c. 637, s. 2; 2002-164, s. 4.4; 2003-294, s. 4.)

§ 131D-10.3A. Mandatory criminal checks.

(a) Effective January 1, 1996, in order to ensure the safety and well-being of any child placed for foster care in a home, the Department shall ensure that the criminal histories of all foster parents, individuals applying for licensure as foster parents, and individuals 18 years of age or older who reside in a family foster home, are checked and, based on the criminal history check, a determination is made as to whether the foster parents, and other individuals required to be checked, are fit for a foster child to reside with them in the home. The Department shall ensure that, as of the effective date of this Article, all individuals required to be checked are checked for county, state, and federal criminal histories.

(b) The Department shall ensure that all individuals who are required to be checked pursuant to subsection (a) of this section are checked upon relicensure for county and State criminal histories.

(c) The Department shall prohibit an individual from providing foster care by denying or revoking the license to provide foster care if an individual required to submit to a criminal history check pursuant to subsection (a) of this section has a criminal history. The Department may prohibit an individual from providing foster care by denying or revoking the license to provide foster care if the Department determines that the safety and well being of a child placed in the home for foster care would be at risk based on other criminal convictions, whether felony or misdemeanor.

(d) The Department of Justice shall provide to the Department the criminal history of the individuals specified in subsection (a) of this section obtained from the State and National Repositories of Criminal Histories as requested by the Department. The Department shall provide to the Department of Justice, along with the request, the fingerprints of the individual to be checked, any additional information required by the Department of Justice, and a form consenting to the check of the criminal record and to the use of fingerprints and other identifying information required by the State or National Repositories signed by the individual to be checked. The fingerprints of the individual to be checked shall be forwarded to the State Bureau of Investigation for a search of the State's criminal history record file, and the State Bureau of Investigation shall forward a set of fingerprints to the Federal Bureau of Investigation for a national criminal history record check.

(e) At the time of application, the individual whose criminal history is to be checked shall be furnished with a statement substantially similar to the following:

"NOTICE

MANDATORY CRIMINAL HISTORY CHECK

NORTH CAROLINA LAW REQUIRES THAT A CRIMINAL HISTORY CHECK BE CONDUCTED ON ALL PERSONS 18 YEARS OF AGE OR OLDER WHO RESIDE IN A LICENSED FAMILY FOSTER HOME.

"Criminal history" includes any county, State, and federal conviction of a felony by a court of competent jurisdiction or pending felony indictment of a crime for child abuse or neglect, spousal abuse, a crime against a child, including child pornography, or for a crime involving violence, including rape, sexual assault, or homicide, other than physical assault or battery; a county, State, or federal conviction of a felony by a court of competent jurisdiction or a pending felony indictment for physical assault, battery, or a drug related offense, if the offense was committed within the past five years; or similar crimes under federal law or under the laws of other states. Your fingerprints will be used to check the criminal history records of the State Bureau of Investigation (SBI) and the Federal Bureau of Investigation (FBI).

If it is determined, based on your criminal history, that you are unfit to have a foster child reside with you, you shall have the opportunity to complete or challenge the accuracy of the information contained in the SBI or FBI identification records.

If licensure is denied or the foster home license is revoked by the Department of Health and Human Services as a result of the criminal history check, if you are a foster parent, or are applying to become a foster parent, you may request a hearing pursuant to Article 3 of Chapter 150B of the General Statutes, the Administrative Procedure Act.

Any person who intentionally falsifies any information required to be furnished to conduct the criminal history is guilty of a Class 2 misdemeanor."

Refusal to consent to a criminal history check is grounds for the Department to deny or revoke a license to provide foster care. Any person who intentionally falsifies any information required to be furnished to conduct the criminal history is guilty of a Class 2 misdemeanor.

(f) The Department shall notify in writing the foster parent and any person applying to be licensed as a foster parent, and that individual's supervising agency of the determination by the Department of whether the foster parent is qualified to provide foster care based on the criminal history of all individuals required to be checked. In accordance with the law regulating the dissemination of the contents of the criminal history file furnished by the Federal Bureau of Investigation, the Department shall not release nor disclose any portion of an individual's criminal history to the foster parent or any other individual required to be checked. The Department shall also notify the individual of the individual's right to review the criminal history information, the procedure for completing or challenging the accuracy of the criminal history, and the foster parent's right to contest the Department's determination.

A foster parent who disagrees with the Department's decision may request a hearing pursuant to Chapter 150B of the General Statutes, the Administrative Procedure Act.

(g) All the information that the Department receives through the checking of the criminal history is privileged information and is not a public record but is for the exclusive use of the Department and those persons authorized under this section to receive the information. The Department may destroy the information after it is used for the purposes authorized by this section after one calendar year.

(h) There is no liability for negligence on the part of a supervising agency, or a State or local agency, or the employees of a State or local agency, arising from any action taken or omission by any of them in carrying out the provisions of this section. The immunity established by this subsection shall not extend to gross negligence, wanton conduct, or intentional wrongdoing that would otherwise be actionable. The immunity established by this subsection shall be deemed to have been waived to the extent of indemnification by insurance, indemnification under Article 31A of Chapter 143 of the General Statutes, and to the extent sovereign immunity is waived under the Torts Claim Act, as set forth in Article 31 of Chapter 143 of the General Statutes.

(i) The Department of Justice shall perform the State and national criminal history checks on individuals required by this section and shall charge the Department a reasonable fee only for conducting the checks of the national criminal history records authorized by this section. The Division of Social Services, Department of Health and Human Services, shall bear the costs of implementing this section. (1995, c. 507, s. 23.26(b); 1997-140, s. 2; 1997-443, ss. 11A.89, 11A.118(a); 2003-304, s. 4; 2007-276, ss. 12, 13.)

§ 131D-10.4. Exemptions.

This Article shall not apply to:

(1) Any residential child-care facility chartered by the laws of the State of North Carolina (or operating under charters of other states which have complied with the corporation laws of North Carolina) which has a plant and assets worth sixty thousand dollars ($60,000) or more and which is owned or operated by a religious denomination or fraternal order and which was in operation before July 1, 1977;

(2) State institutions for emotionally disturbed or delinquent children, the mentally ill, mentally retarded, and substance abusers;

(3) Secure detention facilities as specified in Part 3 of Article 13 of Chapter 143B of the General Statutes;

(4) Licensable facilities subject to the rules of the Commission for Mental Health, Developmental Disabilities, and Substance Abuse Services as specified in Article 2 of Chapter 122C of the General Statutes;

(5) Persons authorized by statute to receive and place children for foster care and adoption in accordance with G.S. 108A-14;

(6) Primarily educational institutions as defined in G.S. 131D-10.2(11); or

(7) Individuals who are related by blood, marriage, or adoption to the child. (1983, c. 637, s. 2; 1985, c. 589, s. 39; 1991, c. 636, s. 19(b); 1998-202, s. 13(ii); 1999-423, s. 6; 2000-137, s. 4(gg); 2011-145, s. 19.1(ll).)

§ 131D-10.5. Powers and duties of the Commission.

In addition to other powers and duties prescribed by law, the Commission shall exercise the following powers and duties:

(1)   Adopt, amend and repeal rules consistent with the laws of this State and the laws and regulations of the federal government to implement the provisions and purposes of this Article;

(2)   Issue declaratory rulings as may be needed to implement the provisions and purposes of this Article;

(3)   Adopt rules governing procedures to appeal Department decisions pursuant to this Article granting, denying, suspending or revoking licenses;

(4)   Adopt criteria for waiver of licensing rules adopted pursuant to this Article;

(5)   Adopt rules on documenting the use of physical restraint in residential child-care facilities;

(6)   Adopt rules establishing personnel and training requirements related to the use of physical restraints and time-out for staff employed in residential child-care facilities; and

(7)   Adopt rules establishing educational requirements, minimum age, relevant experience, and criminal record status for executive directors and staff employed by child placing agencies and residential child care facilities. (1983, c. 637, s. 2; 2000-129, s. 2(a); 2007-30, s. 2; 2009-188, s. 2.)

§ 131D-10.5A. Collection of data on use of restraints in residential child-care facilities.

A residential child-care facility that employs physical restraint of a child shall collect data on the use of the restraint. The data shall reflect for each incidence, the type of procedure used, the length of time employed, alternatives considered or employed, and the effectiveness of the procedure or alternative employed. The facility shall analyze the data on at least a quarterly basis to monitor effectiveness, determine trends, and take corrective action where necessary. The facility shall make the data available to the Department upon request. Nothing in this subsection abrogates State or federal law or requirements pertaining to the confidentiality, privilege, or other prohibition against disclosure of information provided to the Department under this subsection. In reviewing data requested under this subsection, the Department shall adhere to State and federal requirements of confidentiality, privilege, and other prohibitions against disclosure and release applicable to the information received under this subsection. (2000-129, s. 2(b).)

§ 131D-10.6. Powers and duties of the Department.

In addition to other powers and duties prescribed by law, the Department shall exercise the following powers and duties:

(1) Investigate applicants for licensure to determine whether they are in compliance with licensing rules adopted by the Commission and the provisions of this Article.

(2) Grant a license when an investigation shows compliance with this Article and Commission rules. The license shall be valid for a period not to exceed 24 months as specified by Commission rules and may be revoked or placed in suspended or provisional status sooner if the Department finds that licensure rules are not being met or upon a finding that the health, safety or welfare of children is threatened.

(3) Administer and enforce the provisions of this Article and the rules of the Commission.

(4) Appoint hearing officers to conduct appeals pursuant to this Article.

(5) Prescribe the form in which application for licensure or a request for waiver of Commission rules shall be submitted.

(6) Inspect facilities and obtain records, documents and other information necessary to determine compliance with the provisions of this Article and Commission rules.

(7) Grant, deny, suspend or revoke a license or a provisional license, in accordance with Commission rules.

(8) Act to grant or deny a request for waiver of Commission rules within 10 business days after its receipt. Grant a waiver for good cause to Commission rules that do not affect the health, safety, or welfare of children in facilities subject to licensure under this Article, in accordance with Commission rules.

(9) Undertake a comprehensive study of the existing procedures for granting or denying an application for licensure or a request for waiver of Commission rules and report to the General Assembly on or before May 1, 1998, regarding its efforts to make the process more efficient and less time-consuming and its recommendations for any changes in the licensing laws or rules. The study shall include the development of a procedure that will ensure that the local Guardian Ad Litem Program is notified by the county department of social services of the request for a waiver if a guardian has been appointed for any child who may be affected by the waiver.

(10) Report annually on October 1 to the Joint Legislative Oversight Committee on Health and Human Services the level of facility compliance with applicable State law governing the use of restraint and time-out in residential child-care facilities. The report shall also include the total number of facilities that reported deaths under this section, the number of deaths reported by each facility, the number of deaths investigated pursuant to this section, and the number found by the investigation to be related to the use of physical restraint or time-out. (1983, c. 637, s. 2; 1997-110, s. 1; 2000-129, s. 5(b); 2003-58, s. 3; 2011-291, s. 2.48.)

§ 131D-10.6A. Training by the Division of Social Services required.

(a) The Division of Social Services, Department of Health and Human Services, shall require a minimum of 30 hours of preservice training for foster care parents either prior to licensure or within six months from the date a provisional license is issued pursuant to G.S.131D-10.3, and a mandated minimum of 10 hours of continuing education for all foster care parents annually after the year in which a license is obtained.

(b) (See Editor's Note) The Division of Social Services shall establish minimum training requirements for child welfare services staff. The minimum training requirements established by the Division are as follows:

(1) Child welfare services workers shall complete a minimum of 72 hours of preservice training before assuming direct client contact responsibilities. In completing this requirement, the Division of Social Services shall ensure that each child welfare worker receives training on family centered practices and State and federal law regarding the basic rights of individuals relevant to the provision of child welfare services, including the right to privacy, freedom from duress and coercion to induce cooperation, and the right to parent.

(2) Child protective services workers shall complete a minimum of 18 hours of additional training that the Division of Social Services determines is necessary to adequately meet training needs.

(3) Foster care and adoption workers shall complete a minimum of 39 hours of additional training that the Division of Social Services determines is necessary to adequately meet training needs.

(4) Child welfare services supervisors shall complete a minimum of 72 hours of preservice training before assuming supervisory responsibilities and a minimum of 54 hours of additional training that the Division of Social Services determines is necessary to adequately meet training needs.

(5) Child welfare services staff shall complete 24 hours of continuing education annually. In completing this requirement, the Division of Social Services shall provide each child welfare services staff member with annual update information on family centered practices and State and federal law regarding the basic rights of individuals relevant to the provision of child welfare services, including the right to privacy, freedom from duress and coercion to induce cooperation, and the right to parent.

The Division of Social Services may grant an exception in whole or in part to the requirement under subdivision (1) of this subsection to child welfare workers who satisfactorily complete or are enrolled in a masters or bachelors program after July 1, 1999, from a North Carolina social work program accredited pursuant to the Council on Social Work Education. The program's curricula must cover the specific preservice training requirements as established by the Division of Social Services.

The Division of Social Services shall ensure that training opportunities are available for county departments of social services and consolidated human service agencies to meet the training requirements of this subsection. (1995, c.

324, s. 23.25; 1997-390, s. 11.1; 1997-443, s. 11A.118(a); 2000-67, s. 11.14(c); 2003-304, s. 4.2.)

§ 131D-10.6B. Report of death.

(a)   A facility licensed under this Article shall notify the Department immediately upon the death of any resident of the facility that occurs within seven days of physical restraint of the resident, and shall notify the Department within three days of the death of any resident of the facility resulting from violence, accident, suicide, or homicide. The Department may assess a civil penalty of not less than five hundred dollars ($500.00) and not more than one thousand dollars ($1,000) against a facility that fails to notify the Department of a death and the circumstances surrounding the death known to the facility. Chapter 150B of the General Statutes governs the assessment of a penalty under this section. A civil penalty owed under this section may be recovered in a civil action brought by the Department or the Attorney General. The clear proceeds of the penalty shall be remitted to the State Treasurer for deposit in accordance with State law.

(b)   Upon receipt of notification from a facility in accordance with subsection (a) of this section, the Department shall notify the State protection and advocacy agency designated under the Developmental Disabilities Assistance and Bill of Rights Act 2000, P.L. 106-402, that a person with a disability has died. The Department shall provide the agency access to the information about each death reported to the agency pursuant to subsection (a) of this section, including information resulting from any investigation of the death by the Department, and from reports received from the Chief Medical Examiner pursuant to G.S. 130A-385. The agency shall use the information in accordance with its powers and duties under applicable State and federal law and regulations.

(c)   If the death of a resident of the facility occurs within seven days of the use of physical restraint, the Department shall initiate immediately an investigation of the death.

(d)   Nothing in this section abrogates State or federal law or requirements pertaining to the confidentiality, privilege, or other prohibition against disclosure of information provided to the Department or the agency. In carrying out the requirements of this section, the Department and the agency shall adhere to State and federal requirements of confidentiality, privilege, and other prohibitions against disclosure and release applicable to the information received under this section. A facility or provider that makes available confidential information in accordance with this section and with State and federal law is not liable for the release of the information.

(e) The Secretary shall establish a standard reporting format for reporting deaths pursuant to this section and shall provide to facilities subject to this section a form for the facility's use in complying with this section. (2000-129, s. 5(a); 2007-323, ss. 19.1(g), (h).)

§ 131D-10.6C. Maintaining a register of licensed foster homes by the Division of Social Services.

(a) The Division of Social Services shall keep a register of all licensed family foster and therapeutic foster homes. The register shall contain the following information:

(1) The name, age, and address of each foster parent.

(2) Repealed by Session Laws 2012-153, s. 7, effective October 1, 2012.

(3) The foster parent's supervising agency.

(4) The number of hours of mandated training completed by the foster parent.

(5) The date of the initial licensure.

(6) The current licensing period.

(7) Any adverse licensing actions.

(8) Repealed by Session Laws 2012-153, s. 7, effective October 1, 2012.

(b) The register shall be a public record under Chapter 132 of the General Statutes. However, the Division, without penalty, may withhold any specific information about a foster parent to the extent the release of the information would likely pose a threat to the health or safety of the foster parent or a foster child. A person who is denied access to information under this section may seek a court order compelling disclosure or copying in accordance with G.S. 132-9(a). Information not specified in subsection (a) of this section shall be considered confidential and not subject to disclosure. (2003-304, s. 5; 2012-153, s. 7.)

§ 131D-10.7. Penalties.

Any person who establishes or provides foster care for children or who receives and places children in residential child-care facilities, family foster homes or adoptive homes without a license shall be guilty of a Class 3 misdemeanor, and upon conviction shall only be punishable by a fine of not more than fifty dollars ($50.00) for the first offense and not more than five hundred dollars ($500.00) for each subsequent offense. Each day of a continuing violation after conviction shall be considered a separate offense. (1983, c. 637, s. 2; 1993, c. 539, s. 955; 1994, Ex. Sess., c. 24, s. 14(c).)

§ 131D-10.8. Injunction.

(a)   Notwithstanding the existence or pursuit of any other remedy, the Department may, in the manner provided by law, maintain an action in the name of the State for injunction or other process against any person to restrain or prevent the establishment, conduct, management or operation of a facility operating without a license or in a manner that threatens the health, safety or welfare of the individuals in the facility.

(b)   If any person shall interfere with the proper performance or duty of the Department in carrying out this Article, the Department may institute an action in the superior court of the county in which the interference occurred for injunctive relief against the continued interference, irrespective of all other remedies at law. (1983, c. 637, s. 2.)

§ 131D-10.9. Administrative and judicial review.

All procedures arising out of this Article, including all notification, hearing and appeal procedures, shall be governed by the appropriate provisions of Chapter

150B of the Administrative Procedure Act. (1983, c. 637, s. 2; 1987, c. 827, s. 243.)

Part 2. A Family for Every Child Initiative.

§ 131D-10.9A. Permanency Innovation Initiative Oversight Committee created.

(a) Creation and Membership. - The Permanency Innovation Initiative Oversight Committee is established. The Committee shall be located administratively in the General Assembly. The Committee shall consist of 11 members serving staggered terms. In making appointments, each appointing authority shall select members who have appropriate experience and knowledge of the issues to be examined by the Committee and shall strive to ensure racial, gender, and geographical diversity among the membership. The initial Committee members shall be appointed on or after July 1, 2013, as follows:

(1) Four members shall be appointed by the General Assembly upon recommendation of the Speaker of the House of Representatives. Of the members appointed under this subdivision, at least one shall be a member of the judiciary who shall serve for a term of two years and at least one shall be a representative from the Children's Home Society of North Carolina who shall serve for a term of three years. One member of the House shall be appointed for a one-year term. The remaining appointee shall serve a one-year term.

(2) Four members shall be appointed by the General Assembly upon the recommendation of the President Pro Tempore of the Senate. Of the members appointed under this subdivision, at least one shall be a representative from the Department of Health and Human Services, Division of Social Services, who shall serve for a term of two years and at least one shall be a representative from The Duke Endowment who shall serve for a term of three years. One member of the Senate shall be appointed for a one-year term. The remaining appointee shall serve a one-year term.

(3) Three members shall be appointed by the Governor. Of the members appointed under this subdivision, at least one shall be a representative from a county department of social services who shall serve for a term of three years and at least one shall be a representative from the University of North Carolina

at Chapel Hill who shall serve for a term of two years. The remaining member shall serve a one-year term.

(b)   Terms. - Upon the expiration of the terms of the initial Committee members, each member shall be appointed for a term of three years and shall serve until a successor is appointed. No member may serve more than two consecutive full terms. A vacancy shall be filled within 30 days by the authority making the initial appointment.

(c)   Purpose and Powers. - The Committee shall:

(1)   Design and implement a data tracking methodology to collect and analyze information to gauge the success of the initiative.

(2)   Develop a methodology to identify short- and long-term cost-savings in the provision of foster care and any potential reinvestment strategies.

(3)   Oversee program implementation to ensure fidelity to the program models identified under subdivisions (1) and (2) of G.S. 131D-10.9B(a).

(4)   Study, review, and recommend other policies and services that may positively impact permanency and well-being outcomes.

(d)   Reports. - The Committee shall report its analysis and any findings and recommendations to the General Assembly by September 15 of each year.

(e)   Organization. - The President Pro Tempore of the Senate and the Speaker of the House of Representatives shall each designate a cochair of the Committee. The Committee shall meet at least once a quarter upon the joint call of the cochairs. A quorum of the Committee is seven members. No action may be taken except by a majority vote at a meeting at which a quorum is present.

(f)   Funding. - From funds available to the General Assembly, the Legislative Services Commission shall allocate monies to fund the work of the Committee. Members of the Committee shall receive subsistence and travel expenses as provided in G.S. 120-3.1 and G.S. 138-5.

(g)   Staff. - The Legislative Services Commission, through the Legislative Services Officer, shall assign professional staff to assist the Committee in its work. Upon the direction of the Legislative Services Commission, the Director of Legislative Assistants of the Senate and of the House of Representatives shall assign clerical staff to the Committee. The expenses for clerical employees shall be borne by the Committee. (2013-360, s. 12C.10(e).)

§ 131D-10.9B. Permanency Innovation Initiative Fund.

(a) There is created the Permanency Innovation Initiative Fund that will support a demonstration project with services provided by Children's Home Society of North Carolina to (i) improve permanency outcomes for children living in foster care through reunification with parents, providing placement or guardianship with other relatives, or adoption, (ii) improve engagement with biological relatives of children in or at risk of entering foster care, and (iii) reduce costs associated with maintaining children in foster care. In implementing these goals, the Permanency Innovation Initiative Fund shall support the following strategies:

(1) Family Finding, which is a program that uses intensive biological family engagement services to discover and engage biological relatives of children living in public foster care to provide permanent emotional and relational support, including adoption, legal guardianship, or legal custody.

(2) Child Specific Adoption Recruitment Services, which is a program that follows the Wendy's Wonderful Kids Model as developed by The Dave Thomas Foundation for Adoption and works with children in public foster care to develop and execute adoption recruitment plans tailored to the needs of the individual child.

(3) Permanency Training Services, which are services delivered by Children's Home Society of North Carolina to assess the readiness of county departments of social services to implement the permanency strategies under subdivisions (1) and (2) of this subsection and provide training services to support the delivery of the services.

(b) This program shall not constitute an entitlement and is subject to the availability of funds.

(c) The Social Services Commission shall adopt rules to implement the provisions of this section. (2013-360, s. 12C.10(e).)

Article 1B.

Licensing of Maternity Homes.

§ 131D-10.10. Licensing of Maternity Homes.

(a) The Department of Health and Human Services shall inspect and license all maternity homes established in the State under rules adopted by the Social Services Commission. The Commission shall adopt rules establishing educational requirements, minimum age, relevant experience, and criminal record status for executive directors and staff employed in maternity homes.

(b) Facilities subject to the provisions of this section shall include:

(1) Institutions or homes maintained for the purpose of receiving pregnant women for care before, during, and after delivery, and

(2) Institutions or lying-in homes maintained for the purpose of receiving pregnant women for care before and after delivery, when delivery takes place in a licensed hospital. (1868-9, c. 170, s. 3; Code, ss. 2332, 2333; Rev., ss. 3914, 3915; 1917, c. 170, s. 1; 1919, c. 46, ss. 1, 2; C.S., s. 5006; 1925, c. 90, ss. 1, 2; 1927, c. 65; 1931, c. 175; 1937, c. 319, s. 2; c. 436, ss. 3, 5; 1941, c. 270, s. 1; 1945, c. 185; 1951, c. 103; c. 1098, s. 2; 1953, c. 117; 1955, c. 269; 1957, c. 100, s. 1; c. 541, s. 7; 1959, c. 684; 1961, c. 51, s. 2; 1965, cc. 391, 1175; 1969, c. 546, s. 1; 1973, c. 476, s. 138; 1981, c. 275, s. 2; 1997-443, s. 11A.118(a); 2007-30, s. 1; 2009-188, s. 1; 2009-462, s. 1(b).)

Article 2.

Local Confinement Facilities.

§ 131D-11. Inspection.

The Department of Health and Human Services shall, as authorized by G.S. 153-51, inspect regularly all local confinement facilities as defined by G.S. 153-50(4) to determine compliance with the minimum standards for local confinement facilities adopted by the Social Services Commission. (1868-9, c. 170, s. 5; Code, s. 2335; Rev., s. 3917; 1917, c. 170, s. 1; C.S., s. 5008; 1957,

c. 86; 1961, c. 186; 1969, c. 546, s. 1; 1973, c. 476, s. 138; 1981, c. 275, s. 2; 1997-443, s. 11A.118(a).)

§ 131D-12. Approval of new facilities.

The Department of Health and Human Services shall, as authorized by G.S. 153-51, approve the plans for the construction or major modification of any local confinement facility. (1868-9, c. 170, s. 5; Code, s. 2335; Rev., s. 3917; 1917, c. 170, s. 1; C.S., s. 5008; 1957, c. 86; 1961, c. 186; 1969, c. 546, s. 1; 1973, c. 476, s. 138; 1981, c. 275, s. 2; 1997-443, s. 11A.118(a).)

§ 131D-13. Failure to provide information.

If the board of commissioners of any county, the chief of police of any municipality, or any officer or employee of any local confinement facility shall fail or refuse to furnish to the Department of Health and Human Services any information about any local confinement facility which is required by law to be furnished, or shall fail to allow the inspection of any such facility, such board or individual shall be guilty of a Class 1 misdemeanor. (1869-70, c. 154, s. 3; Code, s. 2341; 1891, c. 491, s. 2; Rev., s. 3566; C.S., s. 5013; 1957, c. 100, s. 1; 1969, c. 546, s. 1; 1973, c. 476, s. 138; 1981, c. 275, s. 2; 1993, c. 539, s. 956; 1994, Ex. Sess., c. 24, s. 14(c); 1997-443, s. 11A.118(a).)

§§ 131D-14 through 131D-18. Reserved for future codification purposes.

Article 3.

Adult Care Home Residents' Bill of Rights.

§ 131D-19. Legislative intent.

It is the intent of the General Assembly to promote the interests and well-being of the residents in adult care homes and assisted living residences licensed pursuant to Part 1 of this Article. It is the intent of the General Assembly that every resident's civil and religious liberties, including the right to independent personal decisions and knowledge of available choices, shall not be infringed and that the facility shall encourage and assist the resident in the fullest possible exercise of these rights. It is the intent of the General Assembly that rules developed by the Social Services Commission to implement Article 1 and Article 3 of Chapter 131D of the General Statutes encourage every resident's quality of life, autonomy, privacy, independence, respect, and dignity and provide the following:

(1) Diverse and innovative housing models that provide choices of different lifestyles that are acceptable, cost-effective, and accessible to all consumers regardless of age, disability, or financial status;

(2) A residential environment free from abuse, neglect, and exploitation;

(3) Available, affordable personal service models and individualized plans of care that are mutually agreed upon by the resident, family, and providers and that include measurable goals and outcomes;

(4) Client assessment, evaluation, and independent case management that enhance quality of life by allowing individual risk-taking and responsibility by the resident for decisions affecting daily living to the greatest degree possible based on the individual's ability; and

(5) Oversight, monitoring, and supervision by State and county governments to ensure every resident's safety and dignity and to assure that every resident's needs, including nursing and medical care needs if and when needed, are being met. (1981, c. 923, s. 1; 1995, c. 535, s. 12; 2009-462, s. 4(g).)

§ 131D-20. Definitions.

As used in this Article, the following terms have the meanings specified:

(1) "Abuse" means the willful or grossly negligent infliction of physical pain, injury or mental anguish, unreasonable confinement, or the willful or grossly negligent deprivation by the administrator or staff of an adult care home of services which are necessary to maintain mental and physical health.

(2) Repealed by Session Laws 1995, c. 535, s. 13, effective October 1, 1995.

(2a) "Adult care home" is an assisted living residence in which the housing management provides 24-hour scheduled and unscheduled personal care services to two or more residents, either directly or, for scheduled needs, through formal written agreement with licensed home care or hospice agencies. Some licensed adult care homes provide supervision to persons with cognitive impairments whose decisions, if made independently, may jeopardize the safety or well-being of themselves or others and therefore require supervision. Medication in an adult care home may be administered by designated, trained staff. Adult care homes that provide care to two to six unrelated residents are commonly called family care homes. Adult care homes and family care homes are subject to licensure by the Division of Health Service Regulation.

(2b) "Assisted living residence" means any group housing and services program for two or more unrelated adults, by whatever name it is called, that makes available, at a minimum, one meal a day and housekeeping services and provides personal care services directly or through a formal written agreement with one or more licensed home care or hospice agencies. The Department may allow nursing service exceptions on a case-by-case basis. Settings in which services are delivered may include self-contained apartment units or single or shared room units with private or area baths. Assisted living residences are to be distinguished from nursing homes subject to provisions of G.S. 131E-102.

(3) "Exploitation" means the illegal or improper use of an aged or disabled resident or his resources for another's profit or advantage.

(4) "Facility" means an adult care home licensed under G.S. 131D-2.4.

(5) "Family care home" means an adult care home having two to six residents. The structure of a family care home may be no more than two stories high and none of the aged or physically disabled persons being served there may be housed in the upper story without provision for two direct exterior ground-level accesses to the upper story.

(6) Repealed by Session Laws 2001-209, s. 1(c), effective June 15, 2001.

(7) Repealed by Session Laws 1995, c. 535, s. 13.

(8) "Neglect" means the failure to provide the services necessary to maintain the physical or mental health of a resident.

(9) "Resident" means an aged or disabled person who has been admitted to a facility. (1981, c. 923, s. 1; 1981 (Reg. Sess., 1982), c. 1282, s. 20.2C; 1983, c. 824, ss. 2, 3, 5, 7, 8; 1995, c. 535, s. 13; 1997-456, s. 21; 2001-209, s. 1(c); 2007-182, s. 1; 2009-462, s. 4(h).)

§ 131D-21. Declaration of residents' rights.

Each facility shall treat its residents in accordance with the provisions of this Article. Every resident shall have the following rights:

(1) To be treated with respect, consideration, dignity, and full recognition of his or her individuality and right to privacy.

(2) To receive care and services which are adequate, appropriate, and in compliance with relevant federal and State laws and rules and regulations.

(3) To receive upon admission and during his or her stay a written statement of the services provided by the facility and the charges for these services.

(4) To be free of mental and physical abuse, neglect, and exploitation.

(5) Except in emergencies, to be free from chemical and physical restraint unless authorized for a specified period of time by a physician according to clear and indicated medical need.

(6) To have his or her personal and medical records kept confidential and not disclosed except as permitted or required by applicable State or federal law.

(7) To receive a reasonable response to his or her requests from the facility administrator and staff.

(8) To associate and communicate privately and without restriction with people and groups of his or her own choice on his or her own or their initiative at any reasonable hour.

(9) To have access at any reasonable hour to a telephone where he or she may speak privately.

(10) To send and receive mail promptly and unopened, unless the resident requests that someone open and read mail, and to have access at his or her expense to writing instruments, stationery, and postage.

(11) To be encouraged to exercise his or her rights as a resident and citizen, and to be permitted to make complaints and suggestions without fear of coercion or retaliation.

(12) To have and use his or her own possessions where reasonable and have an accessible, lockable space provided for security of personal valuables. This space shall be accessible only to the resident, the administrator, or supervisor-in-charge.

(13) To manage his or her personal needs funds unless such authority has been delegated to another. If authority to manage personal needs funds has been delegated to the facility, the resident has the right to examine the account at any time.

(14) To be notified when the facility is issued a provisional license or notice of revocation of license by the North Carolina Department of Health and Human Services and the basis on which the provisional license or notice of revocation of license was issued. The resident's responsible family member or guardian shall also be notified.

(15) To have freedom to participate by choice in accessible community activities and in social, political, medical, and religious resources and to have freedom to refuse such participation.

(16) To receive upon admission to the facility a copy of this section.

(17) To not be transferred or discharged from a facility except for medical reasons, the residents' own or other residents' welfare, nonpayment for the stay, or when the transfer is mandated under State or federal law. The resident shall be given at least 30 days' advance notice to ensure orderly transfer or discharge, except in the case of jeopardy to the health or safety of the resident or others in the home. The resident has the right to appeal a facility's attempt to transfer or discharge the resident pursuant to rules adopted by the Medical Care Commission, and the resident shall be allowed to remain in the facility until

resolution of the appeal unless otherwise provided by law. The Medical Care Commission shall adopt rules pertaining to the transfer and discharge of residents that offer protections to residents for safe and orderly transfer and discharge. (1981, c. 923, s. 1; 1983, c. 824, s. 13; 1983 (Reg. Sess., 1984), c. 1076; 1997-443, s. 11A.118(a); 1999-334, s. 1.6; 2000-111, s. 3; 2011-272, s. 3; 2011-314, s. 5.)

§ 131D-21.1. Peer review.

It is not a violation of G.S. 131D-21(6) for medical records to be disclosed to a private peer review committee if:

(1) The peer review committee has been approved by the Department;

(2) The purposes of the peer review committee are to:

a. Survey facilities to verify a high level of quality care through evaluation and peer assistance;

b. Resolve written complaints in a responsible and professional manner; and

c. Develop a basic knowledge of care and standards useful in establishing a means of measuring quality of care; and

(3) The peer review committee keeps such records confidential. (1983, c. 816, s. 1.)

§ 131D-21.2. Quality assurance, medical, or peer review committees.

(a) A member of a duly appointed quality assurance, medical, or peer review committee shall not be subject to liability for damages in any civil action on account of any act, statement, or proceeding undertaken, made, or performed within the scope of the functions of the committee, if the committee member acts without malice or fraud, and if such peer review committee is approved and operates in accordance with G.S. 131D-21.1.

(b) The proceedings of a quality assurance, medical, or peer review committee, the records and materials it produces and the materials it considers shall be confidential and not considered public records within the meaning of G.S. 132-1, " 'Public records' defined", and shall not be subject to discovery or introduction into evidence in any civil action against an adult care home or a provider of professional health services that results from matters that are the subject of evaluation and review by the committee. No person who was in attendance at a meeting of the committee shall be required to testify in any civil action as to any evidence or other matters produced or presented during the proceedings of the committee or as to any findings, recommendations, evaluations, opinions, or other actions of the committee or its members. However, information, documents, or records otherwise available are not immune from discovery or use in a civil action merely because they were presented during proceedings of the committee. Documents otherwise available as public records within the meaning of G.S. 132-1 do not lose their status as public records merely because they were presented or considered during proceedings of the committee. A member of the committee or a person who testifies before the committee may testify in a civil action but cannot be asked about the person's testimony before the committee or any opinions formed as a result of the committee hearings. (2004-149, s. 2.3; 2006-264, s. 65.)

§ 131D-22. Transfer of management responsibilities.

Any representative authorized in writing by a resident to manage his financial affairs, any resident's legal guardian as appointed by a court, or any resident's attorney-in-fact as specified in the power of attorney agreement may sign any documents required by this Article, perform any other act, and receive or furnish any information required by this Article. (1981, c. 923, s. 1; 1983, c. 824, s. 14.)

§ 131D-23. No waiver of rights.

No facility may require a resident to waive the rights specified in G.S. 131D-21. (1981, c. 923, s. 1.)

§ 131D-24. Notice to resident.

(a) A copy of the declaration of the residents' rights shall be posted conspicuously in a public place in all facilities. A copy of the declaration of residents' rights shall be furnished to the resident upon admittance to the facility, to all residents currently residing in the facility, to a representative payee of the resident, or to any person designated in G.S. 131D-22, and if requested to the resident's responsible family member or guardian. Receipts for the declaration of rights signed by these persons shall be retained in the facility's files. The declaration of rights shall be included as part of the facility's admission policies and procedures.

(b) The address and telephone number of the section in the Department of Health and Human Services responsible for the enforcement of the provisions of this Article shall be posted and distributed with copies of G.S. 131D-21. The address and telephone number of the county social services department, and the appropriate person or office of the Department of Health and Human Services shall also be posted and distributed. (1981, c. 923, s. 1; 1997-443, s. 11A.118(a).)

§ 131D-25. Implementation.

Responsibility for implementing the provisions of this Article shall rest with the administrator of the facility. Each facility shall provide appropriate training to staff to implement the declaration of residents' rights included in G.S. 131D-21. (1981, c. 923, s. 1.)

§ 131D-26. Enforcement and investigation.

(a) The Department of Health and Human Services shall be responsible for the enforcement of the provisions of this Article. Specifically, the department of social services in the county in which the facility is located and the Department of Health and Human Services, shall be responsible for enforcing the provisions of the declaration of the residents' rights. The director of the county department of social services shall monitor the implementation of the declaration of the residents' rights and shall also investigate any complaints or grievances pertaining to violations of the declaration of rights.

(a1)   When the department of social services in the county in which a facility is located receives a complaint alleging a violation of the provisions of this Article pertaining to patient care or patient safety, the department of social services shall initiate an investigation as follows:

(1)   Immediately upon receipt of the complaint if the complaint alleges a life-threatening situation.

(2)   Within 24 hours if the complaint alleges abuse of a resident as defined by G.S. 131D-20(1).

(3)   Within 48 hours if the complaint alleges neglect of a resident as defined by G.S. 131D-20(8).

(4)   Within two weeks in all other situations.

The investigation shall be completed within 60 days. The requirements of this section are in addition to and not in lieu of any investigatory requirements for adult protective services pursuant to Article 6 of Chapter 108A of the General Statutes.

(b)   If upon investigation, it is found that any of the provisions of the declaration of rights has been violated, the director of the county department of social services or a designee must orally inform the administrator immediately of the specific violations, what must be done to correct them, and set a date by which the violations must be corrected. This same information must be confirmed in writing to the administrator by the county director or a designee within 10 working days following the investigation. A copy of the letter shall be sent to the Department of Health and Human Services.

(c)   Upon receiving requests for assistance in resolving complaints from the county department of social services, the Department of Health and Human Services shall ensure compliance with the provisions of this Article.

(d)   The county director of social services shall annually make a report to the Department of Health and Human Services about the number of substantiated violations of G.S. 131D-21, the nature of the violations, and the number of violations referred to the Department of Health and Human Services for resolution. (1981, c. 923, s. 1; 1983, c. 824, ss. 15, 16; 1997-443, s. 11A.118(a); 1999-334, s. 1.8; 2007-444, s. 5(b).)

§ 131D-27. Confidentiality.

The Department of Health and Human Services is authorized to inspect residents' records maintained at the facility when necessary to investigate any alleged violation of the declaration of the residents' rights. The Department of Health and Human Services shall maintain the confidentiality of all persons who register complaints with the Department of Health and Human Services and of all records inspected by the Department of Health and Human Services. (1981, c. 923, s. 1; 1997-443, s. 11A.118(a).)

§ 131D-28. Civil action.

Every resident shall have the right to institute a civil action for injunctive relief to enforce the provisions of this Article. The Department of Health and Human Services, a general guardian, or any person appointed ad litem pursuant to law, may institute an action pursuant to this section on behalf of the resident or residents. Any agency or person above named may enforce the rights of the resident specified in G.S. 131D-21 which the resident himself is unable to enforce. (1981, c. 923, s. 1; 1997-443, s. 11A.118(a).)

§ 131D-29. Revocation of license.

The Department of Health and Human Services shall have the authority to revoke a license issued under G.S. 131D-2.4 in any case where it finds that there has been a substantial failure to comply with the provisions of this Article.

Such revocation shall be effected by mailing to the licensee by registered or certified mail, or by personal service of, a notice setting forth the particular reasons for such action. Such revocation shall become effective 20 days after the mailing or service of the notice, unless the applicant or licensee, within such 20-day period, shall give written notice to the Department of Health and Human Services requesting a hearing, in which case the notice shall be deemed to be suspended. If a hearing has been requested, the licensee shall be given a prompt and fair hearing pursuant to the Administrative Procedure Act. At any time at or prior to the hearing, the Department of Health and Human Services may rescind the notice of revocation upon being satisfied that the reasons for the revocation have been or will be removed. (1981, c. 923, s. 1; 1997-443, s. 11A.118(a); 2009-462, s. 4(i).)

§ 131D-30. Repealed by Session Laws 1987, c. 600, s. 1.

§ 131D-31. Adult care home community advisory committees.

(a) Statement of Purpose. - It is the intention of the General Assembly that community advisory committees work to maintain the intent of the Adult Care Home Residents' Bill of Rights within the licensed adult care homes in this State. It is the further intent of the General Assembly that the committees promote community involvement and cooperation with adult care homes to ensure quality care for the elderly and disabled adults.

(b) Establishment and Appointment of Committees. -

(1) A community advisory committee shall be established in each county that has at least one licensed adult care home, shall serve all the homes in the county, and shall work with each of these homes for the best interests of the residents. In a county that has one, two, or three adult care homes with 10 or more beds, the committee shall have five members.

(2) In a county with four or more adult care homes with 10 or more beds, the committee shall have one additional member for each adult care home with 10 or more beds in excess of three, and may have up to five additional members at the discretion of the county commissioners, not to exceed a maximum of 25 members. In each county with four or more adult care homes with 10 or more beds, the committee shall establish a subcommittee of no more than five members and no fewer than three members from the committee for each adult care home in the county. Each member must serve on at least one subcommittee.

(3) In counties with no adult care homes with 10 or more beds, the committee shall have five members. Regardless of how many members a particular community advisory committee is required to have, at least one member of each committee shall be a person involved in the area of mental retardation.

(4) The boards of county commissioners are encouraged to appoint the Adult Care Home Community Advisory Committees. Of the members, a minority (not less than one-third, but as close to one-third as possible) shall be chosen from among persons nominated by a majority of the chief administrators of adult care homes in the county. If the adult care home administrators fail to make a nomination within 45 days after written notification has been sent to them requesting a nomination, these appointments may be made without nominations. If the county commissioners fail to appoint members to a committee by July 1, 1983, the appointments shall be made by the Assistant Secretary for Aging, Department of Health and Human Services, no sooner than 45 days after nominations have been requested from the adult care home administrators, but no later than October 1, 1983. In making appointments, the Assistant Secretary for Aging shall follow the same appointment process as that specified for the County Commissioners.

(c) Joint Nursing and Adult Care Home Community Advisory Committees. - Appointment to the Nursing Home Community Advisory Committees shall preclude appointment to the Adult Care Home Community Advisory Committees except where written approval to combine these committees is obtained from the Assistant Secretary for Aging, Department of Health and Human Services. Where this approval is obtained, the Joint Nursing and Adult Care Home Community Advisory Committee shall have the membership required of Nursing Home Community Advisory Committees and one additional member for each adult care home with 10 or more beds licensed in the county. In counties with no adult care homes with 10 or more beds, there shall be one additional member for every four other types of adult care homes in the county. In no case shall the number of members on the Joint Nursing and Adult Care Home Community Advisory Committee exceed 25. Each member shall exercise the statutory rights and responsibilities of both Nursing Home Committees and Adult Care Home Committees. In making appointments to this joint committee, the county commissioners shall solicit nominations from both nursing and adult care home administrators for the appointment of approximately (but no more than) one-third of the members.

(d) Terms of Office. - Each committee member shall serve an initial term of one year. Any person reappointed to a second or subsequent term in the same county shall serve a two-or three-year term at the county commissioners' discretion to ensure staggered terms of office.

(e) Vacancies. - Any vacancy shall be filled by appointment of a person for a one-year term. If this vacancy is in a position filled by an appointee nominated by the chief administrators of adult care homes within the county, then the county commissioners shall fill the vacancy from persons nominated by a majority of the chief administrators. If the adult care home administrators fail to make a nomination by registered mail within 45 days after written notification has been sent to them requesting a nomination, this appointment may be made without nominations. If the county commissioners fail to fill a vacancy, the vacancy may be filled by the Assistant Secretary for Aging, Department of Health and Human Services no sooner than 45 days after the commissioners have been notified of the appointment or vacancy.

(f) Officers. - The committee shall elect from its members a chair, to serve a one-year term.

(g) Minimum Qualifications for Appointment. - Each member must be a resident of the county which the committee serves. No person or immediate family member of a person with a financial interest in a home served by the committee, or employee or governing board member of a home served by the committee, or immediate family member of a resident in a home served by the committee may be a member of that committee. Any county commissioner who is appointed to the committee shall be deemed to be serving on the committee in an ex officio capacity. Members of the committee shall serve without compensation, but may be reimbursed for actual expenses incurred by them in the performance of their duties. The names of the committee members and the date of expiration of their terms shall be filed with the Division of Aging, Department of Health and Human Services.

(h) Training. - The Division of Aging, Department of Health and Human Services, shall develop training materials, which shall be distributed to each committee member. Each committee member must receive training as specified by the Division of Aging prior to exercising any power under G.S. 131D-32. The Division of Aging, Department of Health and Human Services, shall provide the committees with information, guidelines, training, and consultation to direct them in the performance of their duties.

(i) Any written communication made by a member of adult care home advisory committee within the course and scope of the member's duties, as specified in G.S. 131D-32, shall be privileged to the extent provided in this subsection. This privilege shall be a defense in a cause of action for libel if the member was acting in good faith and the statements and communications do not amount to intentional wrongdoing.

To the extent that any adult care home advisory committee or any member is covered by liability insurance, that committee or member shall be deemed to have waived the qualified immunity herein to the extent of indemnification by insurance. (1981, c. 923, s. 1; 1983, c. 88, s. 1; 1987, c. 682, s. 2; 1995, c. 535, s. 14; 1997-176, s. 2; 1997-443, s. 11A.118(a).)

§ 131D-32. Functions of adult care home community advisory committees.

(a)   The committee shall serve as the nucleus for increased community involvement with adult care homes and their residents.

(b)   The committee shall promote community education and awareness of the needs of aging and disabled persons who reside in adult care homes, and shall work towards keeping the public informed about aspects of long-term care and the operation of adult care homes in North Carolina.

(c)   The committee shall develop and recruit volunteer resources to enhance the quality of life for adult care home residents.

(d)   The committee shall establish linkages with the adult care home administrators and the county department of social services for the purpose of maintaining the intent of the Adult Care Home Residents' Bill of Rights.

(e)   Each committee shall apprise itself of the general conditions under which the persons are residing in the homes, and shall work for the best interests of the persons in the homes. This may include assisting persons who have grievances with the home and facilitating the resolution of grievances at the local level. The identity of any complainant or resident involved in a complaint shall not be disclosed except as permitted under the Older Americans Act of 1965, as amended, 42 U.S.C. § 3001 et seq. The committee shall notify the enforcement agency of all verified violations of the Adult Care Home Residents' Bill of Rights.

(f)   The committee or subcommittee may communicate through the committee chair with the Department of Health and Human Services, the county department of social services, or any other agency in relation to the interest of any resident.

(g) Each committee shall quarterly visit the adult care homes with 10 or more beds it serves. For each official quarterly visit, a majority of the committee members shall be present. A minimum of three members of the committee shall make at least one visit annually to each other type of adult care home licensed in the county. In addition, each committee may visit the adult care homes it serves whenever it deems it necessary to carry out its duties. In counties with subcommittees, the subcommittee assigned to a home shall perform the duties of the committee under this subsection, and a majority of the subcommittee members must be present for any visit. When visits are made to group homes for developmentally disabled adults, rules concerning confidentiality as adopted by the Commission for Mental Health, Developmental Disabilities, and Substance Abuse Services shall apply.

(h) The individual members of the committee shall have the right between 10:00 a.m. and 8:00 p.m. to enter the facility the committee serves in order to carry out the members' responsibilities. In a county where subcommittees have been established, this right of access shall be limited to members of the subcommittee which serves that home. A majority of the committee or subcommittee members shall be present to enter the facility at other hours. Before entering any adult care home, the committee or members of the committee shall identify themselves to the person present at the facility who is in charge of the facility at that time.

(i) The committee shall prepare reports as required by the Department of Health and Human Services containing an appraisal of the problems of adult care homes facilities as well as issues affecting long-term care in general. Copies of the report shall be sent to the board of county commissioners, county department of social services and the Division of Aging.

(j) Nothing contained in this section shall be construed to require the expenditure of any county funds to carry out the provisions in this section. (1981, c. 923, s. 1; 1983, c. 88, s. 2; 1991, c. 636, s. 19(b); 1995, c. 254, s. 6; c. 535, s. 15; 1997-443, s. 11A.118(a).)

§ 131D-33: Repealed by Session Laws 1983, c. 824, s. 19.

§ 131D-34. Penalties; remedies.

(a) Violation Classification and Penalties. - The Department of Health and Human Services shall impose an administrative penalty in accordance with provisions of this Article on any facility which is found to be in violation of requirements of G.S. 131D-21 or applicable State and federal laws and regulations. Citations for violations shall be classified and penalties assessed according to the nature of the violation as follows:

(1) "Type A1 Violation" means a violation by a facility of the regulations, standards, and requirements set forth in G.S. 131D-21 or applicable State or federal laws and regulations governing the licensure or certification of a facility which results in death or serious physical harm, abuse, neglect, or exploitation. The person making the findings shall do the following:

a. Orally and immediately inform the facility of the Type A1 Violation and the specific findings.

a1. Require a written plan of protection regarding how the facility will immediately abate the Type A1 Violation in order to protect residents from further risk or additional harm.

b. Within 15 working days of the investigation, send a report of the findings to the facility.

c. Require a plan of correction to be submitted to the Department, based on the written report of the findings, that describes steps the facility will take to achieve and maintain compliance.

The Department shall impose a civil penalty in an amount not less than five hundred dollars ($500.00) nor more than ten thousand dollars ($10,000) for each Type A1 Violation in facilities licensed for six or fewer beds. The Department shall impose a civil penalty in an amount not less than one thousand dollars ($1,000) nor more than twenty thousand dollars ($20,000) for each Type A1 Violation in facilities licensed for seven or more beds. Where a facility has failed to correct a Type A1 Violation, the Department shall assess the facility a civil penalty in the amount of up to one thousand dollars ($1,000) for each day that the violation continues beyond the time specified for correction by the Department or its authorized representative. The Department or its authorized representative shall determine whether the violation has been corrected.

(1a) "Type A2 Violation" means a violation by a facility of the regulations, standards, and requirements set forth in G.S. 131D-21 or applicable State or federal laws and regulations governing the licensure or certification of a facility which results in substantial risk that death or serious physical harm, abuse, neglect, or exploitation will occur. The person making the findings shall do the following:

a.   Orally and immediately inform the facility of the Type A2 Violation and the specific findings.

b.   Require a written plan of protection regarding how the facility will immediately abate the Type A2 Violation in order to protect clients or residents from further risk or additional harm.

c.   Within 15 working days of the investigation, send a report of the findings to the facility.

d.   Require a plan of correction to be submitted to the Department, based on the written report of the findings, that describes steps the facility will take to achieve and maintain compliance.

The violation or violations shall be corrected within the time specified for correction by the Department or its authorized representative. The Department may or may not assess a penalty taking into consideration the compliance history, preventative measures, and response to previous violations by the facility. Where a facility has failed to correct a Type A2 Violation, the Department shall assess the facility a civil penalty in the amount of up to one thousand dollars ($1,000) for each day that the deficiency continues beyond the time specified for correction by the Department or its authorized representative. The Department or its authorized representative shall determine whether the violation has been corrected.

(1b)   "Past Corrected Type A1 or Type A2 Violation" means either (i) the violation was not previously identified by the Department or its authorized representative or (ii) the violation was discovered by the facility and was self-reported, but in either case the violation has been corrected. In determining whether a penalty should be assessed under this section, the Department shall consider the following factors:

a.   Preventive systems in place prior to the violation.

b.   Whether the violation or violations were abated immediately.

c. Whether the facility implemented corrective measures to achieve maintain compliance.

d. Whether the facility's system to ensure compliance is maintained and continues to be implemented.

e. Whether the regulatory area remains in compliance.

(2) "Type B Violation" means a violation by a facility of the regulations, standards and requirements set forth in G.S. 131D-21 or applicable State or federal laws and regulations governing the licensure or certification of a facility which is detrimental to the health, safety, or welfare of any resident, but which does not result in substantial risk that death or serious physical harm, abuse, neglect, or exploitation will occur. The person making the findings shall do the following:

a. Orally and immediately inform the facility of the Type B Violation and the specific findings.

b. Require a written plan of protection regarding how the facility will immediately abate the Type B Violation in order to protect residents from further risk or additional harm.

c. Within 15 working days of the investigation, send a report of the findings to the facility.

d. Require a plan of correction to be submitted to the Department, based on the written report of the findings, that describes steps the facility will take to achieve and maintain compliance.

Where a facility has failed to correct a Type B Violation within the time specified for correction by the Department or its authorized representative, the Department shall assess the facility a civil penalty in the amount of up to four hundred dollars ($400.00) for each day that the violation continues beyond the date specified for correction without just reason for such failure. The Department or its authorized representative shall ensure that the violation has been corrected.

(3) Repeat Violations. - The Department shall impose a civil penalty which is treble the amount assessed under subsection (a) of this section when a facility under the same management or ownership has received a citation during

the previous 12 months for which the appeal rights are exhausted and penalty payment is expected or has occurred, and the current violation is for the same specific provision of a statute or regulation for which it received a violation during the previous 12 months. The counting of the 12-month period shall be tolled during any time when the facility is being operated by a court-appointed temporary manager pursuant to Article 4 of this Chapter.

(b) Repealed by Session Laws 2011-249, s. 2, effective June 23, 2011.

(c) Factors to Be Considered in Determining Amount of Initial Penalty. - In determining the amount of the initial penalty to be imposed under this section, the Department shall consider the following factors:

(1) There is substantial risk that serious physical harm, abuse, neglect, or exploitation will occur;

(1a) Serious physical harm, abuse, neglect, or exploitation, without substantial risk for resident death, did occur;

(1b) Serious physical harm, abuse, neglect, or exploitation, with substantial risk for resident death, did occur;

(1c) A resident died;

(1d) A resident died and there is substantial risk to others for serious physical harm, abuse, neglect, or exploitation;

(1e) A resident died and there is substantial risk for further resident death;

(2) The reasonable diligence exercised by the licensee to comply with G.S. 131E-256 and G.S. 131D-40 and other applicable State and federal laws and regulations;

(2a) Efforts by the licensee to correct violations;

(3) The number and type of previous violations committed by the licensee within the past 36 months; and

(4) Repealed by Session Laws 2011-249, s. 2, effective June 23, 2011;

(5) The number of residents put at risk by the violation.

(c1) The facts found to support the factors in subsection (c) of this section shall be the basis in determining the amount of the penalty. The Department shall document the findings in written record and shall make the written record available to all affected parties including:

(1) The penalty review committee;

(2) The local department of social services who is responsible for oversight of the facility involved;

(3) The licensee involved;

(4) The residents affected; and

(5) The family member who serves as a responsible party or those who have legal authority on behalf of the affected resident.

(c2) Local county departments of social services and Division of Health Service Regulation personnel shall submit proposed penalty recommendations to the Department within 45 days of the citation of a violation.

(d) The Department shall impose a civil penalty of fifty dollars ($50.00) per day on any facility which refuses to allow an authorized representative of the Department to inspect the premises and records of the facility.

(d1) The Department shall impose a civil penalty on any applicant for licensure who provides false information or omits information on the portion of the licensure application requesting information on owners, administrators, principals, or affiliates of the facility. The amount of the penalty shall be as is prescribed for a Type A1 Violation.

(e) Any facility wishing to contest a penalty shall be entitled to an administrative hearing as provided in Chapter 150B of the General Statutes. A petition for a contested case shall be filed within 30 days after the Department mails a notice of penalty to a licensee. At least the following specific issues shall be addressed at the administrative hearing:

(1) The reasonableness of the amount of any civil penalty assessed, and

(2) The degree to which each factor has been evaluated pursuant to subsection (c) of this section to be considered in determining the amount of an initial penalty.

If a civil penalty is found to be unreasonable or if the evaluation of each factor is found to be incomplete, the administrative law judge may order that the penalty be adjusted accordingly.

(f) Any penalty imposed by the Department of Health and Human Services under this section shall commence on the date the violation was identified.

(g) The Secretary may bring a civil action in the superior court of the county wherein the violation occurred to recover the amount of the administrative penalty whenever a facility:

(1) Which has not requested an administrative hearing fails to pay the penalty within 60 days after being notified of the penalty, or

(2) Which has requested an administrative hearing fails to pay the penalty within 60 days after receipt of a written copy of the decision as provided in G.S. 150B-36.

(g1) In lieu of assessing all or some of the administrative penalty, the Secretary may order a facility to provide staff training if the training is:

(1) Specific to the violation;

(2) Approved by the Department of Health and Human Services; and

(3) Taught by someone approved by the Department.

(h) The Secretary shall establish a penalty review committee within the Department, which shall meet as often as needed, but no less frequently than once each quarter of the year, to review administrative penalties assessed pursuant to this section and pursuant to G.S. 131E-129 as follows:

(1) The Secretary shall administer the work of the Committee and provide public notice of its meetings via Web site, and provide direct notice to the following parties involved in the penalties the Committee will be reviewing:

a. The licensed provider, who upon receipt of the notice, shall post the notice of the scheduled Penalty Review Committee meeting in a conspicuous place available to residents, family members, and the public;

b. The local department of social services that is responsible for oversight of the facility involved;

c. The residents affected; and

d. Those individuals lawfully designated by the affected resident to make health care decisions for the resident.

(2) The Secretary shall ensure that the Nursing Home/Adult Care Home Penalty Review Committee established by this subsection is comprised of nine members. At least one member shall be appointed from each of the following categories:

a. A licensed pharmacist;

b. A registered nurse experienced in long term care;

c. A representative of a nursing home;

d. A representative of an adult care home; and

e. Two public members. One shall be a "near" relative of a nursing home patient, chosen from a list prepared by the Office of State Long Term Care Ombudsman, Division of Aging, Department of Health and Human Services. One shall be a "near" relative of a rest home patient, chosen from a list prepared by the Office of State Long Term Care Ombudsman, Division of Aging, Department of Health and Human Services. For purposes of this subdivision, a "near" relative is a spouse, sibling, parent, child, grandparent, or grandchild.

(3) Neither the pharmacist, nurse, nor public members appointed under this subsection nor any member of their immediate families shall be employed by or own any interest in a nursing home or adult care home.

(4) Repealed by Session Laws 2005-276, s. 10.40A(l), effective July 1, 2005.

(4a) Repealed by Session Laws 2007-544, s. 1, effective October 1, 2007.

(4b) Prior to serving on the Committee, each member shall complete a training program provided by the Department of Health and Human Services that covers standards of care and applicable State and federal laws and regulations governing facilities licensed under Chapter 131D and Chapter 131E of the General Statutes.

(5) Each member of the Committee shall serve a term of two years. The initial terms of the members shall commence on August 3, 1989. The Secretary shall fill all vacancies. Unexcused absences from three consecutive meetings constitute resignation from the Committee.

(6) The Committee shall be cochaired by:

a. One member of the Department outside of the Division of Health Service Regulation; and

b. One member who is not affiliated with the Department.

(i) The clear proceeds of civil penalties provided for in this section shall be remitted to the State Treasurer for deposit in accordance with State law. (1987, c. 600, s. 3; 1989, c. 556, s. 1; 1991, c. 66, s. 1; c. 572, s. 3; 1993, c. 390, s. 4; 1993 (Reg. Sess., 1994), c. 698, s. 1; 1995, c. 535, s. 16; 1995 (Reg. Sess., 1996), c. 602, s. 1; 1997-431, s. 1; 1997-443, s. 11A.118(a); 1998-215, s. 78(a); 2005-276, s. 10.40A(l); 2007-182, ss. 1, 1.1; 2007-544, s. 1; 2011-249, s. 2; 2011-398, s. 45.)

§ 131D-34.1. Report of death of resident.

(a) An adult care home shall notify the Department of Health and Human Services immediately upon the death of any resident that occurs in the adult care home or that occurs within 24 hours of the resident's transfer to a hospital if the death occurred within seven days of the adult care home's use of physical restraint or physical hold of the resident, and shall notify the Department of Health and Human Services within three days of the death of any resident of the adult care home resulting from violence, accident, suicide, or homicide. The Department may assess a civil penalty of not less than five hundred dollars ($500.00) and not more than one thousand dollars ($1,000) against a facility that fails to notify the Department of a death and the circumstances surrounding the death known to the facility. Chapter 150B of the General Statutes governs the assessment of a penalty under this section. A civil penalty owed under this section may be recovered in a civil action brought by the Department or the Attorney General. The clear proceeds of the penalty shall be remitted to the State Treasurer for deposit in accordance with State law.

(b) Upon receipt of notification from an adult care home in accordance with subsection (a) of this section, the Department of Health and Human Services shall notify the State protection and advocacy agency designated under the Developmental Disabilities Assistance and Bill of Rights Act 2000, P.L. 106-402, that a person with a disability has died. The Department shall provide the agency access to the information about each death reported pursuant to subsection (a) of this section, including information resulting from any investigation of the death by the Department and from reports received from the Chief Medical Examiner pursuant to G.S. 130A-385. The agency shall use the information in accordance with its powers and duties under applicable State and federal law and regulations.

(c) If the death of a resident of the adult care home occurs within seven days of the adult care home's use of physical restraint or physical hold, the Department shall initiate immediately an investigation of the death.

(d) Nothing in this section abrogates State or federal law or requirements pertaining to the confidentiality, privilege, or other prohibition against disclosure of information provided to the Department or the agency. In carrying out the requirements of this section, the Department and the agency shall adhere to State and federal requirements of confidentiality, privilege, and other prohibitions against disclosure and release applicable to the information received under this section. A facility or provider that makes available confidential information in accordance with this section and with State and federal law is not liable for the release of the information.

(e) The Secretary shall establish a standard reporting format for reporting deaths pursuant to this section and shall provide to facilities subject to this section a form for the facility's use in complying with this section. (2000-129, s. 6(a); 2007-323, ss. 19.1(i), 19.1(j).)

Article 4.

Temporary Management of Adult Care Homes.

§ 131D-35. Temporary management of adult care homes.

The provisions of Article 13 of Chapter 131E are incorporated by reference in this Article. (1993, c. 390, s. 3; 1995, c. 535, s. 18.)

§§ 131D-36 through 131D-39. Reserved for future codification purposes.

Article 5.

Miscellaneous Provisions.

§ 131D-40. Criminal history record checks required for certain applicants for employment.

(a) Requirement; Adult Care Home. - An offer of employment by an adult care home licensed under this Chapter to an applicant to fill a position that does not require the applicant to have an occupational license is conditioned on consent to a criminal history record check of the applicant. If the applicant has been a resident of this State for less than five years, then the offer of employment is conditioned on consent to a State and national criminal history record check of the applicant. The national criminal history record check shall include a check of the applicant's fingerprints. If the applicant has been a resident of this State for five years or more, then the offer is conditioned on consent to a State criminal history record check of the applicant. An adult care home shall not employ an applicant who refuses to consent to a criminal history record check required by this section. Within five business days of making the conditional offer of employment, an adult care home shall submit a request to the Department of Justice under G.S. 114-19.10 to conduct a State or national criminal history record check required by this section, or shall submit a request to a private entity to conduct a State criminal history record check required by this section. Notwithstanding G.S. 114-19.10, the Department of Justice shall return the results of national criminal history record checks for employment positions not covered by Public Law 105-277 to the Department of Health and Human Services, Criminal Records Check Unit. Within five business days of receipt of the national criminal history of the person, the Department of Health and Human Services, Criminal Records Check Unit, shall notify the adult care home as to whether the information received may affect the employability of the applicant. In no case shall the results of the national criminal history record check be shared with the adult care home. Adult care homes shall make available upon request verification that a criminal history check has been completed on any staff covered by this section. All criminal history information received by the home is confidential and may not be disclosed, except to the applicant as provided in subsection (b) of this section.

(a1)   Requirement; Contract Agency of Adult Care Home. - An offer of employment by a contract agency of an adult care home licensed under this Chapter to an applicant to fill a position that does not require the applicant to have an occupational license is conditioned upon consent to a criminal history record check of the applicant. If the applicant has been a resident of this State for less than five years, then the offer of employment is conditioned on consent to a State and national criminal history record check of the applicant. The national criminal history record check shall include a check of the applicant's fingerprints. If the applicant has been a resident of this State for five years or more, then the offer is conditioned on consent to a State criminal history record check of the applicant. A contract agency of an adult care home shall not employ an applicant who refuses to consent to a criminal history record check required by this section. Within five business days of making the conditional offer of employment, a contract agency of an adult care home shall submit a request to the Department of Justice under G.S. 114-19.10 to conduct a State or national criminal history record check required by this section, or shall submit a request to a private entity to conduct a State criminal history record check required by this section. Notwithstanding G.S. 114-19.10, the Department of Justice shall return the results of national criminal history record checks for employment positions not covered by Public Law 105-277 to the Department of Health and Human Services, Criminal Records Check Unit. Within five business days of receipt of the national criminal history of the person, the Department of Health and Human Services, Criminal Records Check Unit, shall notify the contract agency of the adult care home as to whether the information received may affect the employability of the applicant. In no case shall the results of the national criminal history record check be shared with the contract agency of the adult care home. Contract agencies of adult care homes shall make available upon request verification that a criminal history check has been completed on any staff covered by this section. All criminal history information received by the contract agency is confidential and may not be disclosed, except to the applicant as provided by subsection (b) of this section.

(b) Action. - If an applicant's criminal history record check reveals one or more convictions of a relevant offense, the adult care home or a contract agency of the adult care home shall consider all of the following factors in determining whether to hire the applicant:

(1) The level and seriousness of the crime.

(2) The date of the crime.

(3) The age of the person at the time of the conviction.

(4) The circumstances surrounding the commission of the crime, if known.

(5) The nexus between the criminal conduct of the person and the job duties of the position to be filled.

(6) The prison, jail, probation, parole, rehabilitation, and employment records of the person since the date the crime was committed.

(7) The subsequent commission by the person of a relevant offense.

The fact of conviction of a relevant offense alone shall not be a bar to employment; however, the listed factors shall be considered by the adult care home or the contract agency of the adult care home. If the adult care home or a contract agency of the adult care home disqualifies an applicant after consideration of the relevant factors, then the adult care home or the contract agency may disclose information contained in the criminal history record check that is relevant to the disqualification, but may not provide a copy of the criminal history record check to the applicant.

(c) Limited Immunity. - An adult care home and an officer or employee of an adult care home that, in good faith, complies with this section is not liable for the failure of the home to employ an individual on the basis of information provided in the criminal history record check of the individual.

(d) Relevant Offense. - As used in this section, "relevant offense" means a county, state, or federal criminal history of conviction or pending indictment of a crime, whether a misdemeanor or felony, that bears upon an individual's fitness to have responsibility for the safety and well-being of aged or disabled persons. These crimes include the criminal offenses set forth in any of the following Articles of Chapter 14 of the General Statutes: Article 5, Counterfeiting and

Issuing Monetary Substitutes; Article 5A, Endangering Executive and Legislative Officers; Article 6, Homicide; Article 7A, Rape and Other Sex Offenses; Article 8, Assaults; Article 10, Kidnapping and Abduction; Article 13, Malicious Injury or Damage by Use of Explosive or Incendiary Device or Material; Article 14, Burglary and Other Housebreakings; Article 15, Arson and Other Burnings; Article 16, Larceny; Article 17, Robbery; Article 18, Embezzlement; Article 19, False Pretenses and Cheats; Article 19A, Obtaining Property or Services by False or Fraudulent Use of Credit Device or Other Means; Article 19B, Financial Transaction Card Crime Act; Article 20, Frauds; Article 21, Forgery; Article 26, Offenses against Public Morality and Decency; Article 26A, Adult Establishments; Article 27, Prostitution; Article 28, Perjury; Article 29, Bribery; Article 31, Misconduct in Public Office; Article 35, Offenses Against the Public Peace; Article 36A, Riots, Civil Disorders, and Emergencies; Article 39, Protection of Minors; Article 40, Protection of the Family; Article 59, Public Intoxication; and Article 60, Computer-Related Crime. These crimes also include possession or sale of drugs in violation of the North Carolina Controlled Substances Act, Article 5 of Chapter 90 of the General Statutes, and alcohol-related offenses such as sale to underage persons in violation of G.S. 18B-302 or driving while impaired in violation of G.S. 20-138.1 through G.S. 20-138.5.

(e) Penalty for Furnishing False Information. - Any applicant for employment who willfully furnishes, supplies, or otherwise gives false information on an employment application that is the basis for a criminal history record check under this section shall be guilty of a Class A1 misdemeanor.

(f) Conditional Employment. - An adult care home may employ an applicant conditionally prior to obtaining the results of a criminal history record check regarding the applicant if both of the following requirements are met:

(1) The adult care home shall not employ an applicant prior to obtaining the applicant's consent for a criminal history record check as required in subsection (a) of this section or the completed fingerprint cards as required in G.S. 114-19.10.

(2) The adult care home shall submit the request for a criminal history record check not later than five business days after the individual begins conditional employment.

(g) Immunity From Liability. - An entity and officers and employees of an entity shall be immune from civil liability for failure to check an employee's history of criminal offenses if the employee's criminal history record check is requested and received in compliance with this section.

(h) For purposes of this section, the term "private entity" means a business regularly engaged in conducting criminal history record checks utilizing public records obtained from a State agency. (1995 (Reg. Sess., 1996), c. 606, s. 2; 1997-125, s. 1; 2000-154, ss. 2.(a), (b); 2004-124, ss. 10.19D(b), (g); 2005-4, ss. 6, 7; 2007-444, s. 3.1; 2012-12, s. 2(uu).)

§ 131D-41: Repealed by Session Laws 2009-462, s. 2, effective October 1, 2009.

§ 131D-42: Repealed by Session Laws 2009-462, s. 2, effective October 1, 2009.

§ 131D-43: Reserved for future codification purposes.

§ 131D-44: Reserved for future codification purposes.

§ 131D-45. Examination and screening for the presence of controlled substances required for applicants for employment in adult care homes.

(a) An offer of employment by an adult care home licensed under this Article to an applicant is conditioned on the applicant's consent to an examination and screening for controlled substances. The examination and screening shall be conducted in accordance with Article 20 of Chapter 95 of the General Statutes. A screening procedure that utilizes a single-use test device may be used for the examination and screening of applicants and may be administered on-site. If the results of the applicant's examination and screening indicate the presence of a controlled substance, the adult care home shall not employ the applicant unless the applicant first provides to the adult care home written verification from the applicant's prescribing physician that every controlled substance identified by the examination and screening is prescribed by that physician to treat the applicant's medical or psychological condition. The verification from the physician shall include the name of the controlled substance, the prescribed dosage and frequency, and the condition for which the substance is prescribed. If the result of an applicant's or employee's examination and screening indicates the presence of a controlled substance, the adult care home may require a second examination and screening to verify the results of the prior examination and screening.

(b) An adult care home may require random examination and screening for controlled substances as a condition of continued employment. If the adult care home has reasonable grounds to believe that an employee is an abuser of a controlled substance, the adult care home may require that employee to undergo examination and screening for controlled substances as a condition of continued employment.

(c) An adult care home and an officer or employee of an adult care home that, in good faith, complies with this section is not liable for the failure of the adult care home to employ or continue the employment of an individual on the basis of the results of an examination and screening of the applicant or employee for controlled substances.

(d) An entity and officers and employees of an entity that perform controlled substance examination and screening in accordance with Article 20 of Chapter 95 of the General Statutes shall be immune from civil liability for conducting or failing to conduct the examination and screening if the examination and screening are requested and received in compliance with this section and with Article 20 of Chapter 95 of the General Statutes.

(e) The results of an examination and screening conducted at the request of an adult care home in accordance with this section are confidential and not a public record under Chapter 132 of the General Statutes. The adult care home shall maintain the confidentiality of all information related to the examination and screening of an applicant for employment or an individual currently employed by the adult care home.

(f) The adult care home shall pay expenses related to controlled substance examination and screening pursuant to this section, except examinee-requested retests. The examinee shall pay all reasonable expenses for retests of confirmed positive results. (2013-167, s. 1.)

Chapter 131E.

Health Care Facilities and Services.

Article 1.

General Provisions.

§ 131E-1. Definitions.

As used in this Chapter, unless the context clearly indicates otherwise:

(1) "Department" means the Department of Health and Human Services.

(2) "Person" means an individual, trust, estate, partnership, or corporation including associations, joint-stock companies, and insurance companies. (1983, c. 775, s. 1; 1997-443, s. 11A.118(a).)

§ 131E-2. Contested case hearing petition time limit.

Except as otherwise provided in this Chapter, a petition for a contested case that is authorized by this Chapter shall be filed in the Office of Administrative Hearings within 30 days after the Department mails written notice of an agency decision to the person filing the petition. This section shall not be construed to create any right to file a petition for a contested case that is not otherwise granted in this Chapter. (1991, c. 143, s. 1, c. 761, s. 23.)

§ 131E-3. Coordination of rules on pathological materials.

The Division of Health Service Regulation, Department of Health and Human Services (Department), shall adopt rules governing the procedures regarding the request for and release of pathological materials made to clinical laboratories within the jurisdiction of the Department. These rules shall be consistent with the North Carolina Hospital Association Best Practices Principles and the College of American Pathologists 2003 Professional Relations Manual and shall be developed in consultation with the North Carolina Medical Board to ensure consistency in procedures governing pathological materials. (2013-43, s. 1.)

§ 131E-4. Reserved for future codification purposes.

Article 2.

Public Hospitals.

Part 1. Municipal Hospitals.

§ 131E-5. Title and purpose.

(a) This Part shall be known and may be cited as the "Municipal Hospital Act."

(b) The purpose of this Part is to authorize municipalities to construct, operate and maintain hospitals and other facilities which furnish hospital, clinical and similar services to the people of this State. It is also the purpose of this Part to authorize municipalities to cooperate with other public and private agencies and with each other. Additionally, it is the purpose of this Part to authorize municipalities to accept assistance from State and federal agencies and from other sources.

(c) This Part provides an additional and alternative method for municipalities to establish facilities that furnish hospital, clinical and similar services. This Part shall not be regarded as repealing any powers now existing under any other law, either general, special or local.

(d) This Part shall be construed liberally to effect its purposes. (1983, c. 775, s. 1.)

§ 131E-6. Definitions.

As used in this Part, unless otherwise specified:

(1) "City", as defined in G.S. 160A-1(2), means a municipal corporation organized under the laws of this State for the better government of the people within its jurisdiction and having the powers, duties, privileges, and immunities conferred by law on cities, towns, and villages. The term "city" does not include counties or municipal corporations organized for a special purpose under any statute or law. The word "city" is interchangeable with the words "town" and "village" and shall mean any city as defined in this subdivision without regard to

the terminology employed in charters, local acts, other portions of the General Statutes, or local customary usage.

(2) "Community general hospital" means a short-term nonfederal hospital that provides diagnostic and therapeutic services to patients for a variety of medical conditions, both surgical and nonsurgical, such services being available for use primarily by residents of the community in which it is located.

(3) "Corporation, foreign or domestic, authorized to do business in North Carolina" means a corporation for profit or having a capital stock which is created and organized under Chapter 55 of the General Statutes or any other general or special act of this State, or a foreign corporation which has procured a certificate of authority to transact business in this State pursuant to Article 10 of Chapter 55 of the General Statutes.

(4) "Hospital facility" means any one or more buildings, structures, additions, extensions, improvements or other facilities, whether or not located on the same site or sites, machinery, equipment, furnishings or other real or personal property suitable for health care or medical care; and includes, without limitation, general hospitals; chronic disease, maternity, mental, tuberculosis and other specialized hospitals; nursing homes, including skilled nursing facilities and intermediate care facilities; adult care homes for the aged and disabled; public health center facilities; housing or quarters for local public health departments; facilities for intensive care and self-care; clinics and outpatient facilities; clinical, pathological and other laboratories; health care research facilities; laundries; residences and training facilities for nurses, interns, physicians and other staff members; food preparation and food service facilities; administrative buildings, central service and other administrative facilities; communication, computer and other electronic facilities; fire-fighting facilities; pharmaceutical and recreational facilities; storage space; X ray, laser, radiotherapy and other apparatus and equipment; dispensaries; utilities; vehicular parking lots and garages; office facilities for hospital staff members and physicians; and such other health and hospital facilities customarily under the jurisdiction of or provided by hospitals, or any combination of the foregoing, with all necessary, convenient or related interests in land, machinery, apparatus, appliances, equipment, furnishings, appurtenances, site preparation, landscaping, and physical amenities.

(4a) "Hospital land" means air and ground rights to real property held either in fee or by lease by a municipality, with all easements, rights-of-way, appurtenances, landscaping, and physical amenities such as utilities, parking lots, and garages, but excluding other improvements to land described in subsection (4) of this section and G.S. 131E-16(15).

(5)   "Municipality" means any county, city, or other political subdivision of this State, or any hospital district created under Part C of this Article.

(6)   "Nonprofit association" or "nonprofit corporation" means any association or corporation from which no part of the net earnings inures or may lawfully inure to the benefit of a private shareholder or individual. (1983, c. 775, s. 1; 1997-233, s. 1.)

§ 131E-7. General powers.

(a)   A municipality shall have all the powers necessary or convenient to carry out the purposes of this Part, including the following powers, which are in addition to the powers granted elsewhere in this Part:

(1)   To construct, equip, operate, and maintain hospital facilities;

(2)   To levy property taxes pursuant to G.S. 153A-149 or G.S. 160A-209 and to allocate those and other revenues whose use is not otherwise restricted by law to fund hospital facilities; a hospital district may levy annually a tax on property having a situs in the district under the rules and according to the procedures prescribed in the Machinery Act, Chapter 105 of the General Statutes, Subchapter II, and a hospital district may allocate those and other revenues whose use is not otherwise restricted by law to fund hospital facilities;

(3)   To issue bonds and notes pursuant to the Local Government Finance Act, Chapter 159 of the General Statutes, for the financing of hospital facilities;

(4)   To use property owned or controlled by the municipality;

(5)   To acquire real or personal property, including existing hospital facilities, by purchase, grant, gift, devise, lease, condemnation, or otherwise;

(6)   To establish a fee schedule for services received from hospital facilities and to make services available regardless of ability to pay.

(b)   A municipality or a public hospital may contract with or enter into any arrangement with other public hospitals or municipalities of this or other states, the State of North Carolina, federal, or public agencies, or with any person, private organization, or nonprofit corporation or association for the provision of health care. The municipality or public hospital may pay for or contribute its share of the cost of any such contract or arrangement from revenues available for these purposes, including revenues rising from the provision of health care.

(c)   Any two or more municipalities may enter into agreements to jointly exercise the powers, privileges, and authorities granted by this Part. These agreements may provide for:

(1)   The appointment of a board, composed of representatives of the parties to the agreement, to supervise and manage a hospital facility;

(2)   The authority and duties of the board and the compensation of its members;

(3)   The proportional share of the costs of acquisition, construction, improvement, maintenance, or operation of hospital facilities;

(4)   The duration, amendment, and termination of the agreement and the disposition of property on termination of the agreement; and

(5)   Any other matters as necessary.

(d)   A municipality may lease any hospital facility, or part, to a nonprofit association on terms and conditions consistent with the purposes of this Part. The municipality will determine the length of the lease. No lease executed under this subsection shall be deemed to convey a freehold interest.

(e)   A municipality shall not sell nor convey any rights of ownership the municipality has in any hospital facility, including the buildings, land and equipment associated with the hospital, to any corporation or other business entity operated for profit, except that nothing herein shall prohibit the sale of surplus buildings, surplus land or surplus equipment by a municipality to any corporation or other business entity operated for profit.

A municipality may lease any hospital facility, or part, to any corporation, foreign or domestic, authorized to do business in North Carolina on terms and conditions consistent with the purposes of this Part and with G.S. 160A-272.

The municipality shall determine the length of the lease; however, no lease under this subsection shall be longer than 10 years, including options to renew or extend the original term of the lease, except that leases of surplus buildings, surplus land or surplus equipment may be for any length of time determined by the municipality. The lease shall provide that the hospital facility will be operated as a community general hospital open to the general public and that the lessee will accept Medicare and Medicaid patients. No lease executed under this subsection shall be deemed to convey a freehold interest. No bonds, notes nor other evidences of indebtedness shall be issued by a municipality to finance equipment for or the acquisition, extension, construction, reconstruction, improvement, enlargement, or betterment of any hospital facility when the facility is leased to a corporation, foreign or domestic, authorized to do business in North Carolina.

For purposes of this subsection, "surplus" means any building, land or equipment which is not required for use in the delivery of necessary health care services by a hospital facility at the time of the sale, conveyance of ownership rights, or lease.

This subsection shall not be construed to affect any pending litigation nor to reflect any legislative intent as to any prior authorized or executed agreements. This subsection shall be effective from January 1, 1984 until June 30, 1984.

(f) In addition to the general and special powers conferred by this Part, a municipality is authorized to exercise powers necessary to implement the powers under this Part. (1983, c. 775, s. 1; 1993, c. 529, s. 5.3; 1995, c. 509, s. 71.)

§ 131E-7.1. Public hospitals' managed care development authorized.

A public hospital as defined in G.S. 159-39(a) may acquire an ownership interest, in whole or in part, in a nonprofit or for-profit managed care company, including a health maintenance organization, physician hospital organization, physician organization, management services organization, or preferred provider organization with which the public hospital is also directly or indirectly a contracting provider. Ownership interest may be evidenced by the ownership or acquired by the purchase of stock. This ownership or acquisition of stock is the exercise of a health care function and is not the investment of idle funds within the meaning of G.S. 159-30 and G.S.159-39(g). (1995 (Reg. Sess., 1996), c. 713, s. 1.)

§ 131E-8. Sale of hospital facilities to nonprofit corporations.

(a)   A municipality as defined in G.S. 131E-6(5) or hospital authority as defined in G.S. 131E-16(14), upon such terms and conditions as it deems wise, with or without monetary consideration, may sell or convey to a nonprofit corporation organized under Chapter 55A of the General Statutes any rights of ownership the municipality or hospital authority has in a hospital facility including the building, land and equipment associated with the hospital, if the nonprofit corporation is legally committed to continue to operate the facility as a community general hospital open to the general public, free of discrimination based upon race, creed, color, sex or national origin. The nonprofit corporation shall also agree, as a condition of the municipality or hospital authority's conveying ownership, to provide such services to indigent patients as the municipality or hospital authority and the nonprofit corporation shall agree. The nonprofit corporation shall further agree that should it fail to operate the facility as a community general hospital open to the general public or should the nonprofit corporation dissolve without a successor nonprofit corporation to carry out the terms and conditions of the agreement of conveyance, all ownership rights in the hospital facility, including the building, land and equipment associated with the hospital, shall revert to the municipality or hospital authority or successor entity originally conveying the hospital.

(b)   When either general obligation bonds or revenue bonds issued for the benefit of the hospital to be conveyed are outstanding at the time of sale or conveyance, then the nonprofit corporation must agree to the following:

By the effective date of sale or conveyance, the nonprofit corporation shall place into an escrow fund money or direct obligations of, or obligations the principal of and interest on which, are unconditionally guaranteed by the United States of America (as approved by the Local Government Commission), the principal of and interest on which, when due and payable, will provide sufficient money to pay the principal of and the interest and redemption premium, if any, on all bonds then outstanding to the maturity date or dates of such bonds or to the date or dates specified for the redemption thereof. The nonprofit corporation shall furnish to the Local Government Commission such evidence as the Commission may require that the securities purchased will satisfy the requirements of this section. A hospital which has placed funds in escrow to retire outstanding general obligation or revenue bonds, as provided in this section, shall not be considered a public hospital, and G.S. 159-39(a)(3) shall be inapplicable to such hospitals.

(c) Any sale or conveyance under this section must be approved by the municipality or hospital authority by a resolution adopted at a regular meeting of the governing body on 10 days' public notice. Notice shall be given by publication describing the hospital facility to be conveyed, the proposed monetary consideration or lack thereof, and the governing body's intent to authorize the sale or conveyance.

(d) Neither G.S. 153A-176 nor Article 12 of Chapter 160A of the General Statutes shall apply to sales or conveyances pursuant to this section.

(e) A sale or conveyance of substantially all the equipment is a sale or conveyance of hospital facility. (1983, c. 775, s. 1; 1989, c. 444.)

§ 131E-8.1. Maintenance of Health Education Facilities.

(a) This section shall apply to all sales and leases of a hospital facility by a municipality or hospital authority where any portion of the facility was constructed with a capital grant from the Area Health Education Centers Program (AHEC).

(b) The municipality or hospital authority shall give specific notice of intent to sell or lease and of any public hearing to the Director of the local AHEC program and the Director of the AHEC Program at the University of North Carolina School of Medicine at Chapel Hill.

(c) The municipality or hospital authority may provide continued access to the identical or equivalent facilities suitable for continuation of AHEC activities, including all services being provided under the existing operating contract. The municipality or hospital authority may convey all ownership rights in the hospital facility, or any part thereof, to the local AHEC Program without monetary consideration. Further, the municipality or hospital authority may reimburse the local AHEC Program for any funds used for the original construction of any office for AHEC provided by AHEC to establish or continue the hospital facility.

(d) No portion of this section shall be construed to alter rights or obligations of the operating contracts between the hospital facility and AHEC. (1983 (Reg. Sess., 1984), c. 1056, s. 1; 1985 (Reg. Sess., 1986), c. 995.)

§ 131E-9. Governing authority of hospital facilities.

(a) The governing body of a municipality may establish by resolution an office, board, or other municipal agency to plan, establish, construct, maintain, or operate a hospital facility. The resolution shall prescribe the powers, duties, compensation, and tenure of the members of the governing authority. The municipality shall remain responsible for the expenses of planning, establishment, construction, maintenance and operation of the hospital facilities.

(b) (1) The county board of commissioners of a county may establish by resolution a county hospital authority to plan, establish, construct, maintain, or operate a hospital facility. The authority shall be referred to as "_____ County Hospital Authority."

(2) The county hospital authority shall consist of six appointed members and one ex officio member.

(3) The appointed members of the authority shall be appointed by the county board of commissioners. All appointed members shall be residents of the county. Three of the members shall be residents of a city in the county and the remaining three members shall not be residents of the same city or cities in which the other three members appointed under this subdivision reside.

(4) For the initial appointments to the county hospital authority, two of the members shall be appointed for a term of three years, two for a term of four years, and two for a term of five years to achieve staggered terms. All subsequent appointments shall be for five-year terms.

(5) The ex officio member of the county hospital authority shall be a member of the county board of commissioners. The ex officio member's term on the hospital authority shall be commensurate with his or her term as a member of the county board of commissioners.

(6) When any member of the county hospital authority resigns or is removed from office before the expiration of the member's term, the county

board of commissioners shall appoint a person to serve the unexpired portion of the term.

(c)   Any authority vested in a county under this Part or any authority or power that may be exercised by a hospital authority under the Hospital Authorities Act, Chapter 131E, Article 2, Part B, may be vested by resolution of the county board of commissioners in a county hospital authority established under this section. However, a county hospital authority shall exercise only the powers and duties prescribed in the county board of commissioners' resolution. The county board of commissioners shall determine in the resolution the compensation, traveling and any other expenses which shall be paid to each member of the county hospital authority. However, the expenses to plan, establish, construct and operate the hospital facility shall remain the responsibility of the county. (1983, c. 775, s. 1.)

§ 131E-10. Condemnation.

Every municipality is authorized to condemn property to carry out the purposes of this Part. In condemning property, a municipality shall proceed in the manner provided in Chapter 40A of the General Statutes or in the charter of the municipality. A municipality or its agents is authorized to enter upon land, provided no unnecessary damage is done, to make surveys and examinations relative to any condemnation proceeding. Notwithstanding the provisions of any other statute or of any applicable municipal charter, the municipality may take possession of property to be condemned at any time after the commencement of the condemnation proceeding. The municipality shall not be precluded from abandonment of the condemnation of property in any case where possession has not taken place. (1983, c. 775, s. 1.)

§ 131E-11. Federal and State aid.

Every municipality or nonprofit association is authorized to accept and disburse federal and State moneys, whether made available by grant, loan, gift or devise, to carry out the purposes of this Part. All federal moneys shall be accepted and disbursed upon the terms and conditions prescribed by the United States, if the terms and conditions are consistent with State law. All State moneys shall be accepted and disbursed upon the terms and conditions prescribed by either or both the State and the North Carolina Medical Care Commission. Unless the terms and conditions provide otherwise, the chief financial officer of the municipality shall deposit all moneys received under this section and keep them in separate trust funds. (1983, c. 775, s. 1.)

§ 131E-12. Public purposes.

The exercise of the powers, privileges, and authorities conferred on municipalities by this Part are public and government functions, exercised for a public purpose and matters of public necessity. In the case of a county, the exercise of the powers, privileges and authorities conferred by this Part is a county function and purpose, as well as a public and governmental function. In the case of any municipality other than a county, the exercise of the powers, privileges, and authorities conferred by this Part is a municipal function and purpose, as well as a public and governmental function. (1983, c. 775, s. 1.)

§ 131E-13. Lease or sale of hospital facilities to or from for-profit or nonprofit corporations or other business entities by municipalities and hospital authorities.

(a)   A municipality or hospital authority as defined in G.S. 131E-16(14), may lease, sell, or convey any hospital facility, or part, to a corporation, foreign or domestic, authorized to do business in North Carolina, subject to these conditions, which shall be included in the lease, agreement of sale, or agreement of conveyance:

(1)   The corporation shall continue to provide the same or similar clinical hospital services to its patients in medical-surgery, obstetrics, pediatrics, outpatient and emergency treatment, including emergency services for the indigent, that the hospital facility provided prior to the lease, sale, or conveyance. These services may be terminated only as prescribed by Certificate of Need Law prescribed in Article 9 of Chapter 131E of the General Statutes, or, if Certificate of Need Law is inapplicable, by review procedure designed to guarantee public participation pursuant to rules adopted by the Secretary of the Department of Health and Human Services.

(2)   The corporation shall ensure that indigent care is available to the population of the municipality or area served by the hospital authority at levels

related to need, as previously demonstrated and determined mutually by the municipality or hospital authority and the corporation.

(3)   The corporation shall not enact financial admission policies that have the effect of denying essential medical services or treatment solely because of a patient's immediate inability to pay for the services or treatment.

(4)   The corporation shall ensure that admission to and services of the facility are available to beneficiaries of governmental reimbursement programs (Medicaid/Medicare) without discrimination or preference because they are beneficiaries of those programs.

(5)   The corporation shall prepare an annual report that shows compliance with the requirements of the lease, sale, or conveyance.

The corporation shall further agree that if it fails to substantially comply with these conditions, or if it fails to operate the facility as a community general hospital open to the general public and free of discrimination based on race, creed, color, sex, or national origin unless relieved of this responsibility by operation of law, or if the corporation dissolves without a successor corporation to carry out the terms and conditions of the lease, agreement of sale, or agreement of conveyance, all ownership or other rights in the hospital facility, including the building, land and equipment associated with the hospital, shall revert to the municipality or hospital authority or successor entity originally conveying the hospital; provided that any building, land, or equipment associated with the hospital facility that the corporation has constructed or acquired since the sale may revert only upon payment to the corporation of a sum equal to the cost less depreciation of the building, land, or equipment.

This section shall not apply to leases, sales, or conveyances of nonmedical services or commercial activities, including the gift shop, cafeteria, the flower shop, or to surplus hospital property that is not required in the delivery of necessary hospital services at the time of the lease, sale, or conveyance.

(b)   In the case of a sale or conveyance, if either general obligation bonds or revenue bonds issued for the benefit of the hospital to be conveyed are outstanding at the time of sale or conveyance, then the corporation shall agree to the following:

By the effective date of sale or conveyance, the corporation shall place into an escrow fund money or direct obligations of, or obligations the principal of and interest on which, are unconditionally guaranteed by the United States of America (as approved by the Local Government Commission), the principal of and interest on which, when due and payable, will provide sufficient money to pay the principal of and the interest and redemption premium, if any, on all bonds then outstanding to the maturity date or dates of such bonds or to the date or dates specified for the redemption thereof. The corporation shall furnish to the Local Government Commission such evidence as the Commission may require that the securities purchased will satisfy the requirements of this section. A hospital which has placed funds in escrow to retire outstanding general obligation or revenue bonds, as provided in this section, shall not be considered a public hospital, and G.S. 159-39(a)(3) shall be inapplicable to such hospitals.

No bonds, notes or other evidences of indebtedness shall be issued by a municipality or hospital authority to finance equipment for or the acquisition, extension, construction, reconstruction, improvement, enlargement, or betterment of any hospital facility if the facility has been sold or conveyed to a corporation, foreign or domestic, authorized to do business in North Carolina.

(c) In the case of a lease, the municipality or hospital authority shall determine the length of the lease. No lease executed under this section shall be deemed to convey a freehold interest. Any sublease or assignment of the lease shall be subject to the conditions prescribed by this section. If the term of the lease is more than 10 years, and either general obligation bonds or revenue bonds issued for the benefit of the hospital to be leased are outstanding at the time of the lease, then the corporation shall agree to the following:

By the effective date of the lease, the corporation shall place into an escrow fund money or direct obligations of, or obligations the principal of and interest on which, are unconditionally guaranteed by the United States of America (as approved by the Local Government Commission), the principal of and interest on which, when due and payable, will provide sufficient money to pay the principal of and the interest and redemption premium, if any, on all bonds then outstanding to the maturity date or dates of such bonds or to the date or dates specified for the redemption thereof. The corporation shall furnish to the Local Government Commission such evidence as the Commission may require that the securities purchased will satisfy the requirements of this section.

No bonds, notes or other evidences of indebtedness shall be issued by a municipality or hospital authority to finance equipment for or the acquisition, extension, construction, reconstruction, improvement, enlargement, or betterment of any hospital facility when the facility is leased to a corporation, foreign or domestic, authorized to do business in North Carolina.

(d)   The municipality or hospital authority shall comply with the following procedures before leasing, selling, or conveying a hospital facility, or part thereof:

(1)   The municipality or hospital authority shall first adopt a resolution declaring its intent to sell, lease, or convey the hospital facility at a regular meeting on 10 days' public notice. Notice shall be given by publication in one or more papers of general circulation in the affected area describing the intent to lease, sell, or convey the hospital facility involved, known potential buyers or lessees, a solicitation of additional interested buyers or lessees and intent to negotiate the terms of the lease or sale. Specific notice, given by certified mail, shall be given to the local office of each state-supported program that has made a capital expenditure in the hospital facility, to the Department of Health and Human Services, and to the Office of State Budget and Management.

(2)   At the meeting to adopt a resolution of intent, the municipality or hospital authority shall request proposals for lease or purchase by direct solicitation of at least five prospective lessees or buyers. The solicitation shall include a copy of G.S. 131E-13.

(3)   The municipality or hospital authority shall conduct a public hearing on the resolution of intent not less than 15 days after its adoption. Notice of the public hearing shall be given by publication at least 15 days before the hearing. All interested persons shall be heard at the public hearing.

(4)   Before considering any proposal to lease or purchase, the municipality or hospital authority shall require information on charges, services, and indigent care at similar facilities owned or operated by the proposed lessee or buyer.

(5)   Not less than 45 days after adopting a resolution of intent and not less than 30 days after conducting a public hearing on the resolution of intent, the municipality or hospital authority shall conduct a public hearing on proposals for lease or purchase that have been made. Notice of the public hearings shall be given by publication at least 10 days before the hearing. The notice shall state that copies of proposals for lease or purchase are available to the public.

(6) The municipality or hospital authority shall make copies of the proposals to lease or purchase available to the public at least 10 days before the public hearing on the proposals.

(7) Not less than 60 days after adopting a resolution of intent, the municipality or hospital authority at a regular meeting shall approve any lease, sale, or conveyance by a resolution. The municipality or hospital authority shall adopt this resolution only upon a finding that the lease, sale, or conveyance is in the public interest after considering whether the proposed lease, sale, or conveyance will meet the health-related needs of medically underserved groups, such as low income persons, racial and ethnic minorities, and handicapped persons. Notice of the regular meeting shall be given at least 10 days before the meeting and shall state that copies of the lease, sale, or conveyance proposed for approval are available.

(8) At least 10 days before the regular meeting at which any lease, sale, or conveyance is approved, the municipality or hospital authority shall make copies of the proposed contract available to the public.

(e) Notwithstanding the provisions of subsections (c) and (d) of this section or G.S. 131E-23, a hospital authority as defined in G.S. 131E-16(14) or a municipality may lease or sublease hospital land to a corporation or other business entity, whether for profit or not for profit, and may participate as an owner, joint venturer, or other equity participant with a corporation or other business entity for the development, construction, and operation of medical office buildings and other health care or hospital facilities, so long as the municipality, hospital authority, or other entity continues to maintain its primary community general hospital facilities as required by subsection (a) of this section.

(f) A municipality or hospital authority may permit or consent to the pledge of hospital land or leasehold estates in hospital land to facilitate the development, construction, and operation of medical office buildings and other health care or hospital facilities. A municipality or hospital authority also may, as lessee, enter into master leases or agreements to fund for temporary vacancies relating to hospital land or hospital facilities for use in the provision of health care.

(g) Neither G.S. 153A-176 nor Article 12 of Chapter 160A of the General Statutes shall apply to leases, subleases, sales, or conveyances under this

Chapter. (1983 (Reg. Sess., 1984), c. 1066, s. 1; 1997-233, s. 2; 1997-443, s. 11A.118(a); 2000-140, s. 93.1(a); 2001-424, s. 12.2(b).)

§ 131E-14. Lease or sale of hospital facilities to certain nonprofit corporations.

If a municipality or hospital authority leases, sells, or conveys a hospital facility, or part, to a nonprofit corporation of which a majority of voting members of its governing body is not appointed or controlled by the municipality or hospital authority, the procedural requirements set forth in G.S. 131E-13(d) shall apply. (1983 (Reg. Sess., 1984), c. 1066, s. 2.)

§ 131E-14.1. Branch facilities.

Notwithstanding anything in this Article, any municipality owning and operating a hospital organized under the provisions of this Part or Part 3 or any nonprofit corporation which leases or operates a hospital facility pursuant to an agreement with the municipality may erect, remodel, enlarge, purchase, finance, and operate branches and related facilities within this State but outside the boundaries of the county subject to the following limitations:

(1) No moneys derived from the exercise by the owning municipality of its power of taxation shall be expended on facilities located outside its boundaries;

(2) No moneys derived from the issuance by the owning municipality of its bonds or notes shall be expended on facilities located outside its boundaries;

(3) The owning municipality shall not possess the power of eminent domain or have the right of condemnation with respect to hospital facilities located outside its boundaries; and

(4) The power conferred on counties by G.S. 153A-169 and G.S. 153A-170 to adopt ordinances regulating the use of county-owned property and parking on county-owned property shall not extend to hospital facilities located outside its boundaries unless the board of commissioners of the county in which the facility is located shall by resolution permit any such ordinance to be applicable within its jurisdiction.

(5), (6) Repealed by Session Laws 1993 (Reg. Sess., 1994), c. 676, s. 1. (1983, c. 578, s. 1; 1993 (Reg. Sess., 1994), c. 676, s. 1.)

§ 131E-14.2. Conflict of interest.

(a) No member of the board of directors or employee of a public hospital, as defined in G.S. 159-39(a), or that person's spouse shall do either of the following:

(1) Acquire any interest, direct or indirect, in any hospital facility or in any property included or planned to be included in a hospital facility.

(2) Have any direct interest in any contract or proposed contract for materials or services to be furnished or used in connection with any hospital facility, except an employment contract for an employee. This restriction shall not apply to any contract, undertaking, or other transaction with a bank or banking institution, savings and loan association or public utility in the regular course of its business provided that the contract, undertaking, or other transaction shall be authorized by the board by specific resolution on which no director having direct interest shall vote.

(b) The fact that a person or that person's spouse owns ten percent (10%) or less stock of a corporation or has a ten percent (10%) or less ownership in any other business entity or is an employee of that corporation or other business entity does not make the person have a "direct interest" as this phrase is used in subsection (a) of this section; provided that, in order for the exception to apply, the contract, undertaking, or other transaction shall be authorized by the board of directors by specific resolution on which no director or employee having an interest, direct or indirect, shall vote.

(c) If a member of the board of directors or an employee of a public hospital or that person's spouse owns or controls an interest, direct or indirect, in any property included or planned to be included in any hospital facility, the member of the board of directors or the employee shall immediately disclose the same in writing to the board and the disclosure shall be entered upon the minutes of the board. Failure to disclose shall constitute misconduct in office and shall be grounds for removal.

(c1)   Subsection (a) of this section shall not apply if the director or employee is not involved in making or administering the contract. A director or employee is involved in administering a contract if the director or employee oversees the performance of or interprets the contract. A director or employee is involved in making a contract if the director or employee participates in the development of specifications or terms or in the preparation or award of the contract. A director or employee is not involved in making or administering a contract solely because of the performance of ministerial duties related to the contract. A director is also involved in making a contract if the board of directors takes action on the contract, whether or not the director actually participates in that action, unless the contract is approved under an exception to this section under which the director is allowed to benefit and is prohibited from voting.

(d)   Subsection (a) of this section shall not apply to any member of the board of directors of a public hospital if (i) the undertaking or contract or series of undertakings or contracts between the public hospital and one of its officials is approved by specific resolution of the board adopted in an open and public meeting and recorded in its minutes; (ii) the official entering into the contract or undertaking with the public hospital does not in an official capacity participate in any way or vote; and (iii) the amount does not exceed twelve thousand five hundred dollars ($12,500) for medically related services and twenty-five thousand dollars ($25,000) for other goods or services within a 12-month period, or the contract is for medically related or administrative services that are provided by a director who serves on the board as an ex officio representative of the hospital medical staff pursuant to a hospital bylaw adopted prior to January 1, 2005, or that are provided by the spouse of that director.

(e)   Subsection (a) of this section shall not apply to any employment relationship between a public hospital and the spouse of a member of the board of directors of the public hospital.

(f)   A contract entered into in violation of this section is void. A contract that is void under this section may continue in effect until an alternative can be arranged when: (i) immediate termination would result in harm to the public health or welfare, and (ii) the continuation is approved as provided in this subsection. A public hospital that is a party to the contract may request approval to continue contracts under this subsection from the chairman of the Local Government Commission. Approval of continuation of contracts under this subsection shall be given for the minimum period necessary to protect the public health or welfare. (2001-409, s. 6; 2005-70, s. 1; 2006-264, s. 64(b).)

Part 2. Hospital Authority.

§ 131E-15. Title and purpose.

(a) This Part shall be known as the "Hospital Authorities Act."

(b) The General Assembly finds and declares that in order to protect the public health, safety, and welfare, including that of low income persons, it is necessary that counties and cities be authorized to provide adequate hospital, medical, and health care and that the provision of such care is a public purpose. Therefore, the purpose of this Part is to provide an alternate method for counties and cities to provide hospital, medical, and health care. (1943, c. 780, ss. 1, 2; 1971, c. 799; 1983, c. 775, s. 1.)

§ 131E-16. Definitions.

As used in this Part, unless otherwise specified:

(1) "Board of county commissioners" means the legislative body charged with governing the county.

(2) "Bonds" means any bonds or notes issued by the hospital authority pursuant to this Part and the Local Government Finance Act, Chapter 159 of the General Statutes.

(3) "City" means any city or town which is, or is about to be, included in the territorial boundaries of a hospital authority when created hereunder.

(4) "City clerk" and "mayor" means the clerk and mayor, respectively, of the city, or the officers thereof charged with the duties customarily imposed on the clerk and mayor, respectively.

(5) "City council" means the legislative body, council, board of commissioners, board of trustees, or other body charged with governing the city or town.

(6) "Commissioner" means one of the members of a hospital authority appointed in accordance with the provisions of this Part.

(7) "Community general hospital" means a short-term nonfederal hospital that provides diagnostic and therapeutic services to patients for a variety of medical conditions, both surgical and nonsurgical, such services being available for use primarily by residents of the community in which it is located.

(8) "Contract" means any agreement of a hospital authority with or for the benefit of an obligee whether contained in a resolution, trust indenture, mortgage, lease, bond or other instrument.

(9) "Corporation, foreign or domestic, authorized to do business in North Carolina" means a corporation for profit or having a capital stock which is created and organized under Chapter 55 of the General Statutes or any other general or special act of this State, or a foreign corporation which has procured a certificate of authority to transact business in this State pursuant to Article 10 of Chapter 55 of the General Statutes.

(10) "County" means the county which is, or is about to be, included in the territorial boundaries of a hospital authority when created hereunder.

(11) "County clerk" and "chairman of the board of county commissioners" means the clerk and chairman, respectively, of the county or the officers thereof charged with the duties customarily imposed on the clerk and chairman, respectively.

(12) "Federal government" means the United States of America, or any agency, instrumentality, corporate or otherwise, of the United States of America.

(13) "Government" means the State and federal governments and any subdivision, agency or instrumentality, corporate or otherwise, of either of them.

(14) "Hospital authority" means a public body and a body corporate and politic organized under the provisions of this Part.

(15) "Hospital facilities" means any one or more buildings, structures, additions, extensions, improvements or other facilities, whether or not located on the same site or sites, machinery, equipment, furnishings or other real or personal property suitable for health care or medical care; and includes, without limitation, general hospitals; chronic disease, maternity, mental, tuberculosis and other specialized hospitals; nursing homes, including skilled nursing facilities and intermediate care facilities; adult care homes for the aged and disabled; public health center facilities; housing or quarters for local public

health departments; facilities for intensive care and self-care; clinics and outpatient facilities; clinical, pathological and other laboratories; health care research facilities; laundries; residences and training facilities for nurses, interns, physicians and other staff members; food preparation and food service facilities; administrative buildings, central service and other administrative facilities; communication, computer and other electronic facilities; fire-fighting facilities; pharmaceutical and recreational facilities; storage space; X ray, laser, radiotherapy and other apparatus and equipment; dispensaries; utilities; vehicular parking lots and garages; office facilities for hospital staff members and physicians; and such other health and hospital facilities customarily under the jurisdiction of or provided by hospitals, or any combination of the foregoing, with all necessary, convenient or related interests in land, machinery, apparatus, appliances, equipment, furnishings, appurtenances, site preparation, landscaping and physical amenities.

(15a) "Hospital land" means air and ground rights to real property held either in fee or by lease by a hospital authority, with all easements, rights-of-way, appurtenances, landscaping, and physical amenities such as utilities, parking lots, and garages, but excluding other improvements to land described in G.S. 131E-6(4) and subsection (15) of this section.

(16) "Municipality" means any county, city, town or incorporated village, other than a city as defined above, which is located within or partially within the territorial boundaries of an authority.

(17) "Real property" means lands, lands under water, structures, and any and all easements, franchises and incorporeal hereditaments and every estate and right therein, legal and equitable, including terms for years and liens by way of judgment, mortgage or otherwise.

(18) "State" means the State of North Carolina. (1943, c. 780, s. 3; 1971, c. 780, s. 22; c. 799; 1983, c. 775, s. 1; 1995, c. 535, s. 19; 1997-233, s. 3.)

§ 131E-17. Creation of a hospital authority.

(a) A hospital authority may be created whenever a city council or a county board of commissioners finds and adopts a resolution finding that it is in the interest of the public health and welfare to create a hospital authority.

(b) After the adoption of a resolution creating a hospital authority, the mayor or the chairman of the county board of commissioners shall appoint commissioners in accordance with G.S. 131E-18.

(c) The commissioners shall be a public body and a body corporate and politic upon the completion of the procedures described in G.S. 131E-19. (1943, c. 780, s. 4; 1971, c. 799; 1983, c. 775, s. 1.)

§ 131E-18. Commissioners.

(a) The mayor or the chairman of the county board shall appoint the commissioners of the authority. There shall be not less than six and not more than 30 commissioners. Upon a finding that it is in the public interest, the commissioners may adopt a resolution increasing or decreasing the number of commissioners by a fixed number; Provided that no decrease in the number of commissioners shall shorten a commissioner's term. A certified copy of the resolution and a list of nominees shall be submitted to the mayor or the chairman of the county board of commissioners for appointments in accordance with the procedures set forth in subsection (d) of this section.

(b) For the initial appointments of commissioners, one-third of the commissioners shall be appointed for a term of one year, one-third for a term of two years, and one-third for a term of three years to achieve staggered terms. All subsequent appointments shall be for three-year terms. A commissioner shall hold office until a successor has been appointed and qualified. Vacancies from resignation or removal from office shall be filled for the unexpired portion of the term.

(c) The mayor or the chairman of the county board of commissioners shall name the first chair of the authority. Thereafter, the commissioners shall elect each subsequent chair from their members. The commissioners shall elect from their members the first vice-chair and all subsequent vice-chairs.

(d) When a commissioner resigns, is removed from office, completes a term of office, or when there is an increase in the number of commissioners, the remaining commissioners shall submit to the mayor or the chairman of the county board of commissioners a list of nominees for appointment to the commission. The mayor or the chairman of the county board of commissioners shall appoint, only from the nominees, the number of commissioners necessary to fill all vacancies. However, the mayor or the chairman of the county board of commissioners may require the commissioners to submit as many additional lists of nominees as he or she may desire.

(e) The mayor shall file with the city clerk, or the chairman of the county board of commissioners shall file with the county clerk, a certificate of appointment or reappointment of a commissioner. The certificate shall be conclusive evidence of the due and proper appointment of the commissioner.

(f) Commissioners shall receive no compensation for their services, but they shall be entitled to reimbursement for necessary expenses, including travel expenses, incurred in the discharge of their duties.

(g) For a county with a population of less than 75,000, according to the most recent decennial federal census, the following exceptions to the provisions of this section shall apply:

(1) The commissioners shall be appointed by the county board of commissioners rather than the chairman of the county board of commissioners;

(2) In making appointments under subsection (d) of this section, the county board of commissioners shall consider the nominations of the commissioners of the authority, but the county board of the commissioners is not bound by the nominations and may choose any qualified person.

The foregoing exceptions shall not apply when a county with a population of less than 75,000 jointly establishes a hospital authority with a city.

(h) A majority of the commissioners shall constitute a quorum. (1943, c. 780, s. 5; 1971, c. 799; 1973, c. 792; 1981, c. 525, s. 1; 1983, c. 775, s. 1.)

§ 131E-19. Incorporation of a hospital authority.

(a) After the commissioners are appointed, they shall present to the Secretary of State an application for incorporation as a hospital authority. The application shall be signed by each of the commissioners and shall set forth:

(1) That the city council or the county board of commissioners has found that it is in the interest of the public health and welfare to create a hospital authority;

(2) That the mayor or the chairman of the county board of commissioners has appointed them as commissioners;

(3) The name and official residence of each of the commissioners;

(4) A certified copy of the appointment evidencing the commissioners' right to office, and the date and place of induction into and taking of office;

(5) That they desire the hospital authority to become a public body and a body corporate and politic under this Part;

(6) The term of office of each of the commissioners;

(7) The name which is proposed for the corporation; and

(8) The location and principal office of the corporation.

The application shall be subscribed and sworn to by each of the commissioners before an officer authorized by the laws of this State to take and certify oaths. This officer shall certify upon the application that he or she personally knows the commissioners and knows them to be the officers as asserted in the application, and that each subscribed to the application and took the oath in the officer's presence.

(b) The Secretary of State shall examine the application. If he or she finds that the name proposed for the corporation is not identical with that of a person or of any other corporation in this State or so nearly similar so as to lead to confusion and uncertainty, the application shall be filed and recorded in the appropriate book of record in the Secretary of State's office. The Secretary of State shall then make and issue to the commissioners a certificate of incorporation pursuant to this Part, under the Seal of the State, and shall record the certificate with the application.

(c) A hospital authority's name or the location or principal office of the corporation may be changed by the adoption of a resolution by the majority of the authority's commissioners. A copy of the resolution, duly verified by the chair and secretary of the commission before an officer authorized by the laws of this State to take and certify oaths, shall be delivered to the Secretary of State, along with a conformed copy. If the Secretary of State finds that the proposed name is not identical with that of a person or any corporation of this State, or so nearly similar as to lead to confusion and uncertainty, the resolution shall be filed and recorded in the appropriate book of record in the Secretary of State's office. A resolution changing the location or principal office of the hospital authority shall be filed and recorded in the appropriate book of record in the Secretary of State's office. The Secretary of State shall then return to the authority the conformed copy, together with a certificate stating that the attached copy is a true copy of the document in the Secretary of State's office, that shows the date of filing.

(d) In any legal proceeding, a copy of the certificate of incorporation, certified by the Secretary of State, shall be admissible in evidence and shall be conclusive proof of its filing and contents and the incorporation of the hospital authority in accordance with this Part. (1943, c. 780, s. 4; 1966, c. 988, s. 1; 1971, c. 799; 1983, c. 775, s. 1.)

§ 131E-20. Boundaries of the authority.

(a) The territorial boundaries of a hospital authority shall include the city or county creating the authority and the area within 10 miles from the territorial boundaries of that city or county. However, a hospital authority may engage in health care activities in a county outside its territorial boundaries pursuant to:

(1) An agreement with a hospital facility if only one hospital currently exists in that county;

(2) An agreement with any hospital if more than one hospital currently exists in that county; or

(3) An agreement with any health care agency if no hospital currently exists in that county.

In no event shall the territorial boundaries of a hospital authority include, in whole or in part, the area of any previously existing hospital authority. All priorities shall be determined on the basis of the time of issuance of the certificates of incorporation by the Secretary of State.

(b) After the creation of an authority, the subsequent existence within its territorial boundaries of more than one city or county shall in no way affect the territorial boundaries of the authority. (1943, c. 780, s. 4; 1971, c. 799; 1983, c. 775, s. 1; 1993, c. 529, s. 6.1.)

§ 131E-21. Conflict of interest.

(a) No commissioner or employee of the hospital authority or that person's spouse shall do either of the following:

(1) Acquire any interest, direct or indirect, in any hospital facility or in any property included or planned to be included in a hospital facility.

(2) Have any interest, direct or indirect, in any contract or proposed contract for materials or services to be furnished or used in connection with any hospital facility, except an employment contract for an employee. The foregoing restriction shall not apply to any contract, undertaking, or other transaction with a bank or banking institution, savings and loan association or public utility in the regular course of its business; Provided that any such contract, undertaking, or other transaction shall be authorized by the commissioners by specific resolution on which no commissioner having an interest, direct or indirect, shall vote.

(b) The fact that a person or that person's spouse owns ten percent (10%) or less stock of a corporation or has a ten percent (10%) or less ownership in any other business entity or is an employee of that corporation or other business entity does not make the person have an "interest, direct or indirect" as this phrase is used in subsection (a) of this section; provided that, in order for the exception to apply, the contract, undertaking or other transaction shall be authorized by the commissioners by specific resolution on which no commissioner or employee having an interest, direct or indirect, shall vote.

(c) If a commissioner or employee of an authority or that person's spouse owns or controls an interest, direct or indirect, in any property included or planned to be included in any hospital facility, the commissioner or employee shall immediately disclose the same in writing to the authority and the disclosure shall be entered upon the minutes of the authority. Failure to disclose shall constitute misconduct in office and shall be grounds for a commissioner's removal from office under G.S. 131E-22.

(d) Subsection (a) of this section shall not apply to any commissioner of a hospital authority if (i) the undertaking or contract or series of undertakings or contracts between the hospital authority and one of its officials is approved by specific resolution of the governing body adopted in an open and public meeting and recorded in its minutes and the amount does not exceed twelve thousand five hundred dollars ($12,500) for medically related services and twenty-five thousand dollars ($25,000) for other goods or services within a 12-month period; and (ii) the official entering into the contract or undertaking with the hospital authority does not in an official capacity participate in any way or vote.

(e)   Subsection (a) of this section shall not apply to any employment relationship between a hospital authority and the spouse of a commissioner of the hospital authority.

(f)   A contract entered into in violation of this section is void. A contract that is void under this section may continue in effect until an alternative can be arranged when: (i) immediate termination would result in harm to the public health or welfare, and (ii) the continuation is approved as provided in this subsection. A hospital authority that is a party to the contract may request approval to continue contracts under this subsection from the chairman of the Local Government Commission. Approval of continuation of contracts under this subsection shall be given for the minimum period necessary to protect the public health or welfare. (1943, c. 780, s. 7; 1971, c. 749; 1983, c. 775, s. 1; 1983 (Reg. Sess., 1984), c. 1058, s. 1; 2001-409, s. 7.)

§ 131E-22. Removal of commissioners.

(a)   The appointing authority, as stated in G.S. 131E-18, may remove a commissioner for inefficiency, neglect of duty, or misconduct in office. A commissioner may be removed only after he or she has been given a copy of the charges and provided the opportunity to be heard in person or by counsel. A commissioner is entitled to at least 10 days after receipt of the notice to prepare for a hearing before the mayor or the chairman of the county.

(b)   An obligee of the authority may file with the mayor or the chairman of the county board of commissioners written charges that the authority is willfully violating the laws of the State or a term, provision, or covenant to any contract to which the authority is a party. The mayor or the chairman of the county board of commissioners shall give each of the commissioners a copy of the charges at least 10 days prior to the hearing on the charges. The commissioners shall be provided an opportunity to be heard in person or by counsel. The mayor or the chairman of the county board of commissioners shall, within 15 days after receipt of the charges, remove any commissioners of the authority who are found to have acquiesced in any willful violation. If a commissioner has not filed a written statement before the hearing with the authority stating his or her objections to or lack of participation in the violation, the commissioner shall be deemed to have acquiesced in a willful violation.

(c)   If, after due and diligent search, a commissioner to whom charges are required to be delivered cannot be found within the county where the authority is located, the charges shall be deemed to be served upon the commissioner when it is mailed to the commissioner at the commissioner's last known address as the same appears on the records of the authority.

(d)   In the event of the removal of any commissioner, the mayor shall file in the office of the city clerk, or the chairman of the county board of commissioners shall file with the county clerk, a record of the proceedings together with the charges against the commissioner and the findings. (1943, c. 780, s. 8; 1971, c. 799; 1983, c. 775, s. 1.)

§ 131E-23. Powers of the authority.

(a)   An authority shall have all powers necessary or convenient to carry out the purposes of this Part, including the following powers, which are in addition to those powers granted elsewhere in this Part:

(1)   To investigate hospital, medical, and health conditions and the means of improving those conditions;

(2)   To determine where inadequate hospital and medical facilities exist;

(3)   To accept donations or money, personal property, or real estate for the benefit of the authority and to take title to the same from any person, firm, corporation or society;

(4)   To acquire by purchase, gift, devise, lease, condemnation, or otherwise any existing hospital facilities;

(5)   To purchase, lease, obtain options upon, or otherwise acquire any real or personal property or any interest therein from any person, firm, corporation, city, county, or government;

(6) To sell, exchange, transfer, assign, or pledge any real or personal property or any interest therein to any person, firm, corporation, city, county or government;

(7) To own, hold, clear and improve property;

(8) To borrow money upon its bonds, notes, debentures, or evidences of indebtedness, as provided for in G.S. 131E-26 and G.S. 131E-27;

(9) To purchase real or personal property pursuant to G.S. 131E-32;

(10) To appoint an administrator of a hospital facility and necessary assistants, and any and all other employees necessary or advisable, to fix their compensation, to adopt necessary rules governing their employment, and to remove employees;

(11) To delegate to its agents or employees any powers or duties as it may deem appropriate;

(12) To employ its own counsel and legal staff;

(13) To adopt, amend and repeal bylaws for the conduct of its business;

(14) To enter into contracts for necessary supplies, equipment, or services for the operation of its business;

(15) To appoint committees or subcommittees as it shall deem advisable, to fix their duties and responsibilities, and to do all things necessary in connection with the construction, repair, reconstruction, management, supervision, control and operation of the authority's business;

(16) To establish procedures for health care providers to secure the privilege of practicing within any hospital operated by the authority pursuant to Part 3 of Article 5 of this Chapter;

(17) To establish reasonable rules governing the conduct of health care providers while on duty in any hospital operated by the facility pursuant to Part 3 of Article 5 of this Chapter;

(18) To provide for the construction, reconstruction, improvement, alteration or repair of any hospital facility, or any part of a facility;

(19) To enter into any contracts or other arrangements with any municipality, other public agency of this or any other State or of the United States, or with any individual, private organization, or nonprofit association for the provision of hospital, clinical, or similar services;

(20) To lease any hospital facilities to or from any municipality, other public agency of this or any other state or of the United States, or to any individual, corporation, or association upon any terms and subject to any conditions as may carry out the purposes of this Part. The authority may provide for the lessee to use, operate, manage and control the hospital facilities, and to exercise designated powers, in the same manner as the authority itself might do;

(21) To act as an agent for the federal, State or local government in connection with the acquisition, construction, operation or management of a hospital facility, or any part thereof;

(22) To arrange with the State, its subdivisions and agencies, and any county or city, to the extent it is within the scope of their respective functions,

a. To cause the services customarily provided by each to be rendered for the benefit of the hospital authority,

b. To furnish, plan, replan, install, open or close streets, roads, alleys, sidewalks or similar facilities and to acquire property, options or property rights for the furnishing of property or services for a hospital facility, and

c. To provide and maintain parks and sewage, water and other facilities for hospital facilities and to lease and rent any of the dwellings or other accommodations or any of the lands, buildings, structures or facilities embraced in any hospital facility and to establish and revise the rents and charges;

(23) To insure the property or the operations of the authority against risks as the authority may deem advisable;

(24) To invest any funds held in reserves or sinking funds, or any funds not required for immediate disbursement, in property or securities in which trustees, guardians, executors, administrators, and others acting in a fiduciary capacity may legally invest funds under their control;

(25) To sue and be sued;

(26) To have a seal and to alter it at pleasure;

(27) To have perpetual succession;

(28) To make and execute contracts and other instruments necessary or convenient to the exercise of the powers of the authority;

(29) To remove vehicles parked on land owned or leased by the hospital authority in areas clearly designated as no parking or restricted parking zones. An owner of a removed vehicle as a condition of regaining possession of the vehicle, shall reimburse the hospital authority for all reasonable costs, not to exceed fifty dollars ($50.00), incidental to the removal and storage of the vehicle provided that the designation of the area as a no parking or restricted parking zone clearly indicates that the owner may be subject to these costs;

(30) To plan and operate hospital facilities;

(31) To provide teaching and instruction programs and schools for medical students, interns, physicians, nurses, technicians and other health care professionals;

(32) To provide and maintain continuous resident physician and intern medical services;

(33) To adopt, amend and repeal rules and regulations governing the admission of patients and the care, conduct, and treatment of patients;

(34) To establish a fee schedule for services received from hospital facilities and make the services available regardless of ability to pay;

(35) To maintain and operate isolation wards for the care and treatment of mental, contagious, or other similar diseases;

(36) To sell a hospital facility pursuant to G.S. 131E-8 or G.S. 131E-13; and

(37) To agree to limitations upon the exercise of any powers conferred upon the hospital authority by this Part in connection with any loan by a government.

(b) A hospital authority may exercise any or all of the powers conferred upon it by this Part, either generally or with respect to any specific hospital facility or facilities, through or by designated agents, including any corporation or corporations which are or shall be formed under the laws of this State.

(c) Expired pursuant to Session Laws 1983, c. 775, s. 1.

(d) No provisions with respect to the acquisition, operation or disposition of property by other public bodies shall be applicable to a hospital authority unless otherwise specified by the General Assembly. (1913, c. 42, s. 15; 1917, c. 268; C.S., s. 7273; 1983, c. 775, s. 1; 1995, c. 509, s. 135.1(l); 1997-456, s. 27; 1999-456, s. 6.)

§ 131E-24. Eminent domain.

(a) A hospital authority may acquire by eminent domain any real property, including fixtures and improvements, which it deems necessary to carry out the purposes of this Part. The hospital authority may exercise the power of eminent domain under the provisions of Chapter 40A of the General Statutes or any other statute now in force or subsequently enacted for the exercise of the power of eminent domain.

(b) No property belonging to any city, town, or county, any government, religious or charitable organization, or to any existing hospital or clinic may be acquired without its consent. No property belonging to a public utility corporation may be acquired without the approval of the commission or other officer or agency, if any, having regulatory power over the corporation.

(c) The right of eminent domain shall not be exercised unless and until a certificate of public convenience and necessity for the facility has been issued by the North Carolina Utilities Commission. The proceedings leading up to issuing of the certificate of public convenience and necessity, and the right of appeal from the proceedings shall be governed by the Public Utilities Act, Chapter 62 of the General Statutes, and the rights under that act are hereby expressly reserved to all interested parties in the proceedings. In addition to the powers now granted by law to the North Carolina Utilities Commission, the Utilities Commission is authorized to investigate and examine all facilities set up or attempted to be set up under this Part and to determine the question of public convenience and necessity for the facility. (1943, s. 780, s. 10; 1971, c. 799; 1981, c. 919, s. 18; 1983, c. 775, s. 1.)

§ 131E-25. Zoning and building laws.

All hospital facilities of the authority shall be subject to the planning, zoning, sanitary and building laws, ordinances and regulations applicable to the locality in which the hospital facility is situated. (1943, c. 780, s. 11; 1971, c. 799; 1983, c. 775, s. 1.)

§ 131E-26. Revenue bonds and notes.

(a)   A hospital authority shall have the power to issue revenue bonds under the Local Government Revenue Bond Act, Chapter 159 of the General Statutes, Article 5, or the bond and revenue anticipation provisions of Chapter 159 of the General Statutes, Article 9, for the purpose of acquiring, constructing, reconstructing, improving, enlarging, bettering, equipping, extending or operating hospital facilities.

(b)   A hospital authority shall have the power to borrow for the purposes above enumerated upon its notes or other evidences of indebtedness, subject to the approval of the Local Government Commission as provided in G.S. 131E-32(c). Such approval shall be required regardless of the amount of any such borrowing. Any borrowing by a hospital authority before the date of ratification of Part 2 of Article 2 of this Chapter, whether or not approved by the Local Government Commission, is valid, ratified and confirmed. (1983, c. 775, s. 1.)

§ 131E-27. Contracts with federal government.

A hospital authority is authorized:

(1)   To borrow money and accept grants from the federal government for or to aid in the construction of a hospital facility;

(2)   To acquire any land acquired by the federal government for the construction of a hospital facility; and

(3)   To acquire, lease or manage any hospital facility constructed or owned by the federal government.

To these ends, a hospital authority is authorized to enter into contracts, mortgages, trust indentures, leases or other agreements giving the federal government the right to supervise and approve the construction, maintenance and operation of the hospital facility. It is the purpose and intent of this Part to authorize every hospital authority to do any and all things necessary to secure the financial aid and cooperation of the federal government in the construction, maintenance, and operation of hospital facilities. (1943, c. 780, s. 19; 1971, c. 799; 1983, c. 775, s. 1.)

§ 131E-28. Tax exemptions.

(a) Hospital authorities shall be exempt from the payment of taxes or fees to the State or any of its subdivisions, or to any officer or employee of the State or any of its subdivisions.

(b) Hospital authority property used for public purposes shall be exempt from all local and municipal taxes and for the purposes of this tax exemption, an authority shall be deemed to be a municipal corporation.

(c) Bonds, notes, debentures, or other evidences of indebtedness of a hospital authority issued under the Local Government Revenue Bond Act, Chapter 159 of the General Statutes, Article 5, or issued pursuant to the bond and revenue anticipation provisions of Chapter 159 of the General Statutes, Article 9, or issued pursuant to G.S. 131E-26(b) or contracted pursuant to G.S. 131E-32 shall at all times be free from taxation by the State or any of its subdivisions, except for inheritance or gift taxes, income taxes on the gain from the transfer of the instruments, and franchise taxes. The interest on the instruments is not subject to taxation as income. (1943, c. 780, s. 21; 1971, c. 799; 1973, c. 695, s. 6; 1977, c. 268; 1983, c. 775, s. 1; 1995, c. 46, s. 13.)

§ 131E-29. Audits and recommendations.

Each hospital authority shall file with the mayor of the city or the chairman of the county board of commissioners at least annually an audit report by a certified public accountant of its activities for the preceding year, and shall make any recommendations necessary to carry out the purposes of this Part. (1943, c. 780, s. 22; 1971, c. 799; 1983, c. 775, s. 1.)

§ 131E-30. Appropriations.

Each year the governing body of a city or county in which the hospital authority is located may appropriate and transfer funds to the authority. The appropriations shall be from the General Fund and may not exceed five percent (5%) of the General Fund. Money appropriated and paid to the hospital authority by a city or county shall be deemed a necessary expense of the city or county. However, the appropriations shall not be deemed to be a revenue of the authority for the purpose of bonds of the hospital authority issued under the Local Government Revenue Bond Act, Chapter 159 of the General Statutes, Article 5. (1943, c. 780, s. 25; 1971, c. 780, s. 23; c. 799; 1983, c. 775, s. 1.)

§ 131E-31. Transfers of property by a city or county to a hospital authority.

(a)   A city or county may lease, sell, convey, or otherwise transfer, with or without consideration or with nominal consideration, any property, whether real or personal or mixed, to a hospital authority whose territorial boundaries include at least part of the city or county. A hospital authority is authorized to accept such lease, transfer, assignment or conveyance and to bind itself to the performance and observation of any agreements and conditions required by the city or county.

(b)   If a city or county sells, conveys, or otherwise irrevocably transfers to a hospital authority property with a market value in excess of two hundred fifty thousand dollars ($250,000), and if the hospital authority accepts this property, the mayor of the city or the chairman of the county board of commissioners shall have the right to name additional commissioners to serve on the authority. The number of additional commissioners shall be such that the proportion of additional commissioners to existing commissioners is approximately equal to the proportion of the total value being transferred to the hospital authority to the total value of property already held by the authority. The determination of the ratios will be made solely by the governing body of the city or county transferring the property to the hospital authority; however, in no event shall fewer than two nor more than nine commissioners be added to the hospital authority. The total number of commissioners shall be increased by the number of commissioners added under this subsection. The times of commencement and expiration of the initial terms of the commissioners being added shall be determined by agreement between the hospital authority and the governing body of the city or county. After the expiration of the initial terms, subsequent terms will be three years. Copies of the agreement setting out the number of persons being added and the terms of each shall be filed with the clerk of the city or the clerk of the county board of commissioners making the transfer and, thereafter, copies of the reports referred to in G.S. 131E-29 shall be filed with the clerk of the city or the clerk of the county board of commissioners. (1943, c. 780, s. 26; 1961, c. 988, s. 2; 1971, c. 799; 1983, c. 775, s. 1.)

§ 131E-32. Purchase money security interests.

(a) An authority shall have the power and authority to purchase real or personal property under installment contracts, purchase money mortgages or deeds of trust, or other instruments, which create in the property purchased a security interest to secure payment of the purchase price and interest thereon. No deficiency judgment may be rendered against any authority for breach of an obligation authorized by this section. Any contract made or entered into by an authority before the date of ratification of Part 2 of Article 2 of this Chapter which would have been valid hereunder is valid, ratified and confirmed.

(b) A hospital authority may contract pursuant to this section in an amount of less than seven hundred fifty thousand dollars ($750,000), adjusted, as hereinafter provided, in any single transaction without the approval of the Local Government Commission: Provided, however, that the approval of the Local Government Commission shall be required for any single contract pursuant to this section if the aggregate dollar amount of all such contracts outstanding after any such single transaction, exclusive of revenue bonds issued pursuant to G.S. 131E-26 and federal contracts entered pursuant to G.S. 131E-27, would exceed ten percent (10%) of the total operating revenues, as hereinafter defined, of the hospital authority for its most recently completed fiscal year as set forth in the audited financial statements of such authority for such fiscal year. The approval of the Local Government Commission shall be required with respect to any single contract pursuant to this section in an amount of seven hundred fifty thousand dollars ($750,000) or more, adjusted as hereinafter provided.

(c) Approval of the Local Government Commission under this section or as required by G.S. 131E-26(b) shall be obtained in accordance with such rules and regulations as the Local Government Commission may prescribe and shall be evidenced by the secretary's certificate on the contract or note or other evidence of indebtedness. In determining whether to approve any such contract or borrowing, the Local Government Commission shall consider whether the hospital authority can demonstrate the financial responsibility and capability of the hospital authority to fulfill its obligations with respect to such contract or borrowing. The Local Government Commission may approve the application without other findings, if it finds that (i) the proposed project or the purpose of the borrowing is necessary and expedient, (ii) the contract or the borrowing, under the circumstances, is preferable to a bond issue for the same purpose, (iii) the sums to fall due under the contract or borrowing are adequate and not excessive for the proposed purpose, (iv) the authority's debt management procedures are good, or that reasonable assurances have been given that its debt will henceforth be managed in strict compliance with law and (v) the authority is not in default on any of its debt service obligations. Any contract or borrowing subject to this subsection requiring the approval of the Local Government Commission that does not bear the secretary's certificate thereon shall be void, and it shall be unlawful for any officer, employee or agent of a hospital authority to make any payments of money thereunder. An order of the Local Government Commission approving any such contract or borrowing shall not be regarded as an approval of the legality of the contract or borrowing in any respect.

(d) The seven hundred fifty thousand dollars ($750,000) amount referred to in G.S. 131E-32(b) shall be in effect from July 15, 1983 through September 30, 1984. For each twelve-month period thereafter, the seven hundred fifty thousand dollar ($750,000) amount shall be the figure in effect for the preceding twelve-month period, adjusted to reflect the change in the preceding twelve-month period in the Department of Commerce Composite Construction Cost Index.

(e) For purposes of G.S. 131E-32(b), the "total operating revenues" of a hospital authority for a fiscal year means patient revenue, less provisions for contractual adjustments, uncompensated care and bad debts, plus other operating revenues, all as determined in accordance with generally accepted accounting principles. (1983, c. 775, s. 1.)

§ 131E-33. Part controlling.

Insofar as the provisions of this Part are inconsistent with the provisions of any other law, the provisions of this Part shall be controlling; however this Part shall not be construed as preventing a city, town, or county from establishing and operating a hospital under the authority of any other law now or hereafter in effect. (1943, c. 780, s. 28; 1971, c. 799; 1983, c. 775, s. 1.)

§ 131E-34: Repealed by Session Laws 2011-326, s. 17, effective June 27, 2011.

§§ 131E-35 through 131E-39. Reserved for future codification purposes.

Part 3. Hospital District Act.

§ 131E-40. Title and purpose.

(a) This Part shall be known as the "Hospital District Act."

(b) It is the purpose of this Part to authorize the creation of hospital districts to furnish hospital, clinical and similar services to the people of this State.

(c) This Part provides an additional and alternative method for the provision of hospital, clinical and similar services.

(d) This Part shall be construed liberally to effect its purposes. (1983, c. 775, s. 1.)

§ 131E-41. Methods of creation of a hospital district.

(a) The voters of an area may petition their county board of commissioners and the North Carolina Medical Care Commission for the creation of a hospital district. All of the area proposed to be included within a hospital district must be located within one county. The petition shall be signed by at least 500 voters of the area described in the petition. However, if the area has less than 1,100 voters, then the minimum number of petitioners shall be 250 voters. The petition shall set forth:

(1) A description of the area to be included within the proposed hospital district;

(2) The names of all municipalities located in whole or in part in the proposed hospital district;

(3) The names of all publicly owned hospitals in the proposed hospital district;

(4) The purpose or purposes sought to be accomplished by the creation of the hospital district; and

(5) The proposed name of the hospital district.

The petition shall be delivered to the county board of commissioners of the county in which the proposed hospital district would be located. If the county board of commissioners approves the creation of the hospital district, they shall have the petition delivered to the North Carolina Medical Care Commission for review under G.S. 131E-42.

(b) In the alternative, the county board of commissioners, in its discretion, may create a hospital district by resolution. This authority exists only when one hospital district already exists in the county, or when a special tax levy for hospital purposes has been authorized or is now authorized with respect to a portion of the county. This power is limited to establishing a hospital district in the area lying outside the existing hospital district or outside the portion of the county in which a hospital tax levy has been or is now authorized. When a county board of commissioners exercises its power under this subsection, all other provisions of this Part shall be applicable, except as modified by this subsection. (1949, c. 766, s. 5; 1953, c. 1045, s. 1; 1959, cc. 877, 1074; 1971, c. 780, s. 37.4; 1973, c. 476, s. 152; c. 494, s. 45; c. 1090, s. 1; 1983, c. 775, s. 1.)

§ 131E-42. Hearing and determination.

(a) After receipt of a petition for the creation of a hospital district that meets the requirements of G.S. 131E-41(a) and that has been approved by the county board of commissioners, the North Carolina Medical Care Commission shall give notice of a hearing on the creation of a hospital district. The notice of hearing shall be posted at the county courthouse door and at three public places within the proposed district. In addition, notice of hearing shall be published at least once for three successive weeks in a newspaper circulating in the proposed district. The notice of hearing shall specify:

(1) The date of hearing which shall not be earlier than 20 days after the first posting and publication of notice;

(2) The location of the hearing, which shall be within the county in which the proposed district would be located; and

(3) That any interested person may appear and be heard at the hearing.

(b) At the time and place specified in the notice of hearing, the North Carolina Medical Care Commission, or its designee, shall hear all interested persons, and, if necessary, adjourn and reconvene at a later time.

(c) After the hearing, the North Carolina Medical Care Commission shall determine if it is in the public interest and beneficial to the residents of the area to create a hospital district, and, if it is, shall adopt a resolution creating the hospital district. The resolution shall define the area to be included in the hospital district. The area shall either be the one described in the petition or a part of that area. However, no municipality, in whole or in part, shall be included in a hospital district unless the governing body of the municipality shall have approved by resolution the inclusion and shall have filed a certified copy of the resolution with the North Carolina Medical Care Commission.

(d) Each hospital district shall be designated by the North Carolina Medical Care Commission as the "_____ Hospital District of _____ County," inserting in the blank spaces a name identifying the locality and the name of the county.

(e) The North Carolina Medical Care Commission shall give notice of the creation of a hospital district. The notice shall be published at least once for two successive weeks in the newspaper in which the notice of hearing required by G.S. 131E-42(a) was published. A notice substantially in the following form, the blanks first being properly filled in, with the printed or written signature of the executive secretary of the North Carolina Medical Care Commission appended, shall be published with the resolution:

The foregoing resolution was passed by the North Carolina Medical Care Commission on the _____ day of _____, _____; it was first published on the _____ day of _____, _____.

Any action or proceeding questioning the validity of the resolution or creation of the _____ Hospital District of _____ County or the inclusion in the district of any of the areas described in the resolution must be commenced within thirty days after the first publication of this resolution.

_____

Secretary

North Carolina Medical

Care Commission.

(1943, c. 766, s. 5; 1951, c. 805; 1953, c. 1045, ss. 1, 2; 1959, c. 877; 1973, c. 476, s. 152; c. 1090, s. 1; 1983, c. 775, s. 1; 1999, c. 456, s. 59.)

§ 131E-43. Limitation of actions.

Any action or proceeding in any court to set aside a resolution of the North Carolina Medical Care Commission creating any hospital district, or questioning the validity of the resolution, or the creation of any hospital district, or the inclusion in the district of any of the territory described in the resolution creating the district, must be commenced within 30 days after the first publication of the resolution and notice required by G.S. 131E-42(e). Thereafter, no right of action or defense founded upon the invalidity of a resolution or the creation of a district or the inclusion of any territory in the district shall be asserted, nor shall the validity of the resolution or the creation of the district or the inclusion of any territory be open to question in any court upon any ground, except in any action or proceeding commenced within the 30-day period. (1949, c. 766, s. 5; 1951, c. 805; 1953, c. 1045, s. 2; 1973, c. 476, s. 152; c. 1090, s. 1; 1983, c. 775, s. 1.)

§ 131E-44. General powers.

(a)   The inhabitants of a hospital district are a body corporate and politic by the name specified by the North Carolina Medical Care Commission. Under that name they:

(1)   Are vested with all the property and rights of property belonging to any corporation;

(2) Have perpetual succession;

(3) May sue or be sued;

(4) May contract;

(5) May acquire any real or personal property;

(6) May hold, invest, sell or dispose of property;

(7) May have a seal and alter and renew it; and

(8) May exercise the powers conferred upon them by this Part.

(b) A hospital district is vested with all the powers necessary or convenient to carry out the purposes of this Part, including the following powers, which are in addition to the powers granted elsewhere:

(1) Those powers granted under the Municipal Hospital Act, Chapter 131E of the General Statutes, Article 2, Part A;

(2) To issue general obligation and revenue bonds and bond anticipation notes pursuant to the Local Government Finance Act, Chapter 159 of the General Statutes;

(3) To issue tax and revenue anticipation notes pursuant to Chapter 159 of the General Statutes, Article 9, Part 2; and

(4) All other powers as are necessary and incidental to the exercise of the powers of this Part. (1971, c. 780, s. 37.4; 1973, c. 476, s. 152; c. 494, s. 45; 1983, c. 775, s. 1.)

§ 131E-45. County taxes.

The county board of commissioners may levy a tax for the financing of the operation, equipment, and maintenance of any hospital operated by the district, including any public or nonprofit hospital, if the tax is approved by a majority of the qualified voters of the hospital district who shall vote on the question of levying the tax. The county board of commissioners shall determine the rate or amount of taxes that will be levied if approved by the voters of the district. The election on the question of levying the tax may be held at any time fixed by the county board of commissioners and shall be conducted in the same manner as bond elections held under G.S. 159-61. (1949, c. 766, s. 5; 1953, c. 1045, s. 6; 1983, c. 775, s. 1.)

§ 131E-46. Referendum on repeal of tax levy.

(a) The board of commissioners of the county in which a hospital district was created under the provisions of this Part may, if a tax levy was authorized by referendum under G.S. 131E-45, call a referendum on the repeal of the authority to levy a tax. Such referendum may be called only if there are no outstanding general obligation bonds of the district.

(b) The question on the ballot shall be:

"[] FOR removal of the right of the board of county commissioners to levy and collect a tax in _____ Hospital District of _____ County,

"[] AGAINST removal of the right of the board of county commissioners to levy and collect a tax in _____ Hospital District of _____ County."

(c) The referendum shall be conducted in the same manner as bond elections held under G.S. 159-61. No new registration of voters shall be required.

(d) If a majority of the votes cast are in favor of the question, then beginning on the first day of the fiscal year following the date of the referendum, the board of county commissioners shall have no authority to levy a tax in the hospital district unless the voters approve under G.S. 131E-45. No referendum may be held within one year of the date of a referendum under this section. (1983, c. 775, s. 1.)

§ 131E-47. Governing body.

The board of county commissioners of the county in which a hospital district is located shall be the governing body of the district. All of the provisions of the

Municipal Hospital Act, Chapter 131E, Article 2, Part 1, shall apply to the hospital district and to the county board of commissioners as the governing body. (1953, c. 1045, s. 7; 1983, c. 775, s. 1.)

Part 4. Limited Liability.

§ 131E-47.1. Limited liability.

(a) A person serving as a director, trustee, or officer of a public hospital as defined in G.S. 159-39, or as a commissioner, member, or officer of a hospital authority established under Part 1 or 2 of this Article, or as a director, trustee, or officer of North Carolina Memorial Hospital, shall be immune individually from civil liability for monetary damages, except to the extent covered by insurance, for any act or failure to act arising out of this service, except where the person:

(1) Is compensated for his services beyond reimbursement for expenses,

(2) Was not acting within the scope of his official duties,

(3) Was not acting in good faith,

(4) Committed gross negligence or willful or wanton misconduct that resulted in the damage or injury,

(5) Derived an improper personal financial benefit from the transaction,

(6) Incurred the liability from the operation of a motor vehicle, or

(7) Is defendant in an action brought under G.S. 55A-28.1 or 55A-28.2.

(b) The immunity in subsection (a) is personal to the directors, trustees, officers, commissioners, and members, and does not immunize the hospital or hospital authority for liability for the acts or omissions of the directors, trustees, or officers. (1987 (Reg. Sess., 1988), c. 1057, s. 1; c. 1100, s. 39.2.)

Article 2A.

Garnishment for Debts Owed Public Hospitals.

§§ 131E-48 through 131E-51: Repealed by Session Laws 2013-382, s. 13.2, effective October 1, 2013, and applicable to hospital and ambulatory surgical facility billings and collections practices occurring on or after that date.

§ 131E-52: Reserved for future codification purposes.

§ 131E-53: Reserved for future codification purposes.

§ 131E-54: Reserved for future codification purposes.

Article 3.

North Carolina Specialty Hospitals.

Part 1. Lenox Baker Children's Hospital.

§§ 131E-55 through 131E-58: Repealed by Session Laws 1987, c. 856, s. 13.

§ 131E-59: Reserved for future codification purposes.

§ 131E-60: Reserved for future codification purposes.

§ 131E-61: Reserved for future codification purposes.

§ 131E-62: Reserved for future codification purposes.

§ 131E-63: Reserved for future codification purposes.

§ 131E-64: Reserved for future codification purposes.

Part 2. Other Programs Controlled by the Department.

§ 131E-65. Alcohol Detoxification Program.

There shall be no reduction of services offered, no contracting of primary services, nor removal of this facility from Buncombe County without prior approval of the General Assembly. (1983, c. 775, s. 1.)

§ 131E-66: Repealed by Session Laws 1985, c. 589, s. 40.

§ 131E-67. Specialty hospitals.

All functions, powers, duties, and obligations heretofore vested in the Board of Directors of the North Carolina Specialty Hospitals and Eastern North Carolina Hospital are hereby transferred to and vested in the Department. All appropriations heretofore made to such Board of Directors or to any of the hospitals are hereby transferred to the Department. The Secretary of the Department shall have the power and duty to adopt rules for the operation of these facilities. (1979, c. 838, s. 46; 1983, c. 775, s. 1.)

§ 131E-68. Reserved for future codification purposes.

§ 131E-69. Reserved for future codification purposes.

Article 4.

Construction and Enlargement of Hospitals.

§ 131E-70. Construction and enlargement of local hospitals.

(a) The Department is authorized to continue surveys of all counties in the State to determine:

(1) The hospital needs of the county;

(2) The economic ability of various areas to support adequate hospital service;

(3) What assistance by the State, if any, is necessary to supplement other available funds; to finance the construction of new hospitals and health centers, additions to existing hospitals and health centers; and to finance equipment necessary to provide adequate hospital service for the citizens of the county;

and to periodically report this information, together with its recommendations, to the Governor, who shall transmit the reports to the General Assembly for any legislative action necessary to ensure an adequate statewide hospital program.

(b) The Department is authorized to act as the agency of the State to develop and administer a statewide plan in accordance with rules adopted by the Medical Care Commission for the construction and maintenance of hospitals, public health centers and related facilities and to receive and administer funds which may be provided by the General Assembly and by the federal government.

(c) The Department is authorized to develop statewide plans for the construction and maintenance of hospitals, medical centers and related facilities, or other plans necessary in order to meet the requirements and receive the benefits of applicable federal legislation.

(d) The Department is authorized to adopt rules to carry out the intent and purposes of this Article.

(e) The Department shall be responsible for doing all acts necessary to authorize the State to receive the full benefits of any federal statutes enacted for the construction and maintenance of hospitals, health centers or allied facilities.

(f) The Medical Care Commission shall make grants-in-aid to counties, cities, towns and subdivisions of government to acquire real estate and construct hospital facilities, including the reconstruction, remodeling or addition to any hospital facilities acquired by municipalities or subdivisions of government for use as community hospitals. These appropriations and funds made available by the State shall be allocated, apportioned and granted for the purposes of this Article and for other purposes in accordance with the rules adopted by the Medical Care Commission. The Medical Care Commission may furnish financial and other types of aid and assistance to any nonprofit hospital owned and operated by a corporation or association, no part of the net earnings of which inures, or may lawfully inure, to the benefit of any private shareholder or individual, upon the same terms and conditions as this aid and financial assistance is granted to municipalities and subdivisions of government.

(g) The Department may make available to any eligible hospital, clinic, or other medical facility operated by the State any unallocated federal sums or balances remaining after all grants-in-aid for local approvable projects made by the Department have been completed, disbursed or encumbered. (1945, c. 1096; 1947, c. 933, ss. 3, 5; 1949, c. 592; 1951, c. 1183, s. 1; 1971, c. 134; 1973, c. 476, s. 152; c. 1090, s. 1; 1979, c. 504, ss. 8, 14; 1983, c. 775, s. 1.)

§§ 131E-71 through 131E-74. Reserved for future codification purposes.

Article 5.

Hospital Licensure Act.

Part 1. Article Title and Definitions.

§ 131E-75. Title; purpose.

(a) This Article shall be known as the "Hospital Licensure Act."

(b) The purpose of this article is to establish hospital licensing requirements which promote public health, safety and welfare and to provide for the development, establishment and enforcement of basic standards for the care and treatment of patients in hospitals. (1947, c. 933, s. 6; 1983, c. 775, s. 1.)

§ 131E-76. Definitions.

As used in this article, unless otherwise specified:

(1) "Commission" means the North Carolina Medical Care Commission.

(1a) "Critical access hospital" means a hospital which has been designated as a critical access hospital by the North Carolina Department of Health and Human Services, Office of Research, Demonstrations and Rural Health

Development. To be designated as a critical access hospital under this subdivision, the hospital must be certified as a critical access hospital pursuant to 42 CFR Part 485 Subpart F. The North Carolina Department of Health and Human Services, Office of Research, Demonstrations, and Rural Health Development may designate a hospital located in a Metropolitan Statistical Area as a rural hospital for the purposes of the critical access hospital program if the hospital is located in a county with twenty-five percent (25%) or more rural residents as defined by the most recent United States decennial census.

(1b) through (1d) Reserved for future codification purposes.

(1e) "Gastrointestinal endoscopy room" means a room used for the performance of procedures that require the insertion of a flexible endoscope into a gastrointestinal orifice to visualize the gastrointestinal lining and adjacent organs for diagnostic or therapeutic purposes.

(2) "Governing body" means the Board of Trustees, Board of Directors, partnership, corporation, association, person or group of persons who maintain and control the hospital. The governing body may or may not be the owner of the properties in which the hospital services are provided.

(3) "Hospital" means any facility which has an organized medical staff and which is designed, used, and operated to provide health care, diagnostic and therapeutic services, and continuous nursing care primarily to inpatients where such care and services are rendered under the supervision and direction of physicians licensed under Chapter 90 of the General Statutes, Article 1, to two or more persons over a period in excess of 24 hours. The term includes facilities for the diagnosis and treatment of disorders within the scope of specific health specialties. The term does not include private mental facilities licensed under Article 2 of Chapter 122C of the General Statutes, nursing homes licensed under G.S. 131E-102, adult care homes licensed under Part 1 of Article 1 of Chapter 131D of the General Statutes, and any outpatient department including a portion of a hospital operated as an outpatient department, on or off of the hospital's main campus, that is operated under the hospital's control or ownership and is classified as Business Occupancy by the Life Safety Code of the National Fire Protection Association as referenced under 42 C.F.R. § 482.41. Provided, however, if the Business Occupancy outpatient location is to be operated within 30 feet of any hospital facility, or any portion thereof, which is classified as Health Care Occupancy or Ambulatory Health Care Occupancy under the Life Safety Code of the National Fire Protection Association, the hospital shall provide plans and specifications to the Department for review and

approval as required for hospital construction or renovations in a manner described by the Department.

(4) "Infirmary" means a unit of a school, or similar educational institution, which has the primary purpose to provide limited short-term health and nursing services to its students.

(5) "Medical review committee" means any of the following committees formed for the purpose of evaluating the quality, cost of, or necessity for hospitalization or health care, including medical staff credentialing:

a. A committee of a state or local professional society.

b. A committee of a medical staff of a hospital.

c. A committee of a hospital or hospital system, if created by the governing board or medical staff of the hospital or system or operating under written procedures adopted by the governing board or medical staff of the hospital or system.

d. A committee of a peer review corporation or organization.

(6) Renumbered.

(6a) "Operating room" means a room used for the performance of surgical procedures requiring one or more incisions and that is required to comply with all applicable licensure codes and standards for an operating room.

(7) "Rural hospital network" means an alliance of members that shall include at least one critical access hospital and one other hospital. To qualify as a rural hospital network, the critical access hospital must submit a comprehensive, written memorandum of understanding to the Department of Health and Human Services, Office of Research, Demonstrations and Rural Health Development, for the Department's approval. The memorandum of understanding must include provisions for patient referral and transfer, a plan for network-wide emergency services, and a plan for sharing patient information and services between hospital members including medical staff credentialing, risk management, quality assurance, and peer review. (1947, c. 933, s. 6; 1949, c. 920, s. 1; 1955, c. 369; 1961, c. 51, s. 1; 1973, c. 476, s. 152; 1983, c. 775, s. 1; 1985, c. 589, s. 41; 1993, c. 321, s. 245; 1995, c. 535, s. 20; 1997-

443, s. 11A.118(a); 2004-149, ss. 1.1, 2.4; 2004-199, s. 49; 2005-346, ss. 1, 2; 2009-462, s. 4(j); 2009-487, s. 4(a).)

Part 2. Hospital Licensure.

§ 131E-77. Licensure requirement.

(a) No person or governmental unit shall establish or operate a hospital in this state without a license. An infirmary is not required to obtain a license under this Part.

(b) The Commission shall prescribe by rule that any licensee or prospective applicant seeking to make specified types of alteration or addition to its facilities or to construct new facilities shall submit plans and specifications before commencement to the Department for preliminary inspection and approval or recommendations with respect to compliance with the applicable rules under this Part.

(c) An applicant for licensing under this Part shall provide information related to hospital operations as requested by the Department. The required information shall be submitted by the applicant on forms provided by the Department and established by rule.

(d) Upon receipt of an application for a license, the Department shall issue a license if it finds that the applicant complies with the provisions of this Article and the rules of the Commission. The Department shall renew each license in accordance with the rules of the Commission. The Department shall charge the applicant a nonrefundable annual base license fee plus a nonrefundable annual per-bed fee as follows:

Facility Type	Number of Beds	Base Fee	Per-Bed Fee
General Acute Hospitals:	1-49 beds	$250.00	$17.50

$17.50	50-99 beds	$350.00
$17.50	100-199 beds	$450.00
$17.50	200-399 beds	$550.00
$17.50	400-699 beds	$750.00
$17.50	700+ beds	$950.00
Other Hospitals: $17.50		$500.00

(e) The Department shall issue the license to the operator of the hospital who shall not transfer or assign it except with the written approval of the Department. The license shall designate the number and types of inpatient beds, the number of operating rooms, and the number of gastrointestinal endoscopy rooms.

(f) The operator shall post the license on the licensed premises in an area accessible to the public. (1947, c. 933, s. 6; 1949, c. 920, ss. 3, 4; 1963, c. 66; 1973, c. 476, s. 152; c. 1090, s. 1; 1975, c. 718, s. 2; 1983, c. 775, s. 1; 2003-284, s. 34.2(a); 2005-276, s. 41.2(b); 2005-346, s. 3; 2009-451, s. 10.76(e); 2011-145, s. 18.10(c); 2011-391, s. 42.1.)

§ 131E-78. Adverse action on a license.

(a) The Department shall have the authority to deny, suspend, revoke, annul, withdraw, recall, cancel, or amend a license in any case when it finds a substantial failure to comply with the provisions of this Part or any rule promulgated under this Part.

(b) Repealed by Session Laws 2007-444, s. 1, effective August 23, 2007.

(b1) The Secretary may suspend the admission of any new patients to specific areas of a hospital or suspend specific services of a hospital licensed under this Article where the conditions of the hospital constitute a substantial failure to comply with the provisions of this Part or any rule adopted under this Part and are dangerous to the health or safety of the patients. When the Secretary suspends admissions or specific services, the suspension shall be limited to the smallest possible components of the hospital. The Department shall provide consultation to assist the hospital in correcting the conditions that led to the suspension in order that the suspension can be lifted at the earliest possible time after the Secretary is satisfied that conditions or circumstances merit removal of the suspension. In determining whether to suspend admissions or services under this subsection, the Secretary shall consider the following factors:

(1) The character and degree of impact of the conditions at the hospital on the health and safety of its patients.

(2) The character and degree of impact that the proposed suspension of admissions or services would have on the functionality of the hospital and the availability of services necessary to the community or to current patients of the hospital.

(3) Whether all other reasonable means for correcting the problem have been exhausted and no less restrictive alternative to suspension of admissions or service exists.

(c) Repealed by Session Laws 2007-444, s. 1, effective August 23, 2007.

(c1) A hospital may contest any adverse action on its license under this section in accordance with Chapter 150B of the General Statutes. (1947, c. 933, s. 6; 1973, c. 476, s. 152; c. 1090, s. 1; 1981, c. 614, ss. 16, 17; 1983, c. 775, s. 1; 1987, c. 827, s. 1; 2007-444, s. 1.)

§ 131E-78.1: Reserved for future codification purposes.

§ 131E-78.2: Reserved for future codification purposes.

§ 131E-78.3: Reserved for future codification purposes.

§ 131E-78.4: Reserved for future codification purposes.

§ 131E-78.5. Designation as primary stroke center.

(a) The Department shall designate as a primary stroke center any hospital licensed under this Article that demonstrates to the Department that the hospital is certified by the Joint Commission or other nationally recognized accrediting body that requires conformance to best practices for stroke care in order to be identified as a primary stroke center. A hospital that is certified by the Joint Commission or other nationally recognized accrediting body that requires conformance to best practices for stroke care in order to be identified as a primary stroke center shall report the certification to the Department within 90 days of receiving that certification. A hospital shall inform the Department of any changes to its certification status within 30 days of any change.

(b) Each hospital designated as a primary stroke center pursuant to this section shall make efforts to coordinate the provision of appropriate acute stroke care with other hospitals licensed in this State through a formal written agreement. The agreement shall, at a minimum, address (i) transportation of acute stroke patients to hospitals designated as primary stroke centers and (ii) acceptance by hospitals designated as primary stroke centers of acute stroke patients initially treated at hospitals that are not capable of providing appropriate stroke care.

(c) The Department shall maintain within the Division of Health Service Regulation, Office of Emergency Services, a list of the hospitals designated as primary stroke centers in accordance with this section and post the list on the Department's Internet Web site. Annually on June 1, the Department shall transmit this list to the medical director of each licensed emergency medical services provider in this State.

(d) A hospital licensed under this Article shall not advertise or hold itself out to the public as a primary stroke center unless certified as a primary stroke center by the Joint Commission or other nationally recognized accrediting body that requires conformance to best practices for stroke care in order to be identified as a primary stroke center.

(e) Nothing in this section shall be construed to do any of the following:

(1) Establish a standard of medical practice for stroke patients.

(2) Restrict in any way the authority of any hospital to provide services authorized under its hospital license.

(f) The Department may adopt rules to implement the provisions of this section. (2013-44, s. 1.)

§ 131E-79. Rules and enforcement.

(a) The Commission shall promulgate rules necessary to implement this Article.

(b) The Department shall enforce this Article and the rules of the Commission. (1947, c. 933, s. 6; 1973, c. 476, s. 152; 1983, c. 775, s. 1.)

§ 131E-79.1. Counseling patients regarding prescriptions.

(a) Any hospital or other health care facility licensed pursuant to this Chapter or Chapter 122C of the General Statutes, health maintenance organization, local health department, community health center, medical office, or facility operated by a health care provider licensed under Chapter 90 of the General Statutes, providing patient counseling by a physician, a registered nurse, or any other appropriately trained health care professional shall be deemed in compliance with the rules adopted by the North Carolina Board of Pharmacy regarding patient counseling.

(b) As used in this section, "patient counseling" means the effective communication of information to the patient or representative in order to improve therapeutic outcomes by maximizing proper use of prescription medications and devices. (1993, c. 529, s. 7.7.)

§ 131E-79.2. Educating parents of newborns regarding pertussis disease.

(a) Each hospital licensed under this Article shall provide to the parents of newborns delivered at the hospital free, medically accurate educational information about pertussis disease and the availability of the tetanus-diphtheria and pertussis (Tdap) vaccine to protect against pertussis disease. The hospital shall provide this educational information to parents during the postpartum period and prior to the mother's discharge from the hospital. As used in this section, "postpartum period" means the period of time between the mother's admittance to the hospital for delivery of the newborn child through the first few hours after childbirth.

(b) The educational information provided to parents pursuant to this section shall include, at a minimum, the most current recommendations of the Centers for Disease Control and Prevention's Advisory Committee on Immunization Practices regarding the use of tetanus-toxoid-diphtheria-acellular pertussis (Tdap) vaccine to reduce the burden of pertussis in infants.

(c) Nothing in this section shall be construed to require a hospital to provide or pay for any vaccination against pertussis disease. (2013-161, s. 1.)

§ 131E-80. Inspections.

(a) The Department shall make or cause to be made inspections as it may deem necessary. Any hospital licensed under this Part shall at all times be subject to inspections by the Department according to the rules of the Commission. Except as provided under G.S. 131E-77(b) of this Part, after the hospital's initial licensing, any location included or added to the hospital's accreditation through an accrediting body approved pursuant to section 1865(a) of the Social Security Act, shall be deemed to be part of the hospital's license; provided, however, that all locations may be subject to inspections which the Department deems necessary to validate compliance with the requirements set forth in this Part.

(b) The Department may delegate to any state officer or agency the authority to inspect hospitals. The Department may revoke this delegated authority at its discretion and make its own inspections.

(c) Authorized representatives of the Department shall have at all times the right of proper entry upon any and all parts of the premises of any place in which entry is necessary to carry out the provisions of this Part or the rules adopted by the Commission; and it shall be unlawful for any person to resist a proper entry by such authorized representative upon any premises other than a private dwelling. However, no representative shall, by this entry onto the premises, endanger the health or well being of any patient being treated in the hospital.

(d) To enable the Department to determine compliance with this Part and the rules promulgated under the authority of this Part and to investigate complaints made against a hospital licensed under this Part, while maintaining the confidentiality of the complainant, the Department shall have the authority to review any writing or other record in any recording medium which pertains to the admission, discharge, medication, treatment, medical condition, or history of persons who are or have been patients of the hospital licensed under this Part and the personnel records of those individuals employed by the licensed hospital. The examinations of these records is permitted notwithstanding the provisions of G.S. 8-53, "Communications between physician and patient," or any other provision of law relating to the confidentiality of communications between physician and patient. Proceedings of medical review committees are exempt from the provisions of this section. The hospital, its employees, and any person interviewed during these inspections shall be immune from liability for damages resulting from the disclosure of any information to the Department. Any confidential or privileged information received from review of records or interviews shall be kept confidential by the Department and not disclosed without written authorization of the patient, employee or legal representative, or unless disclosure is ordered by a court of competent jurisdiction. The Department shall institute appropriate policies and procedures to ensure that this information shall not be disclosed without authorization or court order. The Department shall not disclose the name of anyone who has furnished information concerning a hospital without the consent of that person. Any officer, administrator, or employee of the Department who willfully discloses confidential or privileged information without appropriate authorization or court order shall be guilty of a Class 3 misdemeanor and upon conviction shall only be fined in the discretion of the court but not in excess of five hundred dollars ($500.00). Neither the names of persons furnishing information nor any confidential or privileged information obtained from records or interviews shall be considered "public records" within the meaning of G.S. 132-1, "Public Records" defined.

(e) Information received by the Commission and the Department through filed reports, license applications, or inspections that are required or authorized by the provisions of this Part, may be disclosed publicly except where this disclosure would violate the confidential relationship existing between physician and patient. However, no such public disclosure shall identify the patient involved without permission of the patient or court order. (1947, c. 933, s. 6;

1973, c. 476, s. 152; c. 1090, s. 1; 1981, c. 586, s. 3; 1983, c. 775, s. 1; 1993, c. 539, s. 957; 1994, Ex. Sess., c. 24, s. 14(c); 2009-487, s. 4(b).)

§ 131E-81. Penalties.

(a) Any person establishing, conducting, managing, or operating any hospital without a license shall be guilty of a Class 3 misdemeanor, and upon conviction shall only be liable for a fine of not more than fifty dollars ($50.00) for the first offense and not more than five hundred dollars ($500.00) for each subsequent offense. Each day of a continuing violation after conviction shall be considered a separate offense.

(b) Except as otherwise provided in this Part, any person who willfully violates any provision of this Part or who willfully fails to perform any act required, or who willfully performs any act prohibited by this Part, shall be guilty of a Class 1 misdemeanor. However, any person who willfully violates any rule adopted by the Commission under this Part or who willfully fails to perform any act required by, or who willfully does any act prohibited by, these rules shall be guilty of a Class 3 misdemeanor. (1947, c. 933, s. 6; 1983, c. 775, s. 1; 1993, c. 539, s. 958; 1994, Ex. Sess., c. 24, s. 14(c).)

§ 131E-82. Injunction.

(a) Notwithstanding the existence or pursuit of any other remedy, the Department may, in the manner provided by law, maintain an action in the name of the State for injunction or other process against any person or governmental unit to restrain or prevent the establishment, conduct, management or operation of a hospital without a license.

(b) If any person shall hinder the proper performance of duty of the Secretary or a representative in carrying out the provisions of this Part, the Secretary may institute an action in the superior court of the county in which the hindrance occurred for injunctive relief against the continued hindrance, irrespective of all other remedies at law.

(c)   Actions under this section shall be in accordance with Article 37 of Chapter 1 of the General Statutes, and Rule 65 of the Rules of Civil Procedure. (1947, c. 933, s. 6; 1973, c. 476, s. 152; 1983, c. 775, s. 1.)

§ 131E-83. Temporary change of hospital bed capacity.

A hospital may temporarily increase its bed capacity by up to ten percent (10%) over its licensed bed capacity by utilizing observation beds for hospital inpatients if the hospital notifies and obtains the approval of the Division of Health Service Regulation. For purposes of this section, "temporarily" means not longer than 60 consecutive days. (2001-410, s. 1; 2007-182, s. 1.)

§ 131E-84. Waiver of rules for hospitals that provide temporary shelter or temporary services during a disaster or emergency.

(a)   The Division of Health Service Regulation may temporarily waive, during disasters or emergencies declared in accordance with Article 1A of Chapter 166A of the General Statutes, any rules of the Commission pertaining to a hospital to the extent necessary to allow the hospital to provide temporary shelter and temporary services requested by the emergency management agency. The Division may identify, in advance of a declared disaster or emergency, rules that may be waived, and the extent to which the rules may be waived, upon a declaration of disaster or emergency in accordance with Article 1A of Chapter 166A of the General Statutes. The Division may also waive rules under this subsection during a declared disaster or emergency upon the request of an emergency management agency and may rescind the waiver if, after investigation, the Division determines the waiver poses an unreasonable risk to the health, safety, or welfare of any of the persons occupying the hospital. The emergency management agency requesting temporary shelter or temporary services shall notify the Division within 72 hours of the time the preapproved waivers are deemed by the emergency management agency to apply.

(b)   As used in this section, "emergency management agency" is as defined in G.S. 166A-19.3. (2007-444, s. 2; 2012-12, s. 2(t).)

Part 3. Hospital Privileges.

§ 131E-85. Hospital privileges and procedures.

(a) The granting or denial of privileges to practice in hospitals to physicians licensed under Chapter 90 of the General Statutes, Article 1, dentists, optometrists, and podiatrists and the scope and delineation of such privileges shall be determined by the governing body of the hospital on a non-discriminatory basis. Such determinations shall be based upon the applicant's education, training, experience, demonstrated competence and ability, and judgment and character of the applicant, and the reasonable objectives and regulations of the hospital, including, but not limited to appropriate utilization of hospital facilities, in which privileges are sought. Nothing in this Part shall be deemed to mandate hospitals to grant or deny to any such individuals or others privileges to practice in hospitals, or to offer or provide any type of care.

(b) The procedures to be followed by a licensed hospital in considering applications of dentists, optometrists, and podiatrists for privileges to practice in such hospitals shall be similar to those applicable to applications of physicians licensed under Chapter 90 of the General Statutes, Article 1. Such procedures shall be available upon request.

(c) In addition to the granting or denial of privileges, the governing body of each hospital may suspend, revoke, or modify privileges.

(d) All applicants or individuals who have privileges shall comply with all applicable medical staff bylaws, rules and regulations, including the policies and procedures governing the qualifications of applicants and the scope and delineation of privileges.

(e) The Department shall not issue or renew a license under this Article unless the applicant has demonstrated that the procedures followed in determining hospital privileges are in accordance with this Part and rules of the Department. (1981, c. 659, s. 10; 1983, c. 775, s. 1; 1987, c. 859, s. 18; 1989, c. 446; 1997-75, s. 2.)

§ 131E-86. Limited privileges.

(a) It shall be unlawful for an individual who is not licensed under Chapter 90 of the General Statutes, Article 1, to admit a patient to a hospital without written proof in accordance with the policy of the governing body of the hospital that a physician licensed under Chapter 90 of the General Statutes, Article 1, who is a member of the medical staff will be responsible for the performance of a basic medical appraisal and for the medical needs of the patient. The governing body of a hospital may waive this requirement for a dentist licensed under Chapter 90 of the General Statutes, Article 2, to the extent authorized by this statute, who has successfully completed a postgraduate program in oral and maxillofacial surgery accredited by the American Dental Association.

(b) The governing body of each hospital shall not grant privileges that exceed the scope of a license. (1983, c. 775, s. 1.)

§ 131E-87. Reports of disciplinary action; immunity from liability.

The chief administrative officer of each licensed hospital in the State shall report to the appropriate occupational licensing board the details, as prescribed by the board, of any revocation, suspension, limitation, or voluntary reduction of privileges of a health care provider to practice in that hospital. Each hospital shall also report to the board its medical staff resignations. Reports concerning physician privileges and resignations shall be made in accordance with G.S. 90-14.13. Any person making a report required by this section shall be immune from any resulting criminal prosecution or civil liability unless the person knew the report was false or acted in reckless disregard of whether the report was false. (1983, c. 775, s. 1; 1987, c. 859, s. 16; 2006-144, s. 9.)

§ 131E-88. Reserved for future codification purposes.

§ 131E-89. Reserved for future codification purposes.

Part 4. Discharge from Hospital.

§ 131E-90. Authority of administrator; refusal to leave after discharge.

The case of a patient who refuses or fails to leave the hospital upon discharge by the attending physician shall be reviewed by two physicians licensed to practice medicine in this State, one of whom may be the attending physician. If in the opinion of the physicians, the patient should be discharged as cured or as no longer needing treatment or for the reason that treatment cannot benefit the patient's case or for other good and sufficient reasons, the patient's refusal to leave shall constitute a trespass. The patient shall be guilty of a Class 3 misdemeanor. (1965, c. 258; 1983, c. 775, s. 1; 1993, c. 539, s. 959; 1994, Ex. Sess., c. 24, s. 14(c).)

§ 131E-91. Fair billing and collections practices for hospitals and ambulatory surgical facilities.

(a) All hospitals and ambulatory surgical facilities licensed pursuant to this Chapter shall, upon request of the patient, present an itemized list of charges to all discharged patients detailing in language comprehensible to an ordinary layperson the specific nature of the charges or expenses incurred by the patient. Patient bills that are not itemized shall include notification to the patient of the right to request, free of charge, an itemized bill. A patient may request an itemized list of charges at any time within three years after the date of discharge or so long as the hospital or ambulatory surgical facility, a collections agency, or another assignee of the hospital or ambulatory surgical facility asserts the patient has an obligation to pay the bill. Each hospital and ambulatory surgical facility shall establish a method for patients to inquire about or dispute a bill.

(b) If a patient has overpaid the amount due to the hospital or ambulatory surgical facility, whether as the result of insurance coverage, patient error, health care facility billing error, or other cause, and the overpayment is not in dispute or on appeal, the hospital or ambulatory surgical facility shall provide the patient with a refund within 45 days of receiving notice of the overpayment.

(c) A hospital or ambulatory surgical facility shall not bill insured patients for charges that would have been covered by their insurance had the hospital or ambulatory surgical facility submitted the claim or other information required to process the claim within the allotted time requirements of the insurer.

(d) Hospitals and ambulatory surgical facilities shall abide by the following reasonable collections practices:

(1) A hospital or ambulatory surgical facility shall not refer a patient's unpaid bill to a collections agency, entity, or other assignee during the pendency of a

patient's application for charity care or financial assistance under the hospital's or ambulatory surgical facility's charity care or financial assistance policies.

(2) A hospital or ambulatory surgical facility shall provide a patient with a written notice that the patient's bill will be subject to collections activity at least 30 days prior to the referral being made.

(3) A hospital or ambulatory surgical facility that contracts with a collections agency, entity, or other assignee shall require the collections agency, entity, or other assignee to inform the patient of the hospital's or ambulatory surgical facility's charity care and financial assistance policies when engaging in collections activity.

(4) A hospital or ambulatory surgical facility shall require a collections agency, entity, or other assignee to obtain the written consent of the hospital or ambulatory surgical facility prior to the collections agency, entity, or other assignee filing a lawsuit to collect the debt.

(5) For debts arising from the provision of care by a hospital or ambulatory surgical center, the doctrine of necessaries as it existed at common law shall apply equally to both spouses, except where they are permanently living separate and apart, but shall in no event create any liability between the spouses as to each other. No lien arising out of a judgment for a debt owed a hospital or ambulatory surgical facility under this section shall attach to the judgment debtors' principal residence, or, if the land upon which the principal residence is located is greater than five acres, then no lien shall attach to the judgment debtors' principal residence and the surrounding five acres, held by them as tenants by the entireties or that was held by them as tenants by the entireties prior to the death of either spouse where the tenancy terminated as a result of the death of either spouse.

(6) For debts arising from the provision of care by a hospital or ambulatory surgical center to a minor, there shall be no execution on or otherwise forced sale of the principal residence of the custodial parent or parents for a judgment obtained for the outstanding debt until such time as the minor is either no longer residing with the custodial parent or parents or until the minor reaches the age of majority, whichever occurs first.

(e) The Commission shall adopt rules to ensure that this section is properly implemented. The Department shall not issue or renew a license under this Article unless the applicant has demonstrated that the requirements of this subsection are being met. (1991, c. 310, s. 1; 2013-382, s. 13.1; 2013-393, s. 2.)

§ 131E-92. Reserved for future codification purposes.

§ 131E-93. Reserved for future codification purposes.

§ 131E-94. Reserved for future codification purposes.

Part 5. Medical Review Committee.

§ 131E-95. Medical review committee.

(a) A member of a duly appointed medical review committee who acts without malice or fraud shall not be subject to liability for damages in any civil action on account of any act, statement or proceeding undertaken, made, or performed within the scope of the functions of the committee.

(b) The proceedings of a medical review committee, the records and materials it produces and the materials it considers shall be confidential and not considered public records within the meaning of G.S. 132-1, " 'Public records' defined", and shall not be subject to discovery or introduction into evidence in any civil action against a hospital, an ambulatory surgical facility licensed under Chapter 131E of the General Statutes, or a provider of professional health services which results from matters which are the subject of evaluation and review by the committee. No person who was in attendance at a meeting of the committee shall be required to testify in any civil action as to any evidence or other matters produced or presented during the proceedings of the committee or as to any findings, recommendations, evaluations, opinions, or other actions of the committee or its members. However, information, documents, or records otherwise available are not immune from discovery or use in a civil action merely because they were presented during proceedings of the committee. Documents otherwise available as public records within the meaning of G.S. 132-1 do not lose their status as public records merely because they were presented or considered during proceedings of the committee. A member of the committee or a person who testifies before the committee may testify in a civil action but cannot be asked about the person's testimony before the committee or any opinions formed as a result of the committee hearings.

(c) Information that is confidential and is not subject to discovery or use in civil actions under this section may be released to a professional standards review organization that performs any accreditation or certification including the Joint Commission on Accreditation of Healthcare Organizations, or to a patient safety organization or its designated contractors. Information released under this subsection shall be limited to that which is reasonably necessary and relevant to the standards review organization's determination to grant or continue accreditation or certification, or the patient safety organization's or its contractors' analysis of patient safety and health care quality. Information released under this subsection retains its confidentiality and is not subject to discovery or use in any civil actions as provided under this section, and the standards review or patient safety organization shall keep the information confidential subject to this section, except as necessary to carry out the organization's patient safety, accreditation, or certification activities. For the purposes of this section, "patient safety organization" means an entity that collects and analyzes patient safety or health care quality data of providers for the purpose of improving patient safety and the quality of health care delivery and includes, but is not limited to, an entity formed pursuant to Public Law No. 109-41. (1973, c. 1111; 1981, c. 725; 1983, c. 775, s. 1; 1999-222, s. 2; 2002-179, s. 19; 2004-149, s. 2.5; 2006-144, s. 3.2.)

Part 6. Risk Management.

§ 131E-96. Risk management programs.

(a) Each hospital shall develop and maintain a risk management program which is designed to identify, analyze, evaluate, and manage risks of injury to patients, visitors, employees, and property through loss reduction and prevention techniques and quality assurance activities, as prescribed in rules promulgated by the Commission.

(b) The Department shall not issue or renew a license under this Article unless the applicant is in compliance with this section. (1987, c. 859, s. 17.)

Part 7. Confidential Information.

§ 131E-97. Confidentiality of patient information.

(a) Medical records compiled and maintained by health care facilities in connection with the admission, treatment, and discharge of individual patients are not public records as defined by Chapter 132 of the General Statutes.

(b) Charges, accounts, credit histories, and other personal financial records compiled and maintained by health care facilities in connection with the admission, treatment, and discharge of individual patients are not public records as defined by Chapter 132 of the General Statutes. (1993 (Reg. Sess., 1994), c. 570, s. 10.)

§ 131E-97.1. Confidentiality of personnel information.

(a) Except as provided in subsection (b) of this section, the personnel files of employees or former employees, and the files of applicants for employment maintained by a public hospital as defined in G.S. 159-39 or maintained by a hospital that has been sold or conveyed pursuant to G.S. 131E-8 are not public records as defined by Chapter 132 of the General Statutes.

(b) Repealed by Session Laws, 1997-517, s. 3.

(c) Information regarding the qualifications, competence, performance, character, fitness, or conditions of appointment of an independent contractor who provides health care services under a contract with a public hospital as defined in G.S. 159-39, or with a hospital which has been sold or conveyed pursuant to G.S. 131E-8, is not a public record as defined by Chapter 132 of the General Statutes. Information regarding a hearing or investigation of a complaint, charge, or grievance by or against an independent contractor who provides health care services under a contract with a public hospital as defined in G.S. 159-39 or with a hospital which has been sold or conveyed pursuant to G.S. 131E-8, is not a public record as defined by Chapter 132 of the General Statutes. Final action making an appointment or discharge or removal by a public hospital having final authority for the appointment or discharge or removal shall be taken in an open meeting, unless otherwise exempted by law. The following information with respect to each independent contractor of health care services of a public hospital, as defined by G.S. 159-39, is a matter of public record: name; age; date of original contract; beginning and ending dates; position title; position descriptions; and total compensation of current and former positions; and the date of the most recent promotion, demotion, transfer, suspension, separation, or other change in position classification. (1993 (Reg. Sess., 1994), c. 570, s. 10; 1995, c. 99, s. 1; c. 509, s. 135.2(q); 1997-517, s. 3.)

§ 131E-97.2. Confidentiality of credentialing information.

Information acquired by a public hospital, as defined in G.S. 159-39, a hospital that has been sold or conveyed pursuant to G.S. 131E-8, a State-owned or State-operated hospital, or by persons acting for or on behalf of a hospital, in connection with the credentialing and peer review of persons having or applying for privileges to practice in the hospital is confidential and is not a public record under Chapter 132 of the General Statutes; provided that information otherwise available to the public shall not become confidential merely because it was acquired by the hospital or by persons acting for or on behalf of the hospital. (1993 (Reg. Sess., 1994), c. 570, s. 10; 1995, c. 509, s. 135.2(r).)

§ 131E-97.3. Confidentiality of competitive health care information.

(a) For the purposes of this section, competitive health care information means information relating to competitive health care activities by or on behalf of hospitals and public hospital authorities. Competitive health care information does not include any of the information hospitals and ambulatory surgical facilities are required to report under G.S. 131E-214.12. Competitive health care information shall be confidential and not a public record under Chapter 132 of the General Statutes; provided that any contract entered into by or on behalf of a public hospital or public hospital authority, as defined in G.S. 159-39, shall be a public record unless otherwise exempted by law, or the contract contains competitive health care information, the determination of which shall be as provided in subsection (b) of this section.

(b) If a public hospital or public hospital authority is requested to disclose any contract which the hospital or hospital authority believes in good faith contains or constitutes competitive health care information, the hospital or hospital authority may either redact the portions of the contract believed to constitute competitive health care information prior to disclosure, or if the entire contract constitutes competitive health care information, refuse disclosure of the contract. The person requesting disclosure of the contract may institute an action pursuant to G.S. 132-9 to compel disclosure of the contract or any redacted portion thereof. In any action brought under this subsection, the issue for decision by the court shall be whether the contract, or portions of the contract withheld, constitutes competitive health care information, and in making its determination, the court shall be guided by the procedures and standards applicable to protective orders requested under Rule 26(c)(7) of the Rules of Civil Procedure. For the purposes of this section, competitive health care information includes, but is not limited to, contracts entered into by or on behalf of a public hospital or public hospital authority to purchase a medical practice. Before rendering a decision, the court shall review the contract in camera and hear arguments from the parties. If the court finds that the contract constitutes or contains competitive health care information, the court may either deny disclosure or may make such other appropriate orders as are permitted under Rule 26(c) of the Rules of Civil Procedure.

(c) Nothing in this section shall be deemed to prevent an elected public body, in closed session, which has responsibility for the hospital, the Attorney General, or the State Auditor from having access to this confidential information. The disclosure to any public entity does not affect the confidentiality of the information. Members of the public entity shall have a duty not to further disclose the confidential information. (1993 (Reg. Sess., 1994), c. 570, s. 10; 2001-516, s. 5; 2007-508, s. 8.5; 2013-382, s. 10.4.)

§ 131E-98. Inmate medical records.

Notwithstanding any other provision of law, a hospital does not breach patient confidentiality by providing the Division of Adult Correction of the Department of Public Safety with the medical records of inmates who receive medical treatment at the hospital while in the custody of the Division. A hospital complying with a request from the Division of Adult Correction of the Department of Public Safety or its agent for a copy of the medical records of an inmate who received medical services while in custody shall be immune from liability in any civil action for the release of the inmate's medical record. (1993, c. 321, s. 178(b); 2011-145, s. 19.1(h).)

Vision Books Order Form

Fax Orders:	1-980-299-5965
Phone Orders:	1-704-898-0770
E-mail Orders:	www.visionbooks.org
Mail Orders:	Vision Books, LLC P.O. Box 42406 Charlotte, NC 28215

Shipp To:
Name_____
Address_____
City_____State_____Zip_____
Phone_____Fax_____
Email_____@_____

Bill To: We can bill a third party on your behalf.
Name_____
Address_____
City_____State_____Zip_____
Phone____(_____)_____Fax_____
Email_____@_____

Pamphlet Number ($15.00 Each)	Qty	Total Cost
_____	_____	_____
_____	_____	_____
_____	_____	_____
_____	_____	_____
_____	_____	_____
_____	_____	_____
_____	_____	_____
<u>Full Volume Set 1-92</u>	<u>92 Pamphlets</u>	<u>1,380.00</u>

Free Shipping & Handling on Full Volume Orders
Add $1.00 Shipping & Handling Per Pamphlet $_____

Total Cost $_____

Thank you for your support. Management!

DID YOU ENJOY THIS BOOK?

Vision Books, LLC would like to hear from you! If you or someone you know has been fasely imprisoned, we would like to hear your story. If the 'North Carolina Criminal Law and Procedure' has had an effect in your life or if you have suggestions, we would like to hear from you. Send your letters to:

Vision Books, LLC
Attn: Staff Writers
P.O. Box 42406
Charlotte, NC 28215
Email: staff@visionbooks.org

Order Additional Copies:

Fax Orders: 1-980-299-5965

Phone Orders: 1-704-898-0770

E-mail Orders: www.visionbooks.org

Mail Orders: Vision Books, LLC
P.O. Box 42406
Charlotte, NC 28215

www.ingramcontent.com/pod-product-compliance
Lightning Source LLC
Chambersburg PA
CBHW051629170526
45167CB00001B/120